KING LEAR

The RSC Shakespeare

Edited by Jonathan Bate and Eric Rasmussen

Chief Associate Editor: Héloïse Sénéchal

Associate Editors: Trey Jansen, Eleanor Lowe, Lucy Munro, Dee Anna Phares, Jan Sewell

King Lear

Textual editing: Eric Rasmussen and Trey Jansen

Introduction and Shakespeare's Career in the Theatre: Jonathan Bate

Commentary: Penelope Freedman and Héloïse Sénéchal

Scene-by-Scene Analysis: Esme Miskimmin

In Performance: Karin Brown (RSC stagings), Jan Sewell (overview), Jonathan Bate (captions)

The Director's Cut (interviews by Jonathan Bate and Kevin Wright): Adrian Noble, Deborah Warner, Trevor Nunn

Editorial Advisory Board

The RSC Shakespeare

WILLIAM SHAKESPEARE

KING LEAR

Edited by
Jonathan Bate and Eric Rasmussen

Introduced by Jonathan Bate

Macmillan

Published by arrangement with Modern Library, an imprint of The Random
House Publishing Group, a division of Random House, Inc.

Published 2009 by
MACMILLAN PUBLISHERS LTD.
registered in England, company number 785998, of Houndmills,
Basingstoke, Hampshire RG21 6XS. Companies and representatives
throughout the world.

ISBN 978-0-230-57614-8   ISBN 978-1-137-00436-9 (eBook)
DOI 10.1007/978-1-137-00436-9

A catalogue record for this book is available from the British Library.

10   9   8   7   6   5   4   3   2   1
18 17 16 15 14 13 12 11 10 09

CONTENTS

INTRODUCTION

AN OLD MAN TOTTERING ABOUT THE STAGE?

'*King Lear*', wrote the early nineteenth-century Romantic poet Percy Bysshe Shelley in his *Defence of Poetry*, 'may be judged to be the most perfect specimen of the dramatic art existing in the world.' For all the Romantics, *Lear* was Shakespeare's most 'sublime' and 'universal' play. John Keats wrote a sonnet 'On sitting down to read *King Lear* once again': having burned his way through the play, he would feel somehow purified and regenerated. For Keats' contemporary, Charles Lamb, Shakespeare's anatomy of the human condition was so profound and tempestuous that the play seemed too vast for the stage. It is the centrepiece of his essay 'On the tragedies of Shakspeare, considered with reference to their fitness for stage representation':

> So to see Lear acted, – to see an old man tottering about the stage with a walking-stick, turned out of doors by his daughters in a rainy night, has nothing in it but what is painful and disgusting. We want to take him into shelter and relieve him. That is all the feeling which the acting of Lear ever produced in me. But the Lear of Shakspeare cannot be acted. The contemptible machinery by which they mimic the storm which he goes out in, is not more inadequate to represent the horrors of the real elements, than any actor can be to represent Lear: they might more easily propose to personate the Satan of Milton upon a stage, or one of Michael Angelo's terrible figures. The greatness of Lear is not in corporal dimension, but in intellectual: the explosions of his passion are terrible as a volcano: they are storms turning up and disclosing to the bottom that sea his mind, with all its vast riches. It is his mind which is laid bare. This case of flesh and blood

seems too insignificant to be thought on; even as he himself neglects it. On the stage we see nothing but corporal infirmities and weakness, the impotence of rage; while we read it, we see not Lear, but we are Lear, – we are in his mind, we are sustained by a grandeur which baffles the malice of daughters and storms; in the aberrations of his reason, we discover a mighty irregular power of reasoning, immethodized from the ordinary purposes of life, but exerting its powers, as the wind blows where it listeth, at will upon the corruptions and abuses of mankind. What have looks, or tones, to do with that sublime identification of his age with that of the *Heavens themselves*, when in his reproaches to them for conniving at the injustice of his children, he reminds them that 'they themselves are old.' What gestures shall we appropriate to this? What has the voice or the eye to do with such things?

For Lamb, the technical necessities of the theatre – the backstage machinery that creates the storm, the actor's repertoire of gestures, looks and vocal variations – are exterior and superficial distractions from the play's inward and remorseless exploration of reason and madness, humankind and nature, the corruptions and abuses of power. Few theatre-lovers would agree with Lamb, but few would deny that the role of Lear presents perhaps the greatest of all challenges to the Shakespearean actor. There is a theatre saying that by the time you're old enough to play it, you are too old to play it.

A generation before the Romantics, Dr Samuel Johnson confessed that even reading the play was almost too much to bear: 'I was many years ago so shocked by Cordelia's death, that I know not whether I ever endured to read again the last scenes of the play till I undertook to revise them as an editor.' The shock for Johnson was both emotional and moral. The death of Cordelia – Shakespeare's boldest alteration of his sources, in all of which she survives – was an extraordinary breach of the principal that Johnson called 'poetical justice', whereby 'A play in which the wicked prosper, and the virtuous miscarry, may doubtless be good, because it is a just representation of the common events of human life: but since all reasonable beings naturally love justice, I cannot easily be persuaded, that the observation of justice makes a play worse; or, that if other excellencies are equal, the audience will not always rise better pleased from the final triumph of persecuted virtue.' It had been in order to impose poetical justice on the play that during the 1680s Nahum Tate, author of the hymn 'While Shepherds Watched Their Flocks by Night', had rewritten *King Lear* with a happy ending, in which Cordelia was married off to Edgar. Johnson had some sympathy with this alteration, which held the stage for a century and a half, whereas for Lamb it was yet one more indication that the theatre was not to be trusted with Shakespeare's sublime vision of universal despair.

THE DIVISION OF THE KINGDOM

Written soon after King James united the thrones of England and Scotland, and performed in his royal presence at Whitehall, *King Lear* reveals the dire consequences of dividing a united kingdom. In principle, the aged Lear's decision to take voluntary retirement does not seem a bad thing: he is losing his grip on matters of state, his daughters and sons-in-law are 'younger strengths' with more energy for government, and, most importantly, the division is intended to prevent a future civil war between rival claimants, which would have been a definite possibility in the absence of a son who would automatically inherit the whole kingdom. But can an anointed king abnegate his role at will? If he does, he certainly should not expect to retain the trappings of power. Goneril and Regan have a case for stripping him of his rowdy, extravagant retinue of one hundred knights.

Lear's mistake is to link the division of the kingdom to a public show of affection. The two older sisters, well versed in the 'glib and oily art' of courtly flattery, tell him what he wants to hear, but Cordelia cannot. She is one of the play's truth-tellers and simply lacks the capacity or the experience to dress her love in fine rhetoric. Lear knows that she loves him best, but we may assume that until this moment her love has always been expressed privately. As youngest and unmarried daughter, Cordelia has probably never spoken publicly before the court. Lear's intention for the opening scene is that it will be Cordelia's coming-out: she is supposed to give public expression to her great love and in return she will be rewarded with the richest portion of the kingdom and the most-prized husband. He does not bargain on her inability to play the role in which he has cast her. Kings and earls do not necessarily have to be blind to true virtue – witness the examples of Kent and France – but Lear, too long used to having his own way and hearing only the words of flatterers, has blinded himself. Only when he has been stripped of the fine clothes and fine words of the court, has heard truth in the mouths of a fool and a (supposed) Bedlam beggar, does he find out what it really means to be human.

Where *Macbeth* and *Othello* are focused tightly upon a single plotline, the action of *Lear* greatly extends the technique of parallel plotting with which Shakespeare had experimented in *Hamlet*, where Laertes and Fortinbras serve as foils to the hero. In *Lear*, the Gloucester family plot is a sustained presence. Gloucester is another father who is blind to the true nature of his children; that blindness leads, in Shakespeare's cruellest literalization of metaphor, to the plucking out of his eyes. Edmund corresponds to the wicked daughters; several of the play's many letters pass between them. It is wholly appropriate that he should end up promised to them both. Like the king's favourite daughter Cordelia, Edgar (who is the king's godson) is unjustly exiled from home and excluded from parental care. It is fitting to the parallel structure of the twin plots that the play ends in the Folio version with him returning to take the reins of power, just as there is a certain, though very different, logic to Nahum Tate's infamous Restoration-period rewrite with a happy ending, in which Edgar is married off to Cordelia.

RIPENESS IS ALL?

Shakespeare never takes one side of a question. In the very opening lines of the play we discover that it is Edmund who has previously been unjustly exiled from home and excluded from parental care. Kent, the play's best judge of character, initially describes Edmund as 'proper': he has the bearing of a gentleman, but his illegitimacy has deprived him of the benefits of society. His first soliloquy makes a good case for the unfairness of a social order that practises primogeniture and stigmatizes bastardy; his discovery near the moment of death that 'Edmund was beloved' is curiously touching. He is not, then, an uncomplicated stage 'Machiavel', an embodiment of pure, unmotivated evil.

Astrology and astronomy were synonymous in the Elizabethan age: the signs of the times were read in the signs of the skies. *King Lear* is a play about bad times. The state drifts rudderless, child turns against parent, the clouds of war gather, the king and all around him totter on the brink of the abyss. So it is that Gloucester blames it all on the stars: 'These late eclipses in the sun and moon portend no good to us'. Edmund, however, disputes this: 'an admirable evasion of whoremaster man, to lay his goatish disposition on the charge of a star!' He argues that things often regarded as the product of the 'natural order' are actually shaped by 'custom' – for him, primogeniture and legitimacy would come into this category. The position articulated here is close to that of the sixteenth-century French essayist Michel de Montaigne in the closing section of his *Apology of Raymond Sebond*: any custom abhorred or outlawed by one nation is sure to be praised or practised by another. But if you have nothing save custom, no divinely sanctioned hierarchy, then where does your value-system come from? Montaigne's answer is blind faith in God, whereas Edmund, like an apologist before the letter for the political philosophy of Thomas Hobbes, commits himself to 'nature' as a principle of survival and self-seeking.

Gloucester's philosophical orientation, meanwhile, turns towards the classical Stoic idea of finding the right timing for death. After his mock suicide, he says 'henceforth I'll bear / Affliction till it do cry out itself / "Enough, enough" and die.' But he cannot sustain this position: when Lear and Cordelia lose the battle, he is found in 'ill thoughts again', wanting to rot. Edgar responds with more Stoic advice: 'Men must endure / Their going hence, even as their coming hither: / Ripeness is all'. But this idea of ripe timing doesn't work out:

by mistiming the revelation of his own identity to Gloucester, Edgar precipitates his father's death.

The play's pattern, then, is of Stoic comfort not working. At the beginning of the fourth act Edgar reflects on his own condition and cheers himself up with thoughts about the worst, but then his father comes on blinded and he is instantly confounded – things are worse than before. If the case of Edgar reveals the deficiency of Stoic comfort, that of Albany demonstrates the inadequacy of belief in divine justice. His credo is that the good shall taste 'the wages of their virtue' and the bad drink from the poisoned 'cup of their deservings'. This scheme works for the bad, but not for the good. In the closing scene, Albany tries to orchestrate events, to make order out of chaos, but each of his resolutions is followed by new disaster: he greets the restored Edgar, then immediately hears the news of Gloucester's death, then the news of the two queens' deaths; then Kent comes on, dying; then in response to the news that Cordelia is to be hanged, Albany says 'The gods defend her!', only for Lear to enter with her in his arms already hanged. The gods have not defended her. Then Albany tries to give power back to Lear – and he promptly dies. Then he tries to persuade Kent and Edgar to divide the kingdom, and Kent promptly goes off to die.

The final lines of the play – given to different speakers in the Quarto and Folio versions of the text – suggest that the lesson has been learnt that Stoic comfort will not do, that it is better to speak what we feel than what we ought to say. The Folio's ascription of this speech to Edgar makes more dramatic sense than the Quarto's to Albany, since Edgar's stripping down in Act 3 is an exposure to feeling, occurring in conjunction with Lear's feeling with and for the poor, which makes him the character better prepared to voice this sentiment.

THIS GREAT STAGE OF FOOLS

The Stoic philosopher tries to be ruled by reason rather than passion. But for the great sixteenth-century humanist Desiderius Erasmus in his *Praise of Folly*, there is inhumanity in the notion that to be wise you must suppress the emotions. The most important thing is to 'feel' – as Gloucester has to learn, to see the world not rationally but 'feelingly'. Erasmus' personification of Folly points out that friendship is among the highest human values, and it depends on emotion. The people who show friendship to Lear (Fool, Kent disguised as Caius, Edgar disguised as Poor Tom and then as Peasant) and to Gloucester (Servants, Old Man) are not the wise or the rich.

We are ruled by our passions and our bodies; we go through life performing a series of different roles of which we are by no means in control. 'All this life of mortal men, what is it else but a certain kind of stage play?', asks Erasmus' Folly. Lear echoes the sentiment: 'When we are born, we cry that we are come / To this great stage of fools.' In the great theatre of the world, with the gods as audience, we are the fools on stage. Under the aspect of Folly, we see that a king is no different from any other man. The trappings of monarchy are but a costume: this is both Folly's and Lear's discovery.

Erasmus' Folly tells us that there are two kinds of madness – one is the thirst for gold, lust and power. That is the madness of Regan, Cornwall, Edmund and the rest. Their madness is what Lear rejects. The second madness is the desirable one, the state of folly in which 'a certain pleasant raving, or error of the mind, delivereth the heart of that man whom it possesseth from all wonted carefulness, and rendreth it divers ways much recreated with new delectation' (*Praise of Folly*, in the sixteenth-century English translation of Sir Thomas Chaloner). This 'error of the mind' is a special gift of the goddess Folly. Thus Lear is happy when his mind is free, when he is running around in his madness like a child on a country holiday: 'Look, look, a mouse! Peace, peace, this piece of toasted cheese will do't.' Lines such as that bring a smile to our faces, not least because the mouse isn't really there. Lear repeats his 'look, look' at the end of his life. Cordelia is dead, but he deceives himself into the belief that she lives – that the feather moves, that her breath mists the looking-glass. His final words are spoken in the delusion that her lips are moving: 'Look on her, look, her lips, / Look there, look there!' Her lips are not moving, just as there is no mouse, but it is better for Lear that he should not know this. Philosophers say that it is miserable to be deceived; Folly replies that it is most miserable 'not to be deceived', for nothing could be further from the truth than the notion that man's happiness resides in things as they actually are. Lear's Fool says that he would fain 'learn to lie'. Lying is destructive in the mouths of Goneril, Regan and Edmund at the beginning of the play, but Cordelia – who has a special bond with the Fool – has to learn to lie. At the beginning, she can only tell the truth (hence her banishment), but later she lies beautifully and generously when Lear says that she has cause to do him wrong, and she replies 'No cause, no cause'.

The closing section of Erasmus' *Praise of Folly* undertakes a serious praise of Christian 'madness'. Christ says that the mystery of salvation is hidden from the wise and given to the simple. He delighted in simple people, fishermen and women. He chose to ride an ass when he could have mounted a lion. The language of his parables is steeped in simple, natural things – lilies, mustardseed, sparrows, a language analogous to that of Lear in his madness. The fundamental folly of Christianity is its demand that you throw away your possessions. Lear pretends to do this in Act 1, but actually he wants to keep 'The name, and all th'addition to a king'. Only when he loses his knights, his clothes and his sanity does he find happiness.

But he also becomes kind. Little things show us this: in Act 1, he's still always giving orders. Even in the storm he continues to make demands: 'come, unbutton here'. But in the end he learns to say 'please' and 'thank you': 'Pray you undo this button. Thank you, sir.' He has begun to learn true manners not at court, but through the love he shows for Poor Tom, the image of unaccommodated man, the image of himself: 'Did'st thou give all to thy daughters? And art thou come to this?' True wisdom comes not in Gloucester's and Edgar's words of Stoic comfort or Albany's hapless faith in divine providence, but in moments of folly and love, as in this exchange:

EDGAR Bless thy five wits!
KENT O pity! Sir, where is the patience now
    That you so oft have boasted to retain?

Patience is the boast of the Stoic. It's a retainer like the hundred knights. To achieve true wisdom, you must let it go. You must let even the wits, the sanity, go. What you must keep are the *pity* and the *blessing*. Pity and blessing are at the very heart of *King Lear*. Pity means the performance of certain deeds, such as showing kindness to strangers. Blessing is a performative speech-act, an utterance that effects an action by the very act of being spoken. Typically blessing is accompanied by a small but forceful *gesture*, a kind of action that is of vital importance on the bare boards of the Shakespearean theatre.

The play ends on a note of apocalypse, millennial doom. A trumpet sounds three times to announce the final showdown. Then when Lear enters with his beloved daughter dead in his arms, loyal Kent asks 'Is this the promised end?' He is thinking of Doomsday, but the line is also a sly allusion on Shakespeare's part: in all previous versions of the Lear story, several of which would have been familiar to members of his audience, Cordelia survives and Lear is restored to the throne. The death of Cordelia is all the more painful because it is not the end 'promised' by previous literary and theatrical tradition.

King Lear is a play full of questions. The big ones go unanswered. The biggest of all is Lear's 'Why should a dog, a horse, a rat, have life, / And thou no breath at all?' In this world, there is no rhyme or reason, no pattern of divine justice. Here again, Shakespeare departs strikingly from his source, the old anonymous play of *King Leir*, in which Christian providence prevails. Shakespeare reimagines his material in a bleak pagan world. In this, he not only looks back to the past, but also anticipates a future that is ours – a time when the old religious hierarchies and moral certainties have been stripped away.

But in a strange way an answer *is* to be found in Edgar's reply to Kent's line about the promised end. A question is answered with a question: 'Or image of that horror?' It's not *really* the end of the world; it's an *image* of the end. Hamlet said that the player holds up a mirror to nature, but in *King Lear* we are again and again reminded that what you see in a mirror is an image, not the thing itself. Gloucester doesn't really jump off the cliff: it's all an elaborate game, designed by Edgar to teach him a lesson. In uncertain times, we need images, games and experiments as ways of trying to make sense of our world. We need plays. That is why, four centuries on, we keep going back to Shakespeare and his dazzling mirror-world in which everyone is a player.

Looked at in one way, the world of *King Lear*, with its images of doom, its mad king, scheming ugly sisters, its fool and its (pretend) mad Bedlam beggar, could not be further from *ordinary life*. But looked at another way, it is an image of ordinary things, but seen in *extremity*. It is a play that has more time for a language of ordinary things – garden waterpots, wrens and toasted cheese – than for the 'glib and oily art' of courtly speech.

So is the whole play, like the 'Dover cliff' scene, an elaborate game designed by Shakespeare to teach us a lesson? Only if we think of it as a lesson in feeling, not in high-minded judgement. To be truly responsive to the play we must, as the final speech has it, 'Speak what we feel, not what we ought to say.' To be human is to *see feelingly*, not to fall back on easy moralizing, the 'ought to say' that characterizes people like Albany. And seeing feelingly is to do with our sympathetic response to the images that confront us, both on the stage and in the great theatre of the world. Lear becomes human when he stops caring about one kind of *image* (the glorious trappings of monarchy) and instead confronts another: the image of raw human being, of a fool and a Bedlam beggar, of poor naked wretches. Come the last trump, the play tells us, we will be judged by our fellow-feeling for the dispossessed, not our status in society. In this, as in so much else, Shakespeare speaks not only for his own age, but for ours.

LEAR Who is it that can tell me who I am?
FOOL Lear's shadow.

1. Robert Armin took over as company clown after Will Kempe left the Chamberlain's Men in 1599. A playwright as well as the author of joke-books, he practised a more intellectual form of comedy than Kempe, full of witty verbal pyrotechnics: his style was given full rein in such parts as Lear's Fool, Feste in *Twelfth Night* and the sour Lavatch in *All's Well that Ends Well*.

ABOUT THE TEXT

Shakespeare endures through history. He illuminates later times as well as his own. He helps us to understand the human condition. But he cannot do this without a good text of the plays. Without editions there would be no Shakespeare. That is why every twenty years or so throughout the last three centuries there has been a major new edition of his complete works. One aspect of editing is the process of keeping the texts up to date – modernizing the spelling, punctuation and typography (though not, of course, the actual words), providing explanatory notes in the light of changing educational practices (a generation ago, most of Shakespeare's classical and biblical allusions could be assumed to be generally understood, but now they can't).

But because Shakespeare did not personally oversee the publication of his plays, editors also have to make decisions about the relative authority of the early printed editions. Half of the sum of his plays only appeared posthumously, in the elaborately produced First Folio text of 1623, the original 'Complete Works' prepared for the press by Shakespeare's fellow-actors, the people who knew the plays better than anyone else. The other half had appeared in print in his lifetime, in the more compact and cheaper form of 'Quarto' editions, some of which reproduced good quality texts, others of which were to a greater or lesser degree garbled and error-strewn. In the case of a few plays there are hundreds of differences between the Quarto and Folio editions, some of them far from trivial.

Who is left in charge at the end of *King Lear?* According to the conventions of Elizabethan and Jacobean tragedy, the senior remaining character speaks the final speech. That is the mark of his assumption of power. Thus Fortinbras rules Denmark at the end of *Hamlet*, Lodovico speaks for Venice at the end of *Othello*, Malcolm rules Scotland at the end of *Macbeth*, and Octavius rules the world at the end of *Antony and Cleopatra*.

So who rules Britain? The answer used to be something like this. As the husband of the king's eldest daughter, Albany is the obvious candidate, but he seems reluctant to take on the role and, with astonishing stupidity given the chaos brought about by Lear's division of the kingdom at the beginning of the play, he proposes to divide the kingdom at the end of the play, suggesting that Kent and Edgar should share power between them. Kent, wise as ever, sees the foolishness of this and gracefully withdraws, presumably to commit suicide or will on the heart attack that he is already sensing. By implication, Edgar, who was the king's godson and is now Duke of Gloucester, is left in charge. So it is that in the Folio text, which is the most authoritative that we have, Edgar speaks the final speech:

> The weight of this sad time we must obey:
> Speak what we feel, not what we ought to say.
> The oldest hath borne most: we that are young
> Shall never see so much, nor live so long.

If we were being very scrupulous, we would have added that there is some uncertainty over the matter, since in the Quarto text it is Albany who speaks the final speech, an ascription that has been followed by many editors since Alexander Pope.

Thanks to the textual scholarship of the late twentieth century, the new answer is something like this. Ah: that's a question over which Shakespeare himself seems to have had some uncertainty. In his original version of the play Albany speaks the final speech and thus rules the realm. But then Shakespeare changed his mind. In his revised version of the play Edgar speaks the final speech and thus rules the realm. We must posit two very different stagings. In the first one, Kent's words of refusal of his half-share in the kingdom would have been accompanied by some gesture of refusal, such as a turning away, on Edgar's part. In the second one, Edgar's speaking of the final speech would have been staged so as to betoken acceptance of Albany's offer. This alteration to the ending marks the climax of Shakespeare's subtle but thoroughgoing revision of the roles of Albany and Edgar in his two versions of *King Lear*. We do not know exactly when the revision took place, but it is a fair assumption that it was as a result of experience in the playhouse and with the collaboration of the company. Presumably there was dissatisfaction on the part of dramatist and/or performers with the way in which the two roles had turned out, so various adjustments were made. Shakespeare's plays were not polished for publication; they were designed as scripts to be worked upon in the theatre. To be cut, added to, and altered.

Until recently, editors were remarkably reluctant to admit this. From the eighteenth century until the 1980s, editions attempted to recover an ideal unitary text, to get as close as they could to 'what Shakespeare wrote'. There was a curious resistance to the idea that Shakespeare wrote one thing, tested it in the theatre, and then wrote another. It was assumed that there was a single *King Lear* and that the editorial task was to reconstruct it. Generations of editors adopted a 'pick and mix' approach to the text, moving between Quarto and Folio readings, making choices on either aesthetic or bibliographic grounds, and creating a composite text that Shakespeare never actually wrote.

How, then, did editors deal with the following awkward fact? *King Lear* exists in two different texts, the Quarto and the Folio. The Quarto has nearly three hundred lines that are not in the Folio; the Folio has over a hundred lines that are not in the Quarto; there are more than eight hundred verbal variants in the parts of the play that the two texts share. The standard editorial response to this difficulty was the claim that the Quarto was some kind of 'Bad Quarto', that is to say a text based on memorial reconstruction by actors, not on Shakespeare's own script (his 'foul papers') or the playhouse script (the 'promptbook'). It was, however, a difficult position to maintain because the Quarto text of Lear, although corrupt in many places, does not have the usual characteristics of memorial reconstruction, the kind of features so apparent in the Bad Quarto of *Hamlet*, such as the actor remembering 'The first verse of the godly ballad / Will tell you all' where Shakespeare wrote 'the first row of the pious chanson will show you more' (*Hamlet*, Act 2 scene 2).

Getting the structure of a line just about right but the actual words nearly all wrong is typical of texts based on memory, but not typical of the textual anomalies in Quarto *Lear*.

In the 1970s the scholar Peter Blayney proved decisively by means of meticulous and highly technical bibliographic investigation that Quarto *King Lear* was not a bad text based on actors' memories but an authoritative one, almost certainly deriving from Shakespeare's own holograph (*The Texts of 'King Lear' and their Origins: vol. 1 Nicholas Okes and the First Quarto*, published 1982). The poor quality of the text was the result of the personnel in the printing shop being unused to setting drama. Thus the fact that much of Shakespeare's verse was set as prose was due to the printer running out of the blocks that were needed to fill in the margins where text was set as verse – Okes' shop didn't have the proper equipment, so the compositors resorted to prose.

Both Quarto and Folio texts are authentically Shakespearean, yet they differ substantially. Logic suggests that Quarto was his first version of the play, Folio his second. The textual variants give us a unique opportunity to see the plays as working scripts.

In the received editorial tradition, there is a very puzzling moment in Act 3 scene 1 where Kent reports to the Gentleman on the division between Albany and Cornwall (3.1.17–42 in many editions). The syntax halfway through the speech is incomprehensible and the content is contradictory: are there merely French spies in the households of great ones or has a French army actually landed in Dover? The confusion comes from editors having conflated alternative scenarios: in Quarto the French army has landed, whereas in Folio there are only spies reporting to France (thus lines 30–42 in conflated texts are Quarto only, 22–29 are Folio only: in the RSC text, compare and contrast 3.1.13–24 and Quarto Passages, 42–55).

The alteration seems to be part of a wider process of diminishing the French connection. In the Quarto we have a scene in which Shakespeare feels compelled to explain away the absence of the King of France – why isn't he leading his own army?

> KENT Why the King of France is so suddenly gone back, know you no reason?
>
> GENTLEMAN Something he left imperfect in the state, which since his coming forth is thought of, which imports to the kingdom so much fear and danger that his personal return was most required and necessary. (Quarto Passages, 160–3)

It is, to say the least, a halting explanation, which is perhaps one reason why Shakespeare cut the whole of this scene, Act 4 scene 3 in the received editorial tradition, from the Folio text. Theatre audiences tend to think most about the things that are mentioned: by drawing attention to the king's absence, the dramatist in a curious way establishes his presence. Better just to keep quiet about him, which is what happens in Folio – since he's not mentioned, the audience forgets him.

Who, then, is to lead the French army? In Quarto, the Gentleman informs Kent that the Marshall of France, Monsieur La Far, has been left in charge. By omitting the scene in question, Folio obliterates Monsieur La Far; it compensates by altering the staging of the next scene (Act 4 scene 4 in the received editorial tradition, Act 4 scene 3 in ours). In Quarto, the scene begins '*Enter Cordelia, Doctor and others*', whereas in Folio it begins '*Enter with Drum and Colours Cordelia, Gentleman and Soldiers*'. Where in Quarto Cordelia is a daughter seeking medical attention for her father, in Folio she is a general leading an army. She has replaced Monsieur La Far. This alteration is part of a broad shift of emphasis from family to state in the revision – Folio makes less of the familial love-trial and more of the fractured internal politics of the divided kingdom. So it is that the later version adds some crucial lines in the opening scene, giving a stronger political justification for the division of the kingdom:

> We have this hour a constant will to publish
> Our daughters' several dowers, that future strife
> May be prevented now. ... (1.1.44–6)

Furthermore, Folio cuts the so-called arraignment of Goneril, the mock-trial in the hovel scene that is the *quid pro quo* for the show-trial of love in the opening scene. This has the effect of retrospectively rendering the opening more political and less personal.

Other Folio cuts include the passage at the end of the blinding scene when loyal servants promise to apply flax and whites of egg to Gloucester's bleeding eye-sockets. When Peter Brook cut this from his famous 1962 RSC production, critics rebuked him for imposing on the play his own theatre of cruelty. But now we know that Brook's cut was made in Shakespeare's own theatre.

A further intensification of the play's moral bleakness is brought about by a series of cuts to Albany's role: his castigations of Goneril in Act 4 scene 2 are severely trimmed back, considerably reducing his moral force. Quarto Albany is a well-developed character who closes the play as a mature and victorious duke assuming responsibility for the kingdom. In Folio he is weaker, he stands by as his wife walks all over both him and the moral order, he avoids responsibility. His ultimate vacation of power is such that the revision ends at the point where my discussion began: with Edgar having no choice but to take over as sustainer of the gored state.

If you look at printers' handbooks from the age of Shakespeare, you quickly discover that one of the first rules was that, whenever possible, compositors were recommended to set their type from existing printed books rather than manuscripts. This was the age before mechanical typesetting, where each individual letter had to be picked out by hand from the compositor's case and placed on a stick (upside down and back to front) before being laid on the press. It was an age of murky rush-light and of manuscripts written in a secretary hand which had dozens of different, hard-to-decipher forms. Printers' lives were a lot easier when they were reprinting existing books rather than struggling with handwritten copy. Easily the quickest way to have created the First Folio would have been simply to reprint those eighteen plays that had already appeared in Quarto and only work from manuscript on the other eighteen.

But that is not what happened. Whenever Quartos were used, playhouse 'promptbooks' were also consulted and stage directions copied in from them. And in the case of several major plays where a reasonably well-printed Quarto was available, *Lear* notable among them, the Folio printers were instructed to work from an alternative, playhouse-derived manuscript. This meant that the whole process of producing the first complete Shakespeare took months, even years, longer than it might have done. But for the men overseeing the project, John Hemings and Henry Condell, friends and fellow-actors who had been remembered in Shakespeare's will, the additional labour and cost were worth the effort for the sake of producing an edition that was close to the practice of the theatre. They wanted all the plays in print so that people could, as they wrote in their prefatory address to the reader, 'read him and again and again', but they also wanted 'the great variety of readers' to work from texts that were close to the theatre-life for which Shakespeare originally intended them. For this reason, the *RSC Shakespeare*, in both *Complete Works* and individual volumes, uses the Folio as base text wherever possible. Significant Quarto variants are, however, noted in the Textual Notes and Quarto-only passages are appended after the text of *King Lear*.

The following notes highlight various aspects of the editorial process and indicate conventions used in the text of this edition:

Lists of Parts are supplied in the First Folio for only six plays, not including *Lear*, so the list at the beginning of the play is provided by the editors, arranged by groups of character. Capitals indicate that part of the name which is used for speech headings in the script (thus 'LEAR, King of Britain').

Locations are provided by the Folio for only two plays. Eighteenth-century editors, working in an age of elaborately realistic stage sets, were the first to provide detailed locations. Given that Shakespeare wrote for a bare stage and often an imprecise sense of place, we have relegated locations to the explanatory notes at the foot of the page, where they are given at the beginning of each scene where the imaginary location is different from the one before. We have emphasized broad geographical settings rather than specifics of the kind that suggest anachronistically realistic staging. We have therefore avoided such niceties as 'another room in the palace'.

Act and Scene Divisions were provided in the Folio in a much more thoroughgoing way than in the Quartos. Sometimes, however, they were erroneous or omitted; corrections and additions supplied by editorial tradition are indicated by square brackets. Five-act division is based on a classical model, and act breaks provided the opportunity to replace the candles in the indoor Blackfriars playhouse which the King's Men used after 1608, but Shakespeare did not necessarily think in terms of a five-part structure of dramatic composition. The Folio convention is that a scene ends when the stage is empty. Nowadays, partly under the influence of film, we tend to consider a scene to be a dramatic unit that ends with either a change of imaginary location or a significant passage of time within the narrative. Shakespeare's fluidity of composition accords well with this convention, so in addition to act and scene numbers we provide a *running scene* count in the right margin at the beginning of each new scene, in the typeface used for editorial directions. Where there is a scene break caused by a momentary bare stage, but the location does not change and extra time does not pass, we use the convention *running scene continues*. There is inevitably a degree of editorial judgement in making such calls, but the system is very valuable in suggesting the pace of the plays.

Speakers' Names are often inconsistent in Folio. We have regularized speech headings, but retained an element of deliberate inconsistency in entry directions, in order to give the flavour of Folio.

Verse is indicated by lines that do not run to the right margin and by capitalization of each line. The Folio printers sometimes set verse as prose, and vice versa (either out of misunderstanding or for reasons of space). We have silently corrected in such cases, although in some instances there is ambiguity, in which case we have leaned towards the preservation of Folio layout. Folio sometimes uses contraction ('turnd' rather than 'turned') to indicate whether or not the final '-ed' of a past participle is sounded, an area where there is variation for the sake of the five-beat iambic pentameter rhythm. We use the convention of a grave accent to indicate sounding (thus 'turnèd' would be two syllables), but would urge actors not to overstress. In cases where one speaker ends with a verse half-line and the next begins with the other half of the pentameter, editors since the late eighteenth century have indented the second line. We have abandoned this convention, since the Folio does not use it, and nor did actors' cues in the Shakespearean theatre. An exception is made when the second speaker actively interrupts or completes the first speaker's sentence.

Spelling is modernized, but older forms are occasionally maintained where necessary for rhythm or aural effect.

Punctuation in Shakespeare's time was as much rhetorical as grammatical. 'Colon' was originally a term for a unit of thought in an argument. The semi-colon was a new unit of punctuation (some of the Quartos lack them altogether). We have modernized punctuation throughout, but have given more weight to Folio punctuation than many editors, since, though not Shakespearean, it reflects the usage of his period. In particular, we have used the colon far more than many editors: it is exceptionally useful as a way of indicating how many Shakespearean speeches unfold clause by clause in a developing argument that gives the illusion of enacting the process of thinking in the moment. We have also kept in mind the origin of punctuation in classical times as a way of assisting the actor and orator: the comma suggests the briefest of pauses for breath, the colon a middling one and a full stop or period a longer pause. Semi-colons, by contrast, belong to an era of punctuation that was only just coming in during Shakespeare's time and that is coming to an end now: we have accordingly only used them where they occur in our copy-texts (and not always then). Dashes are sometimes used for parenthetical interjections where the Folio has brackets. They are also used for interruptions and changes in train of thought. Where a change of addressee occurs within a speech, we have used a dash preceded by a full stop (or occasionally another form of punctuation). Often the identity of the respective addressees is obvious from the context. When it is not, this has been indicated in a marginal stage direction.

Entrances and Exits are fairly thorough in Folio, which has accordingly been followed as faithfully as possible. Where characters are omitted or corrections are necessary, this is indicated by square brackets (e.g. '[*and Attendants*]'). *Exit* is sometimes silently normalized to *Exeunt* and *Manet* anglicized to 'remains'. We trust Folio positioning of entrances and exits to a greater degree than most editors.

Editorial Stage Directions such as stage business, asides, indications of addressee and of characters' position on the gallery stage are only used sparingly in Folio. Other editions mingle directions of this kind with original Folio and Quarto directions, sometimes marking them by means of square brackets. We have sought to distinguish what could be described as *directorial* interventions of this kind from Folio-style directions (either original or supplied) by placing them in the right margin in a different typeface. There is a degree of subjectivity about which directions are of which kind, but the procedure is intended as a reminder to the reader and the actor that Shakespearean stage directions are often dependent upon editorial inference alone and are not set in stone. We also depart from editorial tradition in sometimes admitting uncertainty and thus printing permissive stage-directions, such as an *Aside?* (often a line may be equally effective as an aside or a direct address – it is for each production or reading to make its own decision) or a *may exit* or a piece of business placed between arrows to indicate that it may occur at various different moments within a scene.

Line Numbers in the left margin are editorial, for reference and to key the explanatory and textual notes.

Explanatory Notes at the foot of each page explain allusions and gloss obsolete and difficult words, confusing phraseology, occasional major textual cruces, and so on. Particular attention is given to non-standard usage, bawdy innuendo and technical terms (e.g. legal and military language). Where more than one sense is given, commas indicate shades of related meaning, slashes alternative or double meanings.

Textual Notes at the end of the play indicate major departures from the Folio. They take the following form: the reading of our text is given in bold and its source given after an equals sign, with 'Q'

indicating one that derives from the principal Quarto, 'F2' one that
derives from the Second Folio of 1632 and 'Ed' one that derives from
the editorial tradition. The rejected Folio ('F') reading is then given.
A selection of Quarto variants and plausible unadopted editorial
readings are also included. Thus, for example, at Act 1 scene 1 line
299 'plighted = F. Q = pleated'. This indicates that we have retained
the Folio reading 'plighted' and that 'pleated' is an interestingly
different reading in the Quarto.

KEY FACTS

MAJOR PARTS: (*with percentage of lines/number of speeches/scenes on stage*) Lear (22%/188/10), Edgar (11%/98/10), Earl of Kent (11%/127/12), Earl of Gloucester (10%/118/12), Edmund (9%/79/9), Fool (7%/58/6), Goneril (6%/53/8), Regan (5%/73/8), Duke of Albany (5%/58/5), Cordelia (3%/31/4), Duke of Cornwall (3%/63/5), Oswald (2%/38/7).

LINGUISTIC MEDIUM: 75% verse, 25% prose.

DATE: 1605–06. Performed at court December 1606; draws on old *Leir* play (published 1605); seems to refer to eclipses of September and October 1605; borrows from books by Samuel Harsnett and John Florio that were published in 1603.

SOURCES: Based on *The True Chronicle Historie of King Leir and his Three Daughters*, an old play of unknown authorship that was in the London theatrical repertoire in the early 1590s, but makes many changes, including alteration of providential Christian to pagan language and the introduction of a tragic ending. The Lear story also appeared in other sources familiar to Shakespeare: *The Mirrour for Magistrates* (edition of 1574), Holinshed's *Chronicles* (1587), and book 2 canto 10 of Edmund Spenser's epic poem *The Faerie Queene* (1590). In all versions of the story before Shakespeare's, there is a 'romance' ending whereby the old king is restored to his daughter Cordelia and to the throne. The Gloucester sub-plot is derived from the story of the Paphlagonian king in book 2 chapter 10 of *The Countess of Pembroke's Arcadia* by Sir Philip Sidney (1590): a blind old man is led to the top of a cliff from where he contemplates suicide because he has been deceived by his bastard son; the good son returns and encounters the bad one in a chivalric duel. The story was intended to exemplify both 'true natural goodness' and 'wretched ungratefulness'; a few chapters later (2.15), Sidney tells of a different credulous king who is tricked into mistrusting his virtuous son. The characters of 'Poor Tom' and the Fool are entirely Shakespearean creations, though some of the language of demonic possession feigned by Edgar is borrowed from Samuel Harsnett's *Declaration of Egregious Popish Impostures* (1603), a work of propaganda about Catholic plots and faked exorcisms which Shakespeare probably read because of the Stratford origins of one of the exorcizing priests, Robert Debdale. The language of the play and some of its philosophical ideas reveal that Shakespeare had also been reading *The Essayes of Montaigne* in John Florio's English translation (1603).

TEXT: Published in Quarto in 1608 under the title *M. William Shakspeare: HIS True Chronicle Historie of the life and death of King LEAR and his three Daughters. With the vnfortunate life of Edgar, sonne and heire to the Earle of Gloster, and his sullen and assumed humor of TOM of Bedlam: As it was played before the Kings Maiestie at Whitehall vpon S. Stephans night in Christmas Hollidayes. By his Maiesties seruants playing vsually at the Gloabe on the Bancke-side.* This text was very poorly printed, partly because its printer (Nicholas Okes) was unaccustomed to setting plays and also because it seems to derive from Shakespeare's own working manuscript, which would have been difficult to read. Quarto includes about 300 lines that are not in the 1623 Folio text, which was entitled 'The Tragedy of King Lear' and has clear signs of derivation from the theatrical playbook (though, to complicate matters, the Folio printing was also influenced by a reprint of the Quarto that appeared in 1619 as one of the ten plays published by Thomas Pavier in an attempt to produce a collected Shakespeare). The Folio in turn has about 100 lines that are not in the Quarto, and nearly 1000 lines have variations of word or phrase. The two early texts thus represent two different stages in the life of the play, with extensive revision having been carried out, either systematically or incrementally. Revisions include diminution of the prominence given to the invading French army (perhaps for political reasons), clarification of Lear's motives for dividing his kingdom, and weakening of the role of Albany (including reassignment from him to Edgar of the play's closing speech, and thus by implication – since it was a convention of Shakespearean tragedy that the new man in power always has the last word – of the right to rule Britain). Among the more striking cuts are the mock trial of Goneril in the hovel and the moment of compassion when loyal servants apply a palliative to Gloucester's bleeding eyes. For centuries, editors have conflated the Quarto and Folio texts, creating a play that Shakespeare never wrote. We endorse the body of scholarship since the 1980s and the new editorial tradition in which Folio and Quarto are regarded as discrete entities. We have edited the more theatrical Folio text, but have corrected its errors (which are plentiful, since much of it was set in type by 'Compositor E', the apprentice who was by far the worst printer in Isaac Jaggard's shop). The influence of Quarto copy on the Folio is of great assistance in making these corrections. Textual notes are perforce more numerous than for any other work by Shakespeare; several hundred Quarto variants are listed. All the most significant Quarto-only passages are printed at the end of the play.

THE TRAGEDY OF KING LEAR

LEAR, King of Britain

GONERIL, Lear's eldest daughter

REGAN, Lear's middle daughter

CORDELIA, Lear's youngest daughter

Duke of ALBANY, Goneril's husband

Duke of CORNWALL, Regan's husband

King of FRANCE, suitor and later husband to Cordelia

Duke of BURGUNDY, suitor to Cordelia

Earl of KENT, later disguised as Caius

Earl of GLOUCESTER

EDGAR, Gloucester's son, later disguised as Poor Tom

EDMUND, Gloucester's illegitimate son

OLD MAN, Gloucester's tenant

CURAN, Gloucester's retainer

Lear's FOOL

OSWALD, Goneril's steward

GENTLEMAN, a Knight serving Lear

GENTLEMAN, attendant on Cordelia

SERVANT of Cornwall

HERALD

CAPTAIN

Knights attendant upon Lear, other Attendants, Messengers, Soldiers, Servants and Trumpeters

Act 1 Scene 1

Enter Kent, Gloucester and Edmund

KENT I thought the king had more affected the Duke of
Albany than Cornwall.

GLOUCESTER It did always seem so to us: but now in the
division of the kingdom it appears not which of the
5   dukes he values most, for qualities are so weighed
that curiosity in neither can make choice of either's
moiety.

KENT Is not this your son, my lord?

GLOUCESTER His breeding, sir, hath been at my charge. I
10   have so often blushed to acknowledge him that now I
am brazed to't.

KENT I cannot conceive you.

GLOUCESTER Sir, this young fellow's mother could;
whereupon she grew round-wombed and had
15   indeed, sir, a son for her cradle ere she had a
husband for her bed. Do you smell a fault?

KENT I cannot wish the fault undone, the issue of it being
so proper.

GLOUCESTER But I have a son, sir, by order of law, some
20   year elder than this, who yet is no dearer in my
account, though this knave came something saucily
to the world before he was sent for: yet was his
mother fair, there was good sport at his making and
the whoreson must be acknowledged.— Do you
25   know this noble gentleman, Edmund?

EDMUND No, my lord.

GLOUCESTER My lord of Kent: remember him hereafter
as my honourable friend.

EDMUND My services to your lordship.

30   **KENT** I must love you, and sue to know you better.

EDMUND Sir, I shall study deserving.

1.1 *Location: the royal court, Britain* **1 affected** favoured **5 qualities** . . . **moiety** their qualities are so
evenly balanced that the most careful scrutiny cannot distinguish between either man's share **9 breeding**
upbringing (plays on the sense of 'conception') **charge** cost (plays on the sense of 'accusation, blame')
11 brazed made brazen, hardened **12 conceive** understand (Gloucester then plays on sense of 'become
pregnant') **15 ere** before **16 fault** transgression/loss of scent during a hunt/vagina **17 undone** plays on
the sense of 'not copulated with' **issue** outcome/child **18 proper** handsome/worthy/rightful **19 by** . . .
law legitimate **some year** about a year **20 dearer** more beloved (plays on the sense of 'more
expensive') **21 account** estimation (plays on the financial sense) **24 whoreson** i.e. bastard (here used
affectionately) **30 sue** entreat, seek **31 deserving** to be worthy of (your esteem)

GLOUCESTER He hath been out nine years, and away he
    shall again. The king is coming.
Sennet. Enter [one bearing a coronet, then] King Lear,
Cornwall, Albany, Goneril, Regan, Cordelia and Attendants
LEAR Attend the lords of France and Burgundy,
35   Gloucester.
GLOUCESTER I shall, my lord.   *Exit*
LEAR Meantime we shall express our darker purpose.
    Give me the map there.   **Kent or an Attendant gives Lear a map**
                      Know that we have divided
    In three our kingdom, and 'tis our fast intent
40   To shake all cares and business from our age,
    Conferring them on younger strengths while we
    Unburdened crawl toward death. Our son of
        Cornwall,
    And you our no less loving son of Albany,
    We have this hour a constant will to publish
45   Our daughters' several dowers, that future strife
    May be prevented now. The princes, France and
        Burgundy,
    Great rivals in our youngest daughter's love,
    Long in our court have made their amorous sojourn
    And here are to be answered. Tell me, my
        daughters —
50   Since now we will divest us both of rule,
    Interest of territory, cares of state —
    Which of you shall we say doth love us most,
    That we our largest bounty may extend
    Where nature doth with merit challenge? Goneril,
55   Our eldest born, speak first.
GONERIL Sir, I love you more than word can wield the
    matter,
    Dearer than eyesight, space and liberty,
    Beyond what can be valued rich or rare,
    No less than life, with grace, health, beauty, honour:
60   As much as child e'er loved or father found:

32 out away (perhaps abroad or in the house of another nobleman; it was common for a nobleman's son to
be educated in the house of another important family)   ***Sennet*** trumpet call signalling a procession   ***bearing***
a coronet carring a small crown denoting inferior rank/wearing a wreath or garland about the head (must be
of material that can be broken in half)   **34 Attend** wait on, look after   **37 darker** secret (with sinister
connotations)   **39 fast intent** firm intention   **40 business** official duties/exertion/anxiety   **42 son** i.e. son-
in-law (like Albany)   **44 constant will** unshakeable intention   **publish** proclaim, make public
45 several dowers individual dowries   **that** so that   **48 sojourn** stay   **51 Interest** possession
53 bounty generosity/gift   **54 nature…challenge** natural affection, combined with merit, makes a claim
56 wield express   **59 grace** virtue

A love that makes breath poor and speech unable:
Beyond all manner of so much I love you.
CORDELIA What shall Cordelia speak? Love and be silent.　*Aside*
LEAR Of all these bounds, even from this line to this,　*Points to the map*
65　With shadowy forests and with champaigns riched,
With plenteous rivers and wide-skirted meads,
We make thee lady. To thine and Albany's issues
Be this perpetual.— What says our second daughter?
Our dearest Regan, wife of Cornwall?
70　**REGAN** I am made of that self-mettle as my sister,
And prize me at her worth. In my true heart,
I find she names my very deed of love:
Only she comes too short, that I profess
Myself an enemy to all other joys
75　Which the most precious square of sense professes,
And find I am alone felicitate
In your dear highness' love.
CORDELIA Then poor Cordelia:　*Aside*
And yet not so, since I am sure my love's
80　More ponderous than my tongue.
LEAR To thee and thine hereditary ever
Remain this ample third of our fair kingdom,
No less in space, validity and pleasure
Than that conferred on Goneril.— Now, our joy,　*To Cordelia*
85　Although our last and least, to whose young love
The vines of France and milk of Burgundy
Strive to be interested, what can you say to draw
A third more opulent than your sisters'? Speak.
CORDELIA Nothing, my lord.
90　**LEAR** Nothing?
CORDELIA Nothing.
LEAR Nothing will come of nothing: speak again.
CORDELIA Unhappy that I am, I cannot heave
My heart into my mouth: I love your majesty
95　According to my bond, no more nor less.

---

61 makes breath poor makes words insufficient/renders one breathless (in the attempt to express it)
unable inadequate　**62 all…much** i.e. all possible expressions of the amount of love　**64 bounds**
territories　**65 shadowy** shady　**champaigns riched** rich open countryside　**66 wide-skirted meads**
extensive meadows　**70 self-mettle** same temperament/same substance ('metal')　**71 prize…worth**
value myself in equal terms　**72 deed** action, performance/bond, legal document　**73 that** in that
75 square of sense guiding principle governing the senses/(physical or mental) region of the senses
76 alone felicitate only happy　**80 ponderous** weighty　**81 hereditary** by inheritance　**83 validity**
value　**86 vines…Burgundy** Lear characterizes France and Burgundy by their assets: vineyards and cattle
pastures　**87 interested** admitted, given a share　**draw** attract/receive, collect/pull forth (as one 'draws
lots')　**95 bond** duty (with connotations both of a binding legal agreement and of restrictive shackles)

LEAR How, how, Cordelia? Mend your speech a little,
    Lest you may mar your fortunes.
CORDELIA Good my lord,
    You have begot me, bred me, loved me:
100   I return those duties back as are right fit,
    Obey you, love you and most honour you.
    Why have my sisters husbands if they say
    They love you all? Happily when I shall wed,
    That lord whose hand must take my plight shall
        carry
105   Half my love with him, half my care and duty:
    Sure I shall never marry like my sisters.
LEAR But goes thy heart with this?
CORDELIA Ay, my good lord.
LEAR So young and so untender?
110 CORDELIA So young, my lord, and true.
LEAR Let it be so: thy truth then be thy dower,
    For by the sacred radiance of the sun,
    The mysteries of Hecate and the night,
    By all the operation of the orbs
115   From whom we do exist and cease to be,
    Here I disclaim all my paternal care,
    Propinquity and property of blood,
    And as a stranger to my heart and me
    Hold thee from this for ever. The barbarous Scythian,
120   Or he that makes his generation messes
    To gorge his appetite, shall to my bosom
    Be as well neighboured, pitied and relieved
    As thou my sometime daughter.
KENT Good my liege—
125 LEAR Peace, Kent:
    Come not between the dragon and his wrath.
    I loved her most, and thought to set my rest
    On her kind nursery.— Hence, and avoid my sight!—   *To Cordelia*

---

96 **Mend** improve 97 **mar** spoil 99 **begot** conceived, fathered **bred** raised, brought up
104 **plight** pledge, promise 109 **untender** hard/cruel (plays on the sense of 'not young') 113 **Hecate** Greek goddess of witchcraft and the moon 114 **operation** movement and astrological influence **orbs** planets 117 **Propinquity...blood** close ties of kinship 119 **this** this time (or Lear gestures towards himself) **Scythian** person from Scythia, an ancient region extending over much of eastern Europe and Asiatic Russia, notorious for its **barbarous** inhabitants 120 **generation** children/own people **messes** small groups of people who eat together/portions of food, meals/disgusting concoctions/troubled, confused conditions 122 **neighboured** treated with hospitable kindness 123 **sometime** former 124 **liege** lord, one to whom feudal duty and service was owed 127 **set my rest** stake everything (card-playing term)/ repose, be at ease 128 **kind** affectionate (in the manner of a family member) **nursery** care **avoid** leave

So be my grave my peace, as here I give
130   Her father's heart from her. Call France. Who stirs?
Call Burgundy.— Cornwall and Albany,
                                    [*Exit Attendant*]
With my two daughters' dowers digest the third.
Let pride, which she calls plainness, marry her.
I do invest you jointly with my power,
135   Pre-eminence, and all the large effects
That troop with majesty. Ourself by monthly course,
With reservation of an hundred knights
By you to be sustained, shall our abode
Make with you by due turn: only we shall retain
140   The name and all th'addition to a king: the sway,
Revenue, execution of the rest,
Belovèd sons, be yours, which to confirm,
This coronet part between you.   *Gives them coronet to break in half*
KENT Royal Lear,
145   Whom I have ever honoured as my king,
Loved as my father, as my master followed,
As my great patron thought on in my prayers—
LEAR The bow is bent and drawn, make from the shaft.
KENT Let it fall rather, though the fork invade
150   The region of my heart: be Kent unmannerly
When Lear is mad. What wouldst thou do, old man?
Think'st thou that duty shall have dread to speak
When power to flattery bows? To plainness honour's
      bound
When majesty falls to folly. Reserve thy state,
155   And in thy best consideration check
This hideous rashness. Answer my life my
      judgement:
Thy youngest daughter does not love thee least,
Nor are those empty-hearted whose low sounds
Reverb no hollowness.
160   **LEAR** Kent, on thy life, no more.

---

130 Who stirs? Get on with it!/Why don't you move?   **132 digest** absorb, incorporate   **133 plainness** frankness, plain speaking   **marry her** be her dowry/get her a husband   **135 large effects** extensive trappings   **136 troop with** accompany   **137 With reservation of** reserving the right to have (legal language)   **138 sustained** maintained, supported   **140 th'addition to** the title and honours of   **sway** authority, rule   **148 make...shaft** avoid the arrow (of my anger)   **149 fork** barbed arrow-head   **151 thou** kings are almost always addressed, respectfully, as 'you'; Kent is **unmannerly** in his use of the familiar 'thou'   **154 Reserve thy state** retain your sovereignty   **155 In...consideration** with wise and careful reflection   **156 Answer...judgement** I'll stake my life on my opinion   **159 Reverb no hollowness** do not reverberate hollowly (i.e. emptily/insincerely)

KENT My life I never held but as pawn
    To wage against thine enemies, ne'er fear to lose it,
    Thy safety being motive.
LEAR Out of my sight!
165 KENT See better, Lear, and let me still remain
    The true blank of thine eye.
LEAR Now, by Apollo—
KENT Now, by Apollo, king,
    Thou swear'st thy gods in vain.
170 LEAR O, vassal! Miscreant!   *Puts his hand on his sword or attacks Kent*
ALBANY and CORDELIA Dear sir, forbear.
KENT Kill thy physician, and thy fee bestow
    Upon the foul disease. Revoke thy gift,
    Or whilst I can vent clamour from my throat,
175   I'll tell thee thou dost evil.
LEAR Hear me, recreant, on thine allegiance hear me!
    That thou hast sought to make us break our vows,
    Which we durst never yet, and with strained pride
    To come betwixt our sentences and our power,
180   Which nor our nature nor our place can bear,
    Our potency made good, take thy reward:
    Five days we do allot thee for provision
    To shield thee from disasters of the world,
    And on the sixth to turn thy hated back
185   Upon our kingdom: if on the next day following
    Thy banished trunk be found in our dominions,
    The moment is thy death. Away! By Jupiter,
    This shall not be revoked.
KENT Fare thee well, king: sith thus thou wilt appear,
190   Freedom lives hence and banishment is here.—
    The gods to their dear shelter take thee, maid,   *To Cordelia*
    That justly think'st, and hast most rightly said.—
    And your large speeches may your deeds approve,   *To Goneril*
    That good effects may spring from words of love.   *and Regan*

---

161 **held** regarded, valued   **pawn** a pledge, surety   162 **wage** deposit as security   166 **blank** centre of a target/line of sight (Kent asks to be the means to help Lear see better)   167 **Apollo** Greek and Roman sun god   170 **vassal** servant/wretch   **Miscreant** villain (literally, 'infidel, unbeliever')   171 **forbear** stop, desist   172 **Kill...disease** i.e. Lear has got things the wrong way round   173 **foul disease** loathsome, festering disease/syphilis   176 **recreant** traitor   177 **That** in that, since   178 **durst** dared   **strained** excessive/unnatural   179 **sentences** pronouncements, decisions   180 **nor...nor** neither...nor   **place** status, rank   181 **potency** power   **made good** being carried into effect/shown to be valid/secured, defended   183 **disasters** misfortunes   186 **trunk** body   187 **Jupiter** supreme Roman god   189 **sith** since   193 **your...approve** may your actions prove the truth of your grand statements

195   Thus Kent, O princes, bids you all adieu.
       He'll shape his old course in a country new.   *Exit*
       Flourish. Enter Gloucester with France and Burgundy,
       Attendants
       CORDELIA Here's France and Burgundy, my noble lord.
       LEAR My lord of Burgundy,
       We first address toward you, who with this king
200   Hath rivalled for our daughter: what in the least
       Will you require in present dower with her,
       Or cease your quest of love?
       BURGUNDY Most royal majesty,
       I crave no more than hath your highness offered,
205   Nor will you tender less.
       LEAR Right noble Burgundy,
       When she was dear to us, we did hold her so,
       But now her price is fallen. Sir, there she stands:
       If aught within that little seeming substance,
210   Or all of it, with our displeasure pieced,
       And nothing more, may fitly like your grace,
       She's there, and she is yours.
       BURGUNDY I know no answer.
       LEAR Will you, with those infirmities she owes,
215   Unfriended, new-adopted to our hate,
       Dowered with our curse and strangered with our
          oath,
       Take her or leave her?
       BURGUNDY Pardon me, royal sir:
       Election makes not up in such conditions.
220   **LEAR** Then leave her, sir, for by the power that made me,
       I tell you all her wealth.— For you, great king,   *To France*
       I would not from your love make such a stray
       To match you where I hate, therefore beseech you
       T'avert your liking a more worthier way
225   Than on a wretch whom nature is ashamed
       Almost t'acknowledge hers.

---

196 **shape . . . course** behave in his usual manner   196 *Flourish* trumpet fanfare signalling the arrival of an important person   200 **rivalled** competed   **in the least** at the lowest   201 **present dower** immediately available dowry   205 **tender** offer   207 **hold her so** consider her to be **dear** (i.e. beloved/ worth a great deal)   209 **aught** anything   **little seeming substance** insignificant (or physically small) thing/one who totally refuses to play a part   210 **pieced** augmented, increased   211 **fitly like** justly please   214 **infirmities** deficiencies   **owes** owns   216 **Dowered with** given as a dowry   **strangered** made a stranger, disowned   219 **Election . . . up** choice is impossible   221 **tell you** inform you of/ enumerate   222 **from . . . stray** stray so far from your love as

FRANCE This is most strange,
    That she whom even but now was your object,
    The argument of your praise, balm of your age,
230   The best, the dearest, should in this trice of time
    Commit a thing so monstrous to dismantle
    So many folds of favour. Sure her offence
    Must be of such unnatural degree
    That monsters it, or your fore-vouched affection
235   Fall into taint, which to believe of her
    Must be a faith that reason without miracle
    Should never plant in me.
CORDELIA I yet beseech your majesty —
    If for I want that glib and oily art
240   To speak and purpose not, since what I will intend
    I'll do't before I speak — that you make known
    It is no vicious blot, murder, or foulness,
    No unchaste action or dishonoured step
    That hath deprived me of your grace and favour,
245   But even for want of that for which I am richer:
    A still-soliciting eye and such a tongue
    That I am glad I have not, though not to have it
    Hath lost me in your liking.
LEAR Better thou hadst
250   Not been born than not t'have pleased me better.
FRANCE Is it but this? A tardiness in nature,
    Which often leaves the history unspoke
    That it intends to do? My lord of Burgundy,
    What say you to the lady? Love's not love
255   When it is mingled with regards that stands
    Aloof from th'entire point. Will you have her?
    She is herself a dowry.
BURGUNDY Royal king,   *To Lear*
    Give but that portion which yourself proposed,
260   And here I take Cordelia by the hand,
    Duchess of Burgundy.
LEAR Nothing: I have sworn: I am firm.

---

228 your object your focus, the object of your sight (the apple of your eye)   **229 argument** theme   **balm** soothing ointment   **230 trice** mere moment   **231 monstrous** unnatural   **dismantle** strip off (the folds of the metaphorical cloth of favour)   **234 monsters it** it becomes monstrous   **fore-vouched** previously sworn   **235 Fall into taint** (must) come under suspicion   **which ... me** i.e. and to believe in all reason that she had committed such a monstrous offence would require a miracle   **239 for** (your anger is) because want lack   **240 purpose not** not intend to do what I say   **242 foulness** wickedness/moral impurity   **245 for which** i.e. for lack of which   **246 still-soliciting** constantly entreating, self-seeking   **251 tardiness in nature** natural slowness   **252 history** account (of an action)   **255 regards ... point** irrelevant concerns

BURGUNDY I am sorry, then, you have so lost a father   *To Cordelia*
That you must lose a husband.
265 CORDELIA Peace be with Burgundy.
Since that respect and fortunes are his love,
I shall not be his wife.
FRANCE Fairest Cordelia, that art most rich being poor,
Most choice forsaken, and most loved despised,
270 Thee and thy virtues here I seize upon:
Be it lawful, I take up what's cast away.   *Takes her hand*
Gods, gods! 'Tis strange that from their cold'st neglect
My love should kindle to inflamed respect.—
Thy dowerless daughter, king, thrown to my chance,
275 Is queen of us, of ours and our fair France:
Not all the dukes of wat'rish Burgundy
Can buy this unprized precious maid of me.—
Bid them farewell, Cordelia, though unkind.
Thou losest here, a better where to find.
280 LEAR Thou hast her, France: let her be thine, for we
Have no such daughter, nor shall ever see
That face of hers again. Therefore be gone
Without our grace, our love, our benison.
Come, noble Burgundy.
               Flourish. Exeunt. [France and the sisters remain]
285 FRANCE Bid farewell to your sisters.
CORDELIA The jewels of our father, with washèd eyes
Cordelia leaves you. I know you what you are,
And like a sister am most loath to call
Your faults as they are named. Love well our father:
290 To your professèd bosoms I commit him,
But yet, alas, stood I within his grace,
I would prefer him to a better place.
So farewell to you both.
REGAN Prescribe not us our duty.
295 GONERIL Let your study
Be to content your lord who hath received you

---

266 **respect and fortunes** status and wealth   269 **Most choice forsaken** most desirable when
rejected   270 **seize upon** take possession of (legal term)   271 **be it lawful** provided it is lawful   272 **their**
may refer to either the gods or to Lear and Burgundy   273 **inflamed** glowing, ardent   274 **thrown…
chance** cast to my luck (gambling metaphor)   276 **wat'rish** well-watered (with rivers)/wet, feeble
277 **unprized** unvalued (may play on a sense of 'priceless')   278 **though unkind** though they are cruel (or
'lacking in natural familial affection')   279 **where** somewhere, place   283 **grace** favour (with
connotations of 'divinely sanctioned mercy')   **benison** blessing   286 **washèd** i.e. wet with tears
289 **as…named** by their true names   290 **your professèd bosoms** i.e. the love you claim to have for
him   **commit** entrust; perhaps with connotations of 'confine (to prison)'   292 **prefer** advance, promote
295 **study** concern, endeavour

At fortune's alms. You have obedience scanted,
And well are worth the want that you have wanted.

CORDELIA Time shall unfold what plighted cunning
hides:

300 Who covers faults, at last with shame derides.
Well may you prosper.

FRANCE Come, my fair Cordelia. *Exit France and Cordelia*

GONERIL Sister, it is not little I have to say of what most
nearly appertains to us both.

305 I think our father will hence tonight.

REGAN That's most certain, and with you: next month
with us.

GONERIL You see how full of changes his age is: the
observation we have made of it hath not been little.

310 He always loved our sister most, and with what poor
judgement he hath now cast her off appears too
grossly.

REGAN 'Tis the infirmity of his age: yet he hath ever but
slenderly known himself.

315 **GONERIL** The best and soundest of his time hath been
but rash. Then must we look from his age to receive
not alone the imperfections of long-engrafted
condition, but therewithal the unruly waywardness
that infirm and choleric years bring with them.

320 **REGAN** Such unconstant starts are we like to have from
him as this of Kent's banishment.

GONERIL There is further compliment of leave-taking
between France and him. Pray you let us sit together:
if our father carry authority with such disposition as

325 he bears, this last surrender of his will but offend us.

REGAN We shall further think of it.

GONERIL We must do something, and i'th'heat. *Exeunt*

---

297 **At fortune's alms** as a charitable gift from fortune   **scanted** stinted, withheld/slighted, neglected
298 **are ... wanted** deserve to be deprived of the love you have failed to show (to others)   299 **plighted
cunning** secret cunning/deceitful promises   300 **Who ... derides** those who hide their faults will in the end
be shamed and mocked   304 **nearly** closely   312 **grossly** obviously   313 **ever** always   314 **slenderly**
slightly   315 **The ... rash** even at his best and healthiest he was impulsive   316 **look** expect   317 **long-
engrafted condition** long-implanted tendencies   318 **therewithal** in addition to that   319 **choleric**
irascible, hot-tempered, impulsive/bilious; one of the four 'humours' or temperaments thought to be related
to an excess of bile in the constitution   320 **unconstant starts** unpredictable fits   322 **compliment**
etiquette, ceremony   323 **sit together** i.e. get together, confer   324 **carry** maintain, manage
disposition frame of mind   325 **last surrender** recent yielding (of authority)   **offend** harm
327 **i'th'heat** immediately

Act 1 Scene 2

Enter Bastard [Edmund]   *With a letter*

EDMUND Thou, nature, art my goddess: to thy law
My services are bound. Wherefore should I
Stand in the plague of custom and permit
The curiosity of nations to deprive me
5   For that I am some twelve or fourteen moonshines
Lag of a brother? Why bastard? Wherefore base?
When my dimensions are as well compact,
My mind as generous, and my shape as true,
As honest madam's issue? Why brand they us
10   With base? With baseness? Bastardy? Base, base?
Who in the lusty stealth of nature take
More composition and fierce quality
Than doth within a dull, stale, tirèd bed,
Go to th'creating a whole tribe of fops
15   Got 'tween a sleep and wake? Well then,
Legitimate Edgar, I must have your land:
Our father's love is to the bastard Edmund
As to th'legitimate — fine word, 'legitimate' —
Well, my legitimate, if this letter speed
20   And my invention thrive, Edmund the base
Shall to th'legitimate. I grow, I prosper:
Now, gods, stand up for bastards!
Enter Gloucester
GLOUCESTER Kent banished thus? And France in choler
    parted?
And the king gone tonight? Prescribed his power,
25   Confined to exhibition? All this done
Upon the gad? Edmund, how now? What news?
EDMUND So please your lordship, none.   *Hides the letter*
GLOUCESTER Why so earnestly seek you to put up that
    letter?
30   **EDMUND** I know no news, my lord.

1.2 *Location: the Earl of Gloucester's residence*   **2 Wherefore** why   **3 Stand in** endure/stand still
under   **4 curiosity** scruples, fussiness   **nations** i.e. society   **5 moonshines** months   **6 Lag of** behind (i.e.
younger than)   **base** illegitimate (also low/unworthy/dishonourable)   **7 dimensions** physical proportions
compact composed   **8 generous** noble   **true** well-proportioned/authentic, true to his father's likeness
9 honest madam's issue a legitimate child   **11 Who** i.e. we bastards who   **take** require/receive
12 More...quality a more complex creation and more vigorous disposition   **14 fops** weak fools
15 Got conceived   **18 As** the same as   **19 speed** succeed   **20 invention** scheme   **21 to th'legitimate**
advance to (or 'take over') the place of the legitimate son; editors sometimes emend this to 'top the
legitimate'   **23 choler** anger   **parted** departed   **24 Prescribed** restricted, limited   **25 exhibition** an
allowance, maintenance   **26 gad** spur of the moment   **28 up** away

GLOUCESTER What paper were you reading?

EDMUND Nothing, my lord.

GLOUCESTER No? What needed, then, that terrible
dispatch of it into your pocket? The quality of
35 nothing hath not such need to hide itself. Let's see:
come, if it be nothing I shall not need spectacles.

EDMUND I beseech you, sir, pardon me: it is a letter from
my brother that I have not all o'er-read; and for so
much as I have perused, I find it not fit for your
40 o'erlooking.

GLOUCESTER Give me the letter, sir.

EDMUND I shall offend either to detain or give it: the
contents, as in part I understand them, are to blame.

GLOUCESTER Let's see, let's see.   *Edmund gives the letter*

45 **EDMUND** I hope for my brother's justification he wrote
this but as an essay or taste of my virtue.

GLOUCESTER *Reads* 'This policy and reverence of age
makes the world bitter to the best of our times, keeps
our fortunes from us till our oldness cannot relish
50 them. I begin to find an idle and fond bondage in the
oppression of aged tyranny, who sways, not as it
hath power, but as it is suffered. Come to me, that of
this I may speak more. If our father would sleep till I
waked him, you should enjoy half his revenue for
55 ever and live the beloved of your brother, Edgar.'
Hum! Conspiracy! 'Sleep till I wake him, you should
enjoy half his revenue.' My son Edgar? Had he a hand
to write this? A heart and brain to breed it in? When
came you to this? Who brought it?

60 **EDMUND** It was not brought me, my lord; there's the
cunning of it: I found it thrown in at the casement of
my closet.

GLOUCESTER You know the character to be your
brother's?

65 **EDMUND** If the matter were good, my lord, I durst swear
it were his, but in respect of that I would fain think it
were not.

GLOUCESTER It is his.

---

33 terrible dispatch fearful and hasty stowing away   **38 for** as for   **40 o'erlooking** reading
46 essay or taste test   **47 policy...age** policy of revering the old (**policy** also suggests the 'strategic
cunning' of the elderly)   **48 the...times** i.e. our youth, our prime   **49 fortunes** inheritance   **relish**
savour, enjoy   **50 idle** useless   **fond** foolish   **51 sways** rules   **52 as...suffered** only insofar as it is
allowed to do so   **61 casement** window   **62 closet** private room   **63 character** handwriting
65 matter subject matter   **66 in...that** given the contents   **fain** willingly

EDMUND It is his hand, my lord, but I hope his heart is
70   not in the contents.

GLOUCESTER Has he never before sounded you in this
business?

EDMUND Never, my lord: but I have heard him oft
maintain it to be fit that, sons at perfect age and
75   fathers declined, the father should be as ward to the
son, and the son manage his revenue.

GLOUCESTER O villain, villain! His very opinion in the
letter! Abhorred villain! Unnatural, detested, brutish
villain! Worse than brutish! Go, sirrah, seek him: I'll
80   apprehend him. Abominable villain, where is he?

EDMUND I do not well know, my lord. If it shall please
you to suspend your indignation against my brother
till you can derive from him better testimony of his
intent, you should run a certain course, where, if you
85   violently proceed against him, mistaking his purpose,
it would make a great gap in your own honour and
shake in pieces the heart of his obedience. I dare
pawn down my life for him, that he hath writ this to
feel my affection to your honour, and to no other
90   pretence of danger.

GLOUCESTER Think you so?

EDMUND If your honour judge it meet, I will place you
where you shall hear us confer of this, and by an
auricular assurance have your satisfaction, and that
95   without any further delay than this very evening.

GLOUCESTER He cannot be such a monster. Edmund,
seek him out: wind me into him, I pray you: frame
the business after your own wisdom. I would unstate
myself to be in a due resolution.

100 EDMUND I will seek him, sir, presently: convey the
business as I shall find means and acquaint you
withal.

---

74 at perfect age being mature   75 declined old/ill   79 sirrah sir (used to social inferiors and children)
80 apprehend arrest   Abominable often, popularly, 'inhuman, unnatural' (from the incorrect belief that
the word was derived from the Latin *ab homine*, i.e. 'away from man')   84 run … course proceed
securely   where whereas   85 proceed perhaps with legal connotations (in keeping with apprehend and
testimony)   88 pawn down pledge   89 feel test, feel out   90 pretence intention, purpose   92 meet
suitable   94 auricular assurance i.e. by hearing for yourself   have your satisfaction resolve yourself of
any doubt   97 wind … him insinuate yourself into his confidence for me   frame devise, arrange
98 unstate … resolution give up my rank and wealth to be resolved on this matter   100 presently
immediately   convey manage, undertake   102 withal therewith

GLOUCESTER These late eclipses in the sun and moon
portend no good to us: though the wisdom of nature
105   can reason it thus and thus, yet nature finds itself
scourged by the sequent effects: love cools, friendship
falls off, brothers divide: in cities, mutinies; in
countries, discord; in palaces, treason; and the bond
cracked 'twixt son and father. This villain of mine
110   comes under the prediction: there's son against
father. The king falls from bias of nature: there's
father against child. We have seen the best of our
time: machinations, hollowness, treachery, and all
ruinous disorders follow us disquietly to our graves.
115   Find out this villain, Edmund: it shall lose thee
nothing. Do it carefully.— And the noble and true-
hearted Kent banished! His offence, honesty! 'Tis
strange.   *Exit*

EDMUND This is the excellent foppery of the world, that
120   when we are sick in fortune — often the surfeits of
our own behaviour — we make guilty of our
disasters the sun, the moon and stars, as if we were
villains on necessity, fools by heavenly compulsion,
knaves,   thieves   and   treachers   by   spherical
125   predominance, drunkards, liars and adulterers by
an enforced obedience of planetary influence, and all
that we are evil in, by a divine thrusting on: an
admirable evasion of whoremaster man, to lay his
goatish disposition on the charge of a star! My father
130   compounded with my mother under the dragon's tail
and my nativity was under Ursa Major, so that it
follows I am rough and lecherous. I should have been
that I am had the maidenliest star in the firmament
twinkled on my bastardizing.

---

103 **late** recent   104 **wisdom of nature** human reason/natural science   106 **scourged** punished
sequent effects subsequent events   111 **bias of nature** natural inclination (a bowling image: the **bias**
refers to the curving path taken by a weighted ball)   115 **it...nothing** i.e. it will advantage you
119 **excellent foppery** supreme foolishness   120 **surfeits** excesses   122 **disasters** misfortunes   123 **on**
i.e. by   124 **treachers** traitors   **spherical predominance** the dominant influence of a particular planet at
one's birth   127 **divine** celestial, supernatural   128 **evasion** shuffling excuse   **whoremaster** i.e.
lecherous, whore-using   129 **goatish** lustful   **charge** responsibility   130 **compounded** had sex
the dragon's tail the constellation Draco   131 **Ursa Major** (constellation of) the Great Bear (or Plough)
132 **rough** cruel, violent   133 **maidenliest** most virginal   **firmament** sky, heavens   134 **bastardizing**
conception out of wedlock

Enter Edgar

135   Pat he comes like the catastrophe of the old comedy:
       my cue is villainous melancholy, with a sigh like Tom
       o'Bedlam.— O, these eclipses do portend these
       divisions! Fa, sol, la, mi.

EDGAR How now, brother Edmund, what serious
140   contemplation are you in?

EDMUND I am thinking, brother, of a prediction I read
       this other day, what should follow these eclipses.

EDGAR Do you busy yourself with that?

EDMUND I promise you, the effects he writes of succeed
145   unhappily. When saw you my father last?

EDGAR The night gone by.

EDMUND Spake you with him?

EDGAR Ay, two hours together.

EDMUND Parted you in good terms? Found you no
150   displeasure in him by word nor countenance?

EDGAR None at all.

EDMUND Bethink yourself wherein you may have
       offended him, and at my entreaty forbear his
       presence until some little time hath qualified the
155   heat of his displeasure, which at this instant so
       rageth in him that with the mischief of your person it
       would scarcely allay.

EDGAR Some villain hath done me wrong.

EDMUND That's my fear. I pray you have a continent
160   forbearance till the speed of his rage goes slower: and,
       as I say, retire with me to my lodging, from whence I
       will fitly bring you to hear my lord speak. Pray ye go.   *Gives a key*
       There's my key: if you do stir abroad, go armed.

EDGAR Armed, brother?

165 EDMUND Brother, I advise you to the best: I am no
       honest man if there be any good meaning toward
       you: I have told you what I have seen and heard, but
       faintly, nothing like the image and horror of it. Pray
       you away.

170 EDGAR Shall I hear from you anon?   *Exit*

---

135 **Pat** on cue   **catastrophe** conclusion   **comedy** play   136 **my cue** could also mean 'designated role'
Tom o'Bedlam i.e. a madman (from the Saint Mary of Bethlehem hospital in London, an institution for the
insane)   138 **divisions** conflicts, discords (plays on the sense of 'musical variations')   **Fa...mi** Edmund
hums a musical scale to himself   142 **this** the   144 **succeed** follow   145 **unhappily** unluckily, by
misfortune   150 **countenance** bearing, demeanour/facial expression   153 **forbear** avoid   154 **qualified**
cooled, lessened   156 **mischief...person** harm caused by your presence   157 **allay** abate, calm
159 **have...forbearance** i.e. restrain yourself and stay away from him   162 **fitly** at an appropriate time
163 **abroad** out of the house   166 **meaning** intention   168 **image and horror** horrific true picture
170 **anon** soon

EDMUND I do serve you in this business.—
A credulous father and a brother noble,
Whose nature is so far from doing harms
That he suspects none: on whose foolish honesty
175   My practices ride easy. I see the business.
Let me, if not by birth, have lands by wit:
All with me's meet that I can fashion fit.   *Exit*

Act 1 Scene 3   *running scene 3*

Enter Goneril and Steward [Oswald]

GONERIL Did my father strike my gentleman for chiding
of his fool?

OSWALD Ay, madam.

GONERIL By day and night he wrongs me: every hour
5   He flashes into one gross crime or other
That sets us all at odds. I'll not endure it.
His knights grow riotous, and himself upbraids us
On every trifle. When he returns from hunting
I will not speak with him: say I am sick.
10   If you come slack of former services
You shall do well: the fault of it I'll answer.

OSWALD He's coming, madam: I hear him.   *Horns within*

GONERIL Put on what weary negligence you please,
You and your fellows: I'd have it come to question:
15   If he distaste it, let him to my sister,
Whose mind and mine, I know, in that are one.
Remember what I have said.

OSWALD Well, madam.

GONERIL And let his knights have colder looks among
20   you: what grows of it, no matter: advise your fellows
so. I'll write straight to my sister, to hold my course.
Prepare for dinner.   *Exeunt*

---

171 **serve** help/trick, deceive   175 **practices** plots   176 **wit** intelligence, ingenuity   177 **meet** fitting
fashion fit shape to my purposes   1.3 *Location: Goneril and the Duke of Albany's residence*
1 **gentleman** man of gentle (i.e. noble) birth attached to a royal household   **chiding** rebuking   5 **flashes**
breaks out   10 **come slack** fall short   11 **answer** be answerable for   14 **fellows** fellow servants
question conflict, a dispute   15 **distaste** dislike   21 **straight** straight away   **to** i.e. and tell her to

Act 1 Scene 4

running scene 3 continues

Enter Kent   *Disguised*

KENT If but as will I other accents borrow,
  That can my speech defuse, my good intent
  May carry through itself to that full issue
  For which I razed my likeness. Now, banished Kent,
5 If thou canst serve where thou dost stand
    condemned,
  So may it come thy master whom thou lov'st,
  Shall find thee full of labours.
Horns within. Enter Lear and Attendants [his Knights]
LEAR Let me not stay a jot for dinner: go get it ready.—
                                              [Exit a Knight]
  How now, what art thou?   *To Kent*
10 **KENT** A man, sir.
LEAR What dost thou profess? What wouldst thou with
  us?
KENT I do profess to be no less than I seem; to serve him
  truly that will put me in trust, to love him that is
15 honest, to converse with him that is wise and says
  little, to fear judgement, to fight when I cannot
  choose and to eat no fish.
LEAR What art thou?
KENT A very honest-hearted fellow, and as poor as the
20 king.
LEAR If thou be'st as poor for a subject as he's for a king,
  thou art poor enough. What wouldst thou?
KENT Service.
LEAR Who wouldst thou serve?
25 **KENT** You.
LEAR Dost thou know me, fellow?
KENT No, sir, but you have that in your countenance
  which I would fain call master.
LEAR What's that?
30 **KENT** Authority.
LEAR What services canst thou do?

1.4   1 as will I perhaps 'as I intend' (but most editors opt for the Quarto 'well' – i.e. 'as well as being
disguised')   **2 defuse** confuse, disorder   **3 full issue** complete outcome   **4 razed my likeness** erased my
true appearance   **8 stay** wait   **11 What…profess?** What is your occupation? (Kent shifts the sense of
profess to 'claim, declare')   **wouldst thou** do you want   **12 us** Lear continues to use the royal plural
pronoun   **16 judgement** i.e. God's judgement/the judgement of fellow men   **cannot choose** have no
other option   **17 to…fish** i.e. only to eat a hearty diet of meat/not to eat fish on Fridays like a Roman
Catholic/not to have sex with prostitutes

KENT I can keep honest counsel, ride, run, mar a curious
tale in telling it, and deliver a plain message bluntly:
that which ordinary men are fit for, I am qualified in,
35   and the best of me is diligence.

LEAR How old art thou?

KENT Not so young, sir, to love a woman for singing, nor
so old to dote on her for anything: I have years on my
back forty-eight.

40   **LEAR** Follow me, thou shalt serve me: if I like thee no
worse after dinner, I will not part from thee yet.—
Dinner, ho, dinner! Where's my knave? My fool? Go
you and call my fool hither.   [*Exit another Knight*]

Enter Steward [Oswald]

You, you, sirrah, where's my daughter?

45   **OSWALD** So please you—   *Exit*

LEAR 'What says the fellow there? Call the clotpoll
back.—   [*Exit another Knight*]
Where's my fool? Ho, I think the world's asleep.—
[*Enter a Knight*]
How now? Where's that mongrel?

KNIGHT He says, my lord, your daughter is not well.

50   **LEAR** Why came not the slave back to me when I called
him?

KNIGHT Sir, he answered me in the roundest manner, he
would not.

LEAR He would not?

55   **KNIGHT** My lord, I know not what the matter is, but to
my judgement your highness is not entertained with
that ceremonious affection as you were wont: there's
a great abatement of kindness appears as well in the
general dependants as in the duke himself also and
60   your daughter.

LEAR Ha? Say'st thou so?

KNIGHT I beseech you pardon me, my lord, if I be
mistaken, for my duty cannot be silent when I think
your highness wronged.

65   **LEAR** Thou but rememb'rest me of mine own conception:
I have perceived a most faint neglect of late, which I

---

32 keep honest counsel keep secrets like an honourable man/keep secrets that are honourable
mar…tale spoil an elaborate story   **38 anything** 'thing' plays on the sense of 'vagina'   **42 knave** rogue/
servant   **45 So if it**   **46 clotpoll** idiot   **50 slave** servant/villain   **52 roundest** bluntest   **56 entertained**
received, treated hospitably   **57 wont** accustomed (to receive)   **59 general dependants** servants as a
whole   **65 rememb'rest** remind   **conception** notion, thought   **66 faint** slight/lazy, half-hearted

have rather blamed as mine own jealous curiosity
than as a very pretence and purpose of unkindness. I
will look further into't. But where's my fool? I have
70   not seen him this two days.

KNIGHT Since my young lady's going into France, sir, the
fool hath much pined away.

LEAR No more of that, I have noted it well.— Go you and
tell my daughter I would speak with her.—

[Exit a Knight]
75   Go you, call hither my fool.—   *[Exit another Knight]*
Enter Steward [Oswald]

O, you sir, you, come you hither, sir. Who am I, sir?

OSWALD My lady's father.

LEAR 'My lady's father'? My lord's knave: you whoreson
dog, you slave, you cur!

80   OSWALD I am none of these, my lord, I beseech your
pardon.

LEAR Do you bandy looks with me, you rascal?   *Strikes him*

OSWALD I'll not be strucken, my lord.

KENT Nor tripped neither, you base football player.   *Trips him*

85   LEAR I thank thee, fellow: thou serv'st me and I'll love
thee.

KENT Come, sir, arise, away! I'll teach you differences:
away, away! If you will measure your lubber's length   *Pushes*
again, tarry: but away, go to. Have you wisdom? So.   *Oswald out*

90   LEAR Now, my friendly knave, I thank thee. There's   *Gives money*
earnest of thy service.

Enter Fool

FOOL Let me hire him too: here's my coxcomb.   *Offers Kent his cap*

LEAR How now, my pretty knave, how dost thou?

FOOL Sirrah, you were best take my coxcomb.   *To Kent*

95   LEAR Why, my boy?

FOOL Why? For taking one's part that's out of favour:
nay, an thou canst not smile as the wind sits, thou'lt
catch cold shortly. There, take my coxcomb. Why,
this fellow has banished two on's daughters and did
100   the third a blessing against his will: if thou follow
him, thou must needs wear my coxcomb.— How

---

67 jealous curiosity mistrustful fastidiousness   **68 very pretence** real intention   **79 cur** dog   **82 bandy** exchange looks as an equal (literally, 'bat to and fro' as in tennis)   **83 strucken** struck, beaten   **84 football** played by the lower classes (unlike tennis)   **87 differences** class distinctions   **88 measure...length** be knocked flat to the floor   **lubber** clumsy lout   **89 tarry** stay   **go to** an expression of impatient dismissal   **91 earnest** part-payment in advance   **92 coxcomb** fool's headgear with a crest like a cock's comb   **93 pretty** fine-looking/clever   **97 an...sits** i.e. if you cannot please those in power   **99 on's** of his   **101 needs** necessarily

now, nuncle? Would I had two coxcombs and two
daughters.

LEAR Why, my boy?

105 **FOOL** If I gave them all my living, I'd keep my coxcombs
myself. There's mine: beg another of thy daughters.

LEAR Take heed, sirrah: the whip.

FOOL Truth's a dog must to kennel: he must be whipped
out when the Lady Brach may stand by th'fire and
110 stink.

LEAR A pestilent gall to me!

FOOL Sirrah, I'll teach thee a speech.

LEAR Do.

FOOL Mark it, nuncle:

115   Have more than thou showest,
       Speak less than thou knowest,
       Lend less than thou owest,
       Ride more than thou goest,
       Learn more than thou trowest,
120   Set less than thou throwest;
       Leave thy drink and thy whore,
       And keep in-a-door,
       And thou shalt have more
       Than two tens to a score.

125 **KENT** This is nothing, fool.

FOOL Then 'tis like the breath of an unfee'd lawyer: you   *To Lear*
gave me nothing for't.— Can you make no use of
nothing, nuncle?

LEAR Why, no, boy: nothing can be made out of nothing.

130 **FOOL** Prithee tell him, so much the rent of his land   *To Kent*
comes to: he will not believe a fool.

LEAR A bitter fool!

FOOL Dost thou know the difference, my boy, between a
bitter fool and a sweet one?

135 **LEAR** No, lad, teach me.

FOOL Nuncle, give me an egg and I'll give thee two
crowns.

LEAR What two crowns shall they be?

---

102 nuncle contraction of 'mine uncle'   **Would** I wish   **105 living** property, possessions   **109 Brach**
bitch   **111 pestilent gall** troublesome irritation   **114 Mark** pay attention to   **117 owest** own
118 goest walk   **119 trowest** believe   **120 Set...throwest** don't stake everything on the throw of the
dice   **123 have...score** i.e. make a profit   **124 score** twenty   **126 unfee'd** unpaid   **127 use**
employment/profit   **137 crowns** coins (the sense then shifts to 'eggshells', 'royal headgear' and 'head')

FOOL Why, after I have cut the egg i'th'middle and eat
140   up the meat, the two crowns of the egg. When thou
       clovest thy crowns i'th'middle and gav'st away both
       parts, thou bor'st thine ass on thy back o'er the dirt:
       thou hadst little wit in thy bald crown when thou
       gav'st thy golden one away. If I speak like myself in
145   this, let him be whipped that first finds it so:
             Fools had ne'er less grace in a year,   *Sings*
             For wise men are grown foppish
             And know not how their wits to wear,
             Their manners are so apish.
150 LEAR When were you wont to be so full of songs, sirrah?
    FOOL I have used it, nuncle, e'er since thou mad'st thy
       daughters thy mothers: for when thou gav'st them
       the rod and put'st down thine own breeches,
             Then they for sudden joy did weep,   *Sings*
155   And I for sorrow sung,
             That such a king should play bo-peep
             And go the fool among.
       Prithee, nuncle, keep a schoolmaster that can teach
       thy fool to lie: I would fain learn to lie.
160 LEAR An you lie, sirrah, we'll have you whipped.
    FOOL I marvel what kin thou and thy daughters are:
       they'll have me whipped for speaking true, thou'lt
       have me whipped for lying, and sometimes I am
       whipped for holding my peace. I had rather be any
165   kind o'thing than a fool. And yet I would not be thee,
       nuncle: thou hast pared thy wit o'both sides and left
       nothing i'th'middle. Here comes one o'the parings.
    Enter Goneril
    LEAR How now, daughter? What makes that frontlet on?
       You are too much of late i'th'frown.
170 FOOL Thou wast a pretty fellow when thou hadst no
       need to care for her frowning: now thou art an O
       without a figure. I am better than thou art now: I am
       a fool, thou art nothing.— Yes, forsooth, I will hold   *To Goneril*

---

140 **meat** edible contents   141 **clovest** split   144 **like myself** i.e. foolishly   146 **grace** favour, patronage
147 **foppish** foolish   149 **apish** silly   151 **used it** made it my custom   153 **rod** punishment cane
156 **bo-peep** a child's game (in which an adult alternately conceals and reveals his or her face)   157 **the
fool among** amongst fools   159 **fain** gladly   160 **An** if   161 **marvel** wonder   166 **pared** trimmed
168 **frontlet** ornamental headband/band worn round forehead at night to smooth wrinkles   172 **figure**
accompanying digit (to make it a number higher than zero)   173 **forsooth** in truth

my tongue, so your face bids me, though you say

175 nothing.

Mum, mum, *Sings*

He that keeps nor crust nor crumb,

Weary of all, shall want some.

That's a shelled peascod. *Points to Lear*

180 **GONERIL** Not only, sir, this your all-licensed fool,

But other of your insolent retinue

Do hourly carp and quarrel, breaking forth

In rank and not-to-be endured riots, sir.

I had thought by making this well known unto you

185 To have found a safe redress, but now grow fearful,

By what yourself too late have spoke and done.

That you protect this course and put it on

By your allowance, which if you should, the fault

Would not scape censure, nor the redresses sleep

190 Which in the tender of a wholesome weal

Might in their working do you that offence,

Which else were shame, that then necessity

Will call discreet proceeding.

FOOL For you know, nuncle,

195 The hedge-sparrow fed the cuckoo so long,

That it's had it head bit off by it young.

So, out went the candle, and we were left darkling.

LEAR Are you our daughter? *To Goneril*

GONERIL I would you would make use of your good

wisdom —

200 Whereof I know you are fraught — and put away

These dispositions which of late transport you

From what you rightly are.

FOOL May not an ass know when the cart draws the

horse?

Whoop, Jug! I love thee.

---

177 nor . . . crumb i.e. no part of the loaf   **178 want some** need something/experience need
179 peascod peapod   **180 all-licensed** licensed to speak entirely freely   **182 carp** complain
183 rank excessive, uncontrolled   **185 safe** certain   **186 too late** all too recently   **187 course** behaviour
put it on encourage it   **189 scape** escape   **redresses sleep** punishments be neglected
190 in . . . proceeding might offend and shame you but which, in the interests of maintaining a healthy
state, must be deemed a prudent course of action   **195 cuckoo** young cuckoo, hatched from an egg its
mother had laid in another bird's nest   **196 it's had it** it had its   **it young** the young cuckoo
197 darkling in darkness   **200 fraught** equipped (literally 'freighted')   **201 dispositions** moods   **204 Jug**
a form of 'Joan', often used as a generic name for a prostitute

205 **LEAR** Does any here know me? This is not Lear.
　　　　Does Lear walk thus? Speak thus? Where are his
　　　　　　eyes?
　　　　Either his notion weakens, his discernings
　　　　Are lethargied — Ha! Waking? 'Tis not so?
　　　　Who is it that can tell me who I am?
210 **FOOL** Lear's shadow.
　　　LEAR Your name, fair gentlewoman?
　　　GONERIL This admiration, sir, is much o'th'savour
　　　　Of other your new pranks. I do beseech you
　　　　To understand my purposes aright:
215 　As you are old and reverend, should be wise.
　　　　Here do you keep a hundred knights and squires,
　　　　Men so disordered, so debauched and bold,
　　　　That this our court, infected with their manners,
　　　　Shows like a riotous inn: epicurism and lust
220 　Makes it more like a tavern or a brothel
　　　　Than a graced palace. The shame itself doth speak
　　　　For instant remedy. Be then desired
　　　　By her, that else will take the thing she begs,
　　　　A little to disquantity your train,
225 　And the remainders, that shall still depend
　　　　To be such men as may besort your age,
　　　　Which know themselves and you.
　　　LEAR Darkness and devils!—
　　　　Saddle my horses, call my train together.—　　　　*To a Servant*
230 　Degenerate bastard! I'll not trouble thee.　　　　　*To Goneril*
　　　　Yet have I left a daughter.
　　　GONERIL You strike my people, and your disordered
　　　　　rabble
　　　　Make servants of their betters.
　　　Enter Albany
　　　LEAR Woe that too late repents!— Is it your will?　　*To Albany*
235 　Speak, sir.— Prepare my horses.　　　　　　　　　*To a Servant*
　　　　Ingratitude, thou marble-hearted fiend,
　　　　More hideous when thou show'st thee in a child
　　　　Than the sea-monster!
　　　ALBANY Pray, sir, be patient.

---

207 notion understanding　**discernings Are lethargied** power of discernment is asleep　**208 Waking?** Am I awake?　**210 shadow** reflection/ghost/shadow cast by the sun/imitator, actor　**212 admiration** air of wonder　**o'th'savour** of the flavour　**215 should** i.e. you should　**217 bold** presumptuous, audacious　**219 epicurism** gluttony/pleasure-seeking　**221 graced** honourable　**speak** call　**222 desired** requested, entreated　**224 disquantity your train** reduce your retinue　**225 depend** be your dependants, serve you　**226 besort** befit, suit　**227 know ... you** i.e. know their place, and yours　**230 Degenerate** having lost the qualities proper to a family member　**234 that** to he who

240 **LEAR** Detested kite, thou liest.   *To Goneril*
       My train are men of choice and rarest parts,
       That all particulars of duty know
       And in the most exact regard support
       The worships of their name. O, most small fault,
245   How ugly didst thou in Cordelia show!
       Which, like an engine, wrenched my frame of nature
       From the fixed place, drew from my heart all love,
       And added to the gall. O Lear, Lear, Lear!
       Beat at this gate, that let thy folly in,   *Hits his head*
250   And thy dear judgement out!— Go, go, my people.
     ALBANY My lord, I am guiltless as I am ignorant
       Of what hath moved you.
     LEAR It may be so, my lord.—
       Hear, nature, hear, dear goddess, hear!
255   Suspend thy purpose if thou didst intend
       To make this creature fruitful:
       Into her womb convey sterility,
       Dry up in her the organs of increase,
       And from her derogate body never spring
260   A babe to honour her: if she must teem,
       Create her child of spleen, that it may live
       And be a thwart disnatured torment to her:
       Let it stamp wrinkles in her brow of youth,
       With cadent tears fret channels in her cheeks,
265   Turn all her mother's pains and benefits
       To laughter and contempt, that she may feel
       How sharper than a serpent's tooth it is
       To have a thankless child!— Away, away!   *Exit*   *Perhaps with*
     ALBANY Now, gods that we adore, whereof comes this? *Kent and Knights*
270 **GONERIL** Never afflict yourself to know more of it,
       But let his disposition have that scope
       As dotage gives it.
     Enter Lear
     LEAR What, fifty of my followers at a clap?
       Within a fortnight?
275 **ALBANY** What's the matter, sir?

---

240 kite bird of prey, scavenger   **241 rarest parts** splendid qualities   **243 in . . . name** uphold the honour
of their names with the most careful consideration (or '. . . in every respect')   **246 engine** piece of
machinery   **248 gall** bitterness   **252 moved** provoked, angered   **258 increase** procreation
259 derogate degenerate, debased   **260 teem** be fertile, have children   **261 spleen** malice   **262 thwart**
perverse, obstinate   **disnatured** unnatural   **264 cadent** falling   **fret** erode, wear   **265 pains** efforts (also
suggests labour pains)   **benefits** kindnesses   **272 dotage** foolish old age   **273 at a clap** with one blow

LEAR I'll tell thee:— Life and death! I am ashamed   *To Goneril*
        That thou hast power to shake my manhood thus,
        That these hot tears, which break from me perforce,
        Should make thee worth them. Blasts and fogs upon
            thee!
280   Th'untented woundings of a father's curse
        Pierce every sense about thee! Old fond eyes,
        Beweep this cause again, I'll pluck ye out
        And cast you, with the waters that you loose,
        To temper clay. Ha? Let it be so.
285   I have another daughter,
        Who, I am sure, is kind and comfortable:
        When she shall hear this of thee, with her nails
        She'll flay thy wolvish visage. Thou shalt find
        That I'll resume the shape which thou dost think
290   I have cast off for ever.
                    Exeunt [Lear, perhaps with Kent and Knights]
GONERIL Do you mark that?
ALBANY I cannot be so partial, Goneril,
        To the great love I bear you—
GONERIL Pray you, content.— What, Oswald, ho!—
295   You, sir, more knave than fool, after your master.   *To Fool*
FOOL Nuncle Lear, nuncle Lear, tarry, take the fool with
        thee.

            A fox, when one has caught her,   *Sings*
            And such a daughter
300   Should sure to the slaughter,
            If my cap would buy a halter:
            So the fool follows after.   *Exit*
GONERIL This man hath had good counsel. A hundred
            knights?
        'Tis politic and safe to let him keep
305   At point a hundred knights: yes, that on every
            dream,
        Each buzz, each fancy, each complaint, dislike,
        He may enguard his dotage with their powers
        And hold our lives in mercy.— Oswald, I say!

---

278 **perforce** by force, uncontrollably   279 **Blasts** violent gusts of winds   280 **Th'untented** the festering
(literally, not probed and cleaned surgically)   281 **fond** foolish/doting   283 **waters...loose** i.e. tears
284 **temper** moisten   **clay** i.e. earth, the ground   286 **kind** benevolent/possessed of natural familial
love   **comfortable** comforting   288 **visage** face   292 **partial** biased   294 **content** content yourself, i.e.
be quiet   301 **halter** hangman's noose   304 **politic** prudent, shrewd   305 **At point** armed and ready
that so that   306 **buzz** rumour   **fancy** whim   307 **enguard** protect, defend   308 **in** at (his)

ALBANY Well, you may fear too far.

310 GONERIL Safer than trust too far:
    Let me still take away the harms I fear,
    Not fear still to be taken. I know his heart.
    What he hath uttered I have writ my sister:
    If she sustain him and his hundred knights
315   When I have showed th'unfitness—
Enter Steward [Oswald]
                          How now, Oswald?
    What, have you writ that letter to my sister?

OSWALD Ay, madam.

GONERIL Take you some company and away to horse:
    Inform her full of my particular fear,
320   And thereto add such reasons of your own
    As may compact it more. Get you gone,
    And hasten your return.—   *[Exit Oswald]*
                       No, no, my lord,
    This milky gentleness and course of yours
    Though I condemn not, yet, under pardon,
325   You are much more at task for want of wisdom
    Than praised for harmful mildness.

ALBANY How far your eyes may pierce I cannot tell:
    Striving to better, oft we mar what's well.

GONERIL Nay, then—
330 ALBANY Well, well, th'event.   *Exeunt*

Act 1 Scene 5   *running scene 3 continues*

Enter Lear, Kent, Gentleman and Fool   *Kent disguised as Caius*

LEAR Go you before to Gloucester with these letters.   *To Kent*
    Acquaint my daughter no further with anything you
    know than comes from her demand out of the letter.
    If your diligence be not speedy, I shall be there afore
5   you.

KENT I will not sleep, my lord, till I have delivered your
    letter.   *Exit*

FOOL If a man's brains were in's heels, were't not in
    danger of kibes?

10 LEAR Ay, boy.

---

311 still always   **312 taken** defeated, captured   **321 compact** confirm, consolidate   **324 under pardon** if you'll pardon my saying so   **325 at task** taken to task, blamed   **330 th'event** the outcome (will tell)
1.5 1 before ahead   **3 demand out of** questions prompted by   **9 kibes** chilblains

FOOL Then, I prithee be merry: thy wit shall not go slip-
    shod.

LEAR Ha, ha, ha!

FOOL Shalt see thy other daughter will use thee kindly,
15   for though she's as like this as a crab's like an apple,
    yet I can tell what I can tell.

LEAR What canst tell, boy?

FOOL She will taste as like this as a crab does to a crab.
    Thou canst tell why one's nose stands i'th'middle
20   on's face?

LEAR No.

FOOL Why, to keep one's eyes of either side's nose, that
    what a man cannot smell out he may spy into.

LEAR I did her wrong—

25 **FOOL** Canst tell how an oyster makes his shell?

LEAR No.

FOOL Nor I neither; but I can tell why a snail has a
    house.

LEAR Why?

30 **FOOL** Why, to put's head in, not to give it away to his
    daughters and leave his horns without a case.

LEAR I will forget my nature. So kind a father!— Be my
    horses ready?

FOOL Thy asses are gone about 'em. The reason why the
35   seven stars are no more than seven is a pretty reason.

LEAR Because they are not eight.

FOOL Yes, indeed: thou wouldst make a good fool.

LEAR To take't again perforce. Monster ingratitude!

FOOL If thou wert my fool, nuncle, I'd have thee beaten
40   for being old before thy time.

LEAR How's that?

FOOL Thou shouldst not have been old till thou hadst
    been wise.

LEAR O, let me not be mad, not mad, sweet heaven!
45   Keep me in temper: I would not be mad!—
    How now, are the horses ready?   *To Gentleman*

GENTLEMAN Ready, my lord.

LEAR Come, boy.

---

11 wit intellect   **slip-shod** in slippers (worn for chilblains)   **14 Shalt** i.e. thou shalt   **15 crab** sour-tasting
crab-apple   **20 on's** of his   **22 side's** side of his   **24 her** i.e. Cordelia (though Goneril is just possible)
34 asses idiots/donkeys (i.e. Lear's servants)   **the seven stars** the Pleiades   **35 pretty** ingenious
38 again back again (refers either to an intention to reclaim sovereignty, or to Goneril's withdrawal of Lear's
privileges)   **45 temper** my right state of mind

FOOL She that's a maid now, and laughs at my
         departure,
50   Shall not be a maid long, unless things be cut shorter.

Exeunt

Act 2 Scene 1

Enter Bastard [Edmund] and Curan, severally

EDMUND Save thee, Curan.
CURAN And you, sir. I have been with your father, and
         given him notice that the Duke of Cornwall and
         Regan his duchess will be here with him this night.
5 EDMUND How comes that?
CURAN Nay, I know not. You have heard of the news
         abroad: I mean the whispered ones, for they are yet
         but ear-kissing arguments?
EDMUND Not I: pray you, what are they?
10 CURAN Have you heard of no likely wars toward 'twixt
         the dukes of Cornwall and Albany?
EDMUND Not a word.
CURAN You may do then in time. Fare you well, sir. *Exit*
EDMUND The duke be here tonight? The better — best!
15   This weaves itself perforce into my business.
         My father hath set guard to take my brother,
         And I have one thing, of a queasy question,
         Which I must act. Briefness and fortune, work!—
Enter Edgar   *Appears above and then enters below*
         Brother, a word: descend, brother, I say!
20   My father watches: O sir, fly this place.
         Intelligence is given where you are hid;
         You have now the good advantage of the night.
         Have you not spoken gainst the Duke of Cornwall?
         He's coming hither, now, i'th'night, i'th'haste,
25   And Regan with him: have you nothing said
         Upon his party gainst the Duke of Albany?
         Advise yourself.

---

49 maid virgin   **50 things** penises   **2.1** *Location: the Earl of Gloucester's residence*   *severally*
separately   **1 Save thee** God save thee (a common greeting)   **7 abroad** out there, in circulation   **ones** i.e.
the news, regarded as plural   **8 ear-kissing arguments** rumoured, whispered topics, not established
truths   **10 toward** impending   **15 perforce** of necessity   **16 queasy question**
dangerous, uncertain nature   **20 watches** is on guard, on the lookout   **21 intelligence** information
24 i'th'haste in haste   **25 have...Albany** i.e. have you spoken in support of Cornwall and against Albany/
have you spoken critically about Cornwall's hostility to Albany   **27 Advise yourself** consider

EDGAR I am sure on't, not a word.

EDMUND I hear my father coming, pardon me:

30　　　In cunning I must draw my sword upon you: *Draws*

Draw, seem to defend yourself. Now quit you well.   *Edgar draws*

Yield: come before my father.— Light, ho, here!—

Fly, brother.— Torches, torches!— So, farewell.

                       Exit Edgar

Some blood drawn on me would beget opinion   *Wounds his arm*

35　　Of my more fierce endeavour: I have seen drunkards

Do more than this in sport.— Father, father!

Stop, stop! No help?

Enter Gloucester and Servants with torches

GLOUCESTER Now, Edmund, where's the villain?

EDMUND Here stood he in the dark, his sharp sword out,

40　　Mumbling of wicked charms, conjuring the moon

To stand auspicious mistress—

GLOUCESTER But where is he?

EDMUND Look, sir, I bleed.

GLOUCESTER Where is the villain, Edmund?

45　EDMUND Fled this way, sir. When by no means he

    could—

GLOUCESTER Pursue him, ho! Go after. [*Exeunt Servants*]

By no means what?

EDMUND Persuade me to the murder of your lordship,

But that I told him the revenging gods

50　　Gainst parricides did all the thunder bend,

Spoke with how manifold and strong a bond

The child was bound to th'father; sir, in fine,

Seeing how loathly opposite I stood

To his unnatural purpose, in fell motion

55　　With his preparèd sword, he charges home

My unprovided body, latched mine arm;

And when he saw my best alarumed spirits,

Bold in the quarrel's right, roused to th'encounter,

Or whether ghasted by the noise I made,

60　　Full suddenly he fled.

---

30 **in cunning** to deceive (Gloucester; though playing on the fact that it is Edgar who is being tricked)
31 **quit you** acquit yourself　34 **beget…endeavour** give the impression that I fought more fiercely **fierce**
violent/brave/zealous　40 **conjuring** invoking　**the moon** i.e. Hecate, goddess of the moon and of
witchcraft　41 **stand auspicious mistress** favour him as his patroness　50 **bend** direct　52 **fine**
conclusion　53 **loathly opposite** deeply opposed, horrified　54 **fell** savage, ruthless　55 **preparèd**
unsheathed　**charges home** makes a direct attack on　56 **unprovided** unprotected　**latched** caught
57 **alarumed** stirred, roused　58 **quarrel's right** rightfulness of my cause　**th'encounter** the fight
59 **ghasted** frightened　60 **Full** very

GLOUCESTER Let him fly far:
    Not in this land shall he remain uncaught,
    And found — dispatch. The noble duke my master,
    My worthy arch and patron, comes tonight:
65   By his authority I will proclaim it,
    That he which finds him shall deserve our thanks,
    Bringing the murderous coward to the stake:
    He that conceals him, death.
EDMUND When I dissuaded him from his intent
70   And found him pight to do it, with curst speech
    I threatened to discover him: he replied,
    'Thou unpossessing bastard, dost thou think,
    If I would stand against thee, would the reposal
    Of any trust, virtue, or worth in thee
75   Make thy words faithed? No: what should I deny —
    As this I would, though thou didst produce
    My very character — I'd turn it all
    To thy suggestion, plot, and damnèd practice,
    And thou must make a dullard of the world,
80   If they not thought the profits of my death
    Were very pregnant and potential spirits
    To make thee seek it.'   *Tucket within*
GLOUCESTER O, strange and fastened villain!
    Would he deny his letter, said he?
85   Hark, the duke's trumpets! I know not where he
        comes.
    All ports I'll bar: the villain shall not scape:
    The duke must grant me that. Besides, his picture
    I will send far and near, that all the kingdom
    May have due note of him, and of my land,
90   Loyal and natural boy, I'll work the means
    To make thee capable.
Enter Cornwall, Regan and Attendants
CORNWALL How now, my noble friend? Since I came
    hither —

---

63 found — dispatch once found, he shall be killed   **64 arch and patron** chief patron   **67 stake** i.e. place of execution   **70 pight** determined   **curst** angry   **71 discover** reveal his plans   **72 unpossessing** unable to take possession of land and property (illegitimate children could not legally inherit)   **73 would stand against** stood against, contradicted   **reposal** placing   **75 faithed** believed   **77 character** handwriting   **78 suggestion** incitement to evil   **practice** scheme   **79 make . . . world** think the world very stupid   **80 not thought** did not think   **profits** i.e. benefits to Edmund   **81 pregnant . . . spirits** fertile and powerful temptations (literally, evil spirits)   ***Tucket*** personal trumpet call, here signalling the arrival of Cornwall   **83 strange** unnatural   **fastened** confirmed, determined   **85 where** why   **86 ports** seaports/ gates of walled towns   **87 picture** could also mean 'description'   **90 natural** naturally loyal and loving to one's family (plays on the sense of 'illegitimate')   **work the means** find a way   **91 capable** able to inherit

Which I can call but now — I have heard
    strangeness.
REGAN If it be true, all vengeance comes too short
95   Which can pursue th'offender. How dost, my lord?
GLOUCESTER O, madam, my old heart is cracked, it's
    cracked!
REGAN What, did my father's godson seek your life?
    He whom my father named? Your Edgar?
GLOUCESTER O, lady, lady, shame would have it hid!
100 REGAN Was he not companion with the riotous knights
    That tended upon my father?
GLOUCESTER I know not, madam: 'tis too bad, too bad.
EDMUND Yes, madam, he was of that consort.
REGAN No marvel, then, though he were ill affected:
105   'Tis they have put him on the old man's death,
    To have th'expense and waste of his revenues.
    I have this present evening from my sister
    Been well informed of them, and with such cautions
    That if they come to sojourn at my house,
110   I'll not be there.
CORNWALL Nor I, assure thee, Regan.—
    Edmund, I hear that you have shown your father
    A child-like office.
EDMUND It was my duty, sir.
115 GLOUCESTER He did bewray his practice and received   *To Cornwall*
    This hurt you see striving to apprehend him.
CORNWALL Is he pursued?
GLOUCESTER Ay, my good lord.
CORNWALL If he be taken, he shall never more
120   Be feared of doing harm: make your own purpose,
    How in my strength you please. For you, Edmund,
    Whose virtue and obedience doth this instant
    So much commend itself, you shall be ours:
    Natures of such deep trust we shall much need:
125   You we first seize on.
EDMUND I shall serve you, sir, truly, however else.
GLOUCESTER For him I thank your grace.
CORNWALL You know not why we came to visit you?

---

101 **tended upon** attended, waited on   103 **consort** company (often pejorative)   104 **though**...
affected if he is ill-disposed   105 **put him on** incited him to   106 **th'expense** the spending
113 **child-like** i.e. obedient, loving   **office** duty/service   115 **bewray** inform on, expose   **his practice**
Edgar's plot   120 **make**...**please** to achieve your ends, use my means and authority in any way you
wish   121 **For** as for   123 **be ours** i.e. work for us, join our household   125 **seize on** take possession of
(legal term)

REGAN Thus out of season, threading dark-eyed night:
130 Occasions, noble Gloucester, of some prize,
Wherein we must have use of your advice:
Our father he hath writ, so hath our sister,
Of differences, which I best thought it fit
To answer from our home: the several messengers
135 From hence attend dispatch. Our good old friend,
Lay comforts to your bosom, and bestow
Your needful counsel to our businesses,
Which craves the instant use.
GLOUCESTER I serve you, madam:
140 Your graces are right welcome.   *Exeunt. Flourish*

Act 2 Scene 2   *running scene 5*

Enter Kent and Steward [Oswald], severally   **Kent disguised as Caius**

OSWALD Good dawning to thee, friend: art of this house?
KENT Ay.
OSWALD Where may we set our horses?
KENT I'th'mire.
5 OSWALD Prithee, if thou lov'st me, tell me.
KENT I love thee not.
OSWALD Why then, I care not for thee.
KENT If I had thee in Lipsbury pinfold, I would make thee
care for me.
10 OSWALD Why dost thou use me thus? I know thee not.
KENT Fellow, I know thee.
OSWALD What dost thou know me for?
KENT A knave, a rascal, an eater of broken meats, a base,
proud, shallow, beggarly, three-suited, hundred-pound,

129 **out of season** inconveniently, unconventionally   **threading** finding a way through (sewing image)   **dark-eyed** quibbling on the idea of a needle's eye   130 **Occasions** events/circumstances   **prize** importance   133 **differences** disputes   134 **from** away from   135 **attend dispatch** wait to be dispatched   138 **craves...use** requires immediate action   2.2 *Location: outside the Earl of Gloucester's residence*   **severally** separately   1 **dawning** it is actually before dawn; we later learn that the moon shines   2 **Ay** in fact, Kent is not a servant at this house; perhaps Kent opens up an opportunity to abuse Oswald   3 **set** put, lodge (Kent plays on the sense of 'fix, make stuck')   4 **mire** mud   5 **if...me** i.e. if you would be so kind (Kent pretends to take the expression literally)   8 **Lipsbury pinfold** the pound for stray animals in Lips-town (i.e. 'between my teeth')   10 **use** treat   12 **for** as   13 **knave** rogue (two lines later the sense shifts to 'servant')   **broken meats** scraps of food   14 **three-suited** servingmen were permitted to have three outfits a year   **hundred-pound** far more than a servingman's income; possibly a contemptuous reference to those who bought knighthoods from James I for £100

15   filthy, worsted-stocking knave, a lily-livered, action-
        taking, whoreson, glass-gazing, super-serviceable
        finical rogue: one-trunk-inheriting slave: one that
        wouldst be a bawd in way of good service, and art
        nothing but the composition of a knave, beggar,
20   coward, pander, and the son and heir of a mongrel
        bitch: one whom I will beat into clamorous whining if
        thou deny'st the least syllable of thy addition.

OSWALD Why, what a monstrous fellow art thou thus to
        rail on one that is neither known of thee nor knows
25   thee!

KENT   What a brazen-faced varlet art thou to deny thou
        knowest me! Is it two days since I tripped up thy
        heels and beat thee before the king? Draw, you
        rogue, for though it be night, yet the moon shines: I'll
30   make a sop o'th'moonshine of you, you whoreson
        cullionly barber-monger. Draw.   *Draws his sword*

OSWALD Away! I have nothing to do with thee.

KENT   Draw, you rascal: you come with letters against
        the king, and take vanity the puppet's part against
35   the royalty of her father: draw, you rogue, or I'll so
        carbonado your shanks: draw, you rascal, come your
        ways.

OSWALD Help, ho! Murder! Help!

KENT   Strike, you slave! Stand, rogue, stand, you neat
40   slave, strike!   *Beats him*

OSWALD Help, ho! Murder! Murder!

*Enter Bastard [Edmund], Cornwall, Regan, Gloucester,
Servants*

EDMUND How now, what's the matter? Part!

KENT   With you, Goodman boy, if you please: come, I'll
        flesh ye: come on, young master.

15 worsted-stocking i.e. servant/unable to afford silk stockings (worsted is a woollen fabric)   **lily-livered**
cowardly, with a bloodless liver (the organ thought to be the seat of strong emotions)
action-taking litigious   **16 whoreson** bastard   **glass-gazing** vain   **glass** mirror   **super-serviceable**
ready to do any kind of service   **17 finical** fussy   **one-trunk-inheriting** owner (or heir to) no more than
would fit in a single trunk   **18 bawd** pimp   **service** plays on the sense of 'sex'   **19 composition**
combination   **20 pander** go-between/pimp   **22 addition** attributes/title/mark of honour added to a coat of
arms (ironic)   **24 rail** rant, heap abuse   **26 varlet** rogue   **28 Draw** draw your sword   **30 sop**
o'th'moonshine i.e. beat you to a pulp (so that you resemble either a soggy piece of bread lying under the
moon's light, or the blancmange pudding called moonshine)   **31 cullionly** rascally   **barber-monger**
frequenter of barbers (i.e. vain fop)   **34 vanity the puppet** i.e. Goneril, imagined as a puppet (or dressed-up
woman) who is the personification of vanity   **36 carbonado** slash diagonally, like meat prepared for
broiling or grilling   **come your ways** come on then   **39 neat** trim, foppish   **43 With you** i.e. I'll fight with
you   **Goodman boy** a contemptuous and belittling form of address (used to Edmund)   **Goodman** a man
below the rank of gentleman   **44 flesh ye** initiate you (into fighting; from the practice of feeding dogs bits of
freshly killed meat in order to excite them for prey)

45   GLOUCESTER Weapons? Arms? What's the matter here?
      CORNWALL Keep peace, upon your lives: he dies that
          strikes again. What is the matter?
      REGAN The messengers from our sister and the king.
      CORNWALL What is your difference? Speak.
50   OSWALD I am scarce in breath, my lord.
      KENT No marvel, you have so bestirred your valour. You
          cowardly rascal, nature disclaims in thee: a tailor
          made thee.
      CORNWALL Thou art a strange fellow — a tailor make a
55   man?
      KENT A tailor, sir: a stone-cutter or a painter could not
          have made him so ill, though they had been but two
          years o'th'trade.
      CORNWALL Speak yet, how grew your quarrel?
60   OSWALD This ancient ruffian, sir, whose life I have
          spared at suit of his grey beard—
      KENT Thou whoreson zed, thou unnecessary letter!—
          My lord, if you will give me leave, I will tread this
          unbolted villain into mortar and daub the wall of a
65   jakes with him.— Spare my grey beard, you wagtail?
      CORNWALL Peace, sirrah!
          You beastly knave, know you no reverence?
      KENT Yes, sir, but anger hath a privilege.
      CORNWALL Why art thou angry?
70   KENT That such a slave as this should wear a sword,
          Who wears no honesty. Such smiling rogues as
              these,
          Like rats, oft bite the holy cords a-twain
          Which are too intrinse t'unloose, smooth every
              passion
          That in the natures of their lords rebel,
75   Being oil to fire, snow to the colder moods,
          Revenge, affirm, and turn their halcyon beaks
          With every gall and vary of their masters,

---

49 difference argument   **51 bestirred your valour** worked up your courage (ironic)   **52 disclaims in** disowns   **tailor made thee** i.e. his only worth lies in his fancy clothes   **57 ill** badly   **61 suit…beard** his own request, because his old age required it   **62 zed…letter** 'z' was regarded as **unnecessary** because 's' could be used instead and there was no 'z' in the Latin alphabet   **64 unbolted** unsifted (plays on the sense of 'unmanly/impotent' – a 'bolt' was a term for the penis)   **65 jakes** privy, toilet   **wagtail** tail-wagger, obsequious person/womanizer   **67 beastly** brutish   **68 a privilege** licence to express itself   **71 honesty** honour, integrity   **72 holy cords** sacred bonds (family or matrimonial ties)   **a-twain** in two   **73 too intrinse t'unloose** too intertwined to be disentangled   **smooth** flatter, indulge   **74 rebel** i.e. against reason   **75 Being…fire** i.e. feed the fire of their masters' passions   **76 halcyon beaks** the kingfisher (**halcyon**) was thought to act as a weather-vane if dried and hung up   **77 gall** irritation   **vary** change

Knowing naught, like dogs, but following.—
A plague upon your epileptic visage!   *To Oswald*
80 Smile you my speeches, as I were a fool?
Goose, if I had you upon Sarum plain,
I'd drive ye cackling home to Camelot.
CORNWALL What, art thou mad, old fellow?
GLOUCESTER How fell you out? Say that.
85 **KENT** No contraries hold more antipathy
Than I and such a knave.
CORNWALL Why dost thou call him knave? What is his
fault?
KENT His countenance likes me not.
CORNWALL No more, perchance, does mine, nor his, nor
hers—
90 **KENT** Sir, 'tis my occupation to be plain:
I have seen better faces in my time
Than stands on any shoulder that I see
Before me at this instant.
CORNWALL This is some fellow
95 Who, having been praised for bluntness, doth affect
A saucy roughness, and constrains the garb
Quite from his nature. He cannot flatter, he:
An honest mind and plain, he must speak truth!
An they will take it, so: if not, he's plain.
100 These kind of knaves I know, which in this plainness
Harbour more craft and more corrupter ends
Than twenty silly ducking observants
That stretch their duties nicely.
KENT Sir, in good faith, in sincere verity,
105 Under th'allowance of your great aspect,
Whose influence, like the wreath of radiant fire
On flickering Phoebus' front—
CORNWALL What mean'st by this?

79 epileptic visage seeing Oswald smiling away his insults, Kent compares his expression to that of an epileptic, grimacing involuntarily   **80 my** at my   **as** as if   **81 Goose** proverbially stupid bird; **cackling** suggests that Oswald may be laughing   **if . . . Camelot** i.e. if I had you at my mercy, I'd send you running home in fright; the exact nature of this reference is unclear, though, as Camelot was sometimes identified with Winchester, some suspect a jibe about a 'Winchester goose' (i.e. a prostitute/venereal disease)   **Sarum** Salisbury, in Wiltshire   **82 Camelot** legendary city that was home to King Arthur   **88 likes** pleases   **90 occupation** habit, business   **96 saucy** insolent   **constrains . . . nature** forces the style (of speaking) away from its true purpose   **99 An** if   **so** so be it   **plain** honest (his excuse for his rudeness)   **101 craft** cunning   **corrupter** corrupt   **102 ducking observants** bowing attendants   **103 stretch . . . nicely** strain to perform their duties to the last detail   **104 verity** truth   **105 th'allowance** the approval   **aspect** face/planetary position (in comparing Cornwall to a powerful planet, Kent mocks a courtier's flattery)   **106 influence** astrological influence   **107 Phoebus** the Greek and Roman sun god   **front** forehead

KENT To go out of my dialect, which you discommend so
110   much. I know, sir, I am no flatterer: he that beguiled
    you in a plain accent was a plain knave, which for
    my part I will not be, though I should win your
    displeasure to entreat me to't.

CORNWALL What was th'offence you gave him?   *To Oswald*
115 **OSWALD** I never gave him any.
    It pleased the king his master very late
    To strike at me, upon his misconstruction:
    When he, compact and flattering his displeasure,
    Tripped me behind, being down, insulted, railed,
120   And put upon him such a deal of man
    That worthied him, got praises of the king
    For him attempting who was self-subdued:
    And, in the fleshment of this dread exploit,
    Drew on me here again.
125 **KENT** None of these rogues and cowards
    But Ajax is their fool.

CORNWALL Fetch forth the stocks!—
    You stubborn ancient knave, you reverent braggart,
    We'll teach you.
130 **KENT** Sir, I am too old to learn.
    Call not your stocks for me: I serve the king,
    On whose employment I was sent to you:
    You shall do small respects, show too bold malice
    Against the grace and person of my master,
135   Stocking his messenger.

CORNWALL Fetch forth the stocks! As I have life and
    honour,
    There shall he sit till noon.

REGAN Till noon? Till night, my lord, and all night too.

KENT Why, madam, if I were your father's dog
140   You should not use me so.

REGAN Sir, being his knave, I will.

---

109 dialect usual manner of speaking   **110 beguiled** deceived   **112 though . . . to't** even if I should incur
your displeasure by refusing (to be a **knave**) when asked   **117 misconstruction** misinterpretation
118 compact colluding (with the king)   **119 being** and I being   **120 deal of man** great show of
manliness   **121 worthied him** earned him honour/made him a hero   **122 attempting . . . self-subdued**
attacking one who offered no resistance   **123 fleshment** excitement of a first success   **dread exploit**
fearsome military enterprise (sarcastic)   **125 None . . . fool** there is not one of these rogues and cowards
who cannot make a fool of a man like **Ajax** (the great Greek warrior was famously stupid; Cornwall is the
subject of this dig)   **127 stocks** instrument of public punishment in which the offender sat with his ankles
and sometimes wrists confined   **128 reverent** old and revered (sarcastic)   **braggart** boaster
133 bold malice impudent hostility   **134 grace** sovereignty   **140 use** treat

Stocks brought out

CORNWALL This is a fellow of the self-same colour
    Our sister speaks of. Come, bring away the stocks!

GLOUCESTER Let me beseech your grace not to do so:
145   The king his master needs must take it ill
    That he so slightly valued in his messenger,
    Should have him thus restrained.

CORNWALL I'll answer that.

REGAN My sister may receive it much more worse
150   To have her gentleman abused, assaulted.   *Kent put in the stocks*

CORNWALL Come, my lord, away.
                Exeunt. [Gloucester and Kent remain]

GLOUCESTER I am sorry for thee, friend: 'tis the duke's
    pleasure,
    Whose disposition all the world well knows
    Will not be rubbed nor stopped. I'll entreat for thee.

155 KENT Pray do not, sir. I have watched and travelled
    hard:
    Some time I shall sleep out, the rest I'll whistle.
    A good man's fortune may grow out at heels.
    Give you good morrow.

GLOUCESTER The duke's to blame in this: 'twill be ill
    taken.   *Exit*

160 KENT Good king, that must approve the common saw,
    Thou out of heaven's benediction com'st
    To the warm sun.   *Pulls out a letter*
    Approach, thou beacon to this under globe,
    That by thy comfortable beams I may
165   Peruse this letter. Nothing almost sees miracles
    But misery. I know 'tis from Cordelia,
    Who hath most fortunately been informed
    Of my obscurèd course, and shall find time
    From this enormous state, seeking to give
170   Losses their remedies. All weary and o'erwatched,
    Take vantage, heavy eyes, not to behold

142 **colour** type   143 **sister** sister-in-law, i.e. Goneril   **away** here/there (Cornwall directs where the stocks are to be placed)   148 **answer** be responsible for   152 **pleasure** will   154 **rubbed** deflected (from bowling where the 'rub' is the obstacle that disrupts the path of the ball)   155 **watched** gone without sleep
157 **out at heels** worn out (literally, coming through one's stockings or shoes; an appropriate phrase for one whose feet are poking out of the stocks)   158 **Give...morrow** Goodbye   160 **approve** prove
saw saying   161 **out...sun** proverbial for going from good to bad; Kent means that Regan will prove worse than Goneril   163 **beacon** i.e. the sun   **this under globe** i.e. the earth   164 **comfortable** comforting, encouraging   165 **Nothing...misery** the miserable are almost the only people to see miracles
168 **obscurèd course** secret (and 'disguised') course of action/dimmed fortunes   169 **From** away from (i.e. in France)   **enormous state** disordered situation (or country)   170 **o'erwatched** worn out by lack of sleep   171 **vantage** advantage

This shameful lodging.
Fortune, goodnight: smile once more, turn thy wheel!   *Sleeps*

Enter Edgar

EDGAR I heard myself proclaimed,
175   And by the happy hollow of a tree
Escaped the hunt. No port is free, no place
That guard and most unusual vigilance
Does not attend my taking. Whiles I may scape,
I will preserve myself, and am bethought
180   To take the basest and most poorest shape
That ever penury in contempt of man
Brought near to beast: my face I'll grime with filth,
Blanket my loins, elf all my hairs in knots,
And with presented nakedness outface
185   The winds and persecutions of the sky.
The country gives me proof and precedent
Of Bedlam beggars, who with roaring voices
Strike in their numbed and mortifièd arms
Pins, wooden pricks, nails, sprigs of rosemary,
190   And with this horrible object, from low farms,
Poor pelting villages, sheepcotes, and mills,
Sometimes with lunatic bans, sometime with prayers,
Enforce their charity. Poor Turlygod, poor Tom!
That's something yet: Edgar I nothing am.   *Exit*

Enter Lear, Fool and Gentleman

195   **LEAR** 'Tis strange that they should so depart from home
And not send back my messengers.
GENTLEMAN As I learned,
The night before there was no purpose in them
Of this remove.
200   **KENT** Hail to thee, noble master!   *Wakes*
LEAR Ha? Mak'st thou this shame thy pastime?
KENT No, my lord.

---

173 **Fortune . . . wheel!** Fortune was traditionally depicted as a woman turning a wheel that raised humans up and cast them down   174 **proclaimed** publicly declared an outlaw   175 **happy** opportune, fortunate   178 **attend my taking** wait to catch me   179 **am bethought** have decided   181 **in . . . man** despising mankind (in particular, man's claim to be superior to beasts)   183 **elf** tangle (into 'elflocks' or messy knots of hair)   184 **presented** openly displayed   187 **Bedlam** the Saint Mary of Bethlehem hospital in London; a number of those who were released became **beggars**   188 **mortifièd** deadened   189 **pricks** spikes   190 **object** sight   **low** humble, lowly   191 **pelting** paltry, insignificant   192 **bans** curses   193 **Poor . . . Tom!** the sorts of cries the beggars would utter; several sixteenth-century accounts refer to beggars calling themselves 'Poor Tom'   **Turlygod** unexplained: perhaps a deliberately nonsensical name   194 **That's something yet** i.e. at least as Poor Tom I have some form of existence   **Edgar . . . am** as Edgar I do not exist/I renounce my identity as Edgar   ***Gentleman*** presumably one of Lear's reduced retinue of knights   195 **they** i.e. Regan and Cornwall

FOOL Ha, ha, he wears cruel garters. Horses are tied by
　　 the heads, dogs and bears by th'neck, monkeys by
205　 th'loins, and men by th'legs: when a man's over-
　　 lusty at legs, then he wears wooden nether-stocks.
LEAR What's he that hath so much thy place mistook
　　 To set thee here?
KENT It is both he and she:
210　 Your son and daughter.
LEAR No.
KENT Yes.
LEAR No, I say.
KENT I say, yea.
215 LEAR By Jupiter, I swear, no.
KENT By Juno, I swear, ay.
LEAR They durst not do't:
　　 They could not, would not do't: 'tis worse than
　　　 murder
　　 To do upon respect such violent outrage.
220　 Resolve me with all modest haste which way
　　 Thou might'st deserve or they impose this usage,
　　 Coming from us.
KENT My lord, when at their home
　　 I did commend your highness' letters to them,
225　 Ere I was risen from the place that showed
　　 My duty kneeling, came there a reeking post,
　　 Stewed in his haste, half breathless, panting forth
　　 From Goneril his mistress salutations,
　　 Delivered letters, spite of intermission,
230　 Which presently they read: on those contents
　　 They summoned up their meiny, straight took horse,
　　 Commanded me to follow and attend
　　 The leisure of their answer, gave me cold looks:
　　 And meeting here the other messenger,
235　 Whose welcome I perceived had poisoned mine —
　　 Being the very fellow which of late

203 **cruel** puns on 'crewel' (i.e. wool used for stockings)　205 **over-lusty at legs** as a servant, too ready to
run away (perhaps plays on the sense of 'too eager for sex')　206 **nether-stocks** stockings　207 **place**
position (as Lear's messenger)　208 **To** as to　210 **son** son-in-law　216 **Juno** wife of Jupiter, the supreme
Roman god　219 **upon respect** upon consideration/against the respect due to a king and his
representatives　220 **Resolve** make clear to, inform　**modest** moderate, reasonable　**which way** why,
how　221 **usage** treatment　222 **Coming from us** when you were sent by me　224 **commend**
deliver　226 **reeking** steaming (with sweat)　**post** messenger　227 **Stewed** hot and drenched in sweat
229 **spite of intermission** in spite of interrupting me/in spite of his halting breath　230 **presently**
immediately　231 **meiny** retinue　**straight** straight away　232 **attend ... answer** wait until they had
time to answer

Displayed so saucily against your highness —
Having more man than wit about me, drew.
He raised the house with loud and coward cries:
240   Your son and daughter found this trespass worth
The shame which here it suffers.

FOOL Winter's not gone yet if the wild geese fly that
way.

Fathers that wear rags   *Sings*
Do make their children blind,
245   But fathers that bear bags
Shall see their children kind.
Fortune, that arrant whore,
Ne'er turns the key to th'poor.
But, for all this, thou shalt have as many dolours for
250   thy daughters as thou canst tell in a year.

LEAR O, how this mother swells up toward my heart!
Hysterica passio, down, thou climbing sorrow:
Thy element's below!— Where is this daughter?

KENT With the earl, sir, here within.

255   LEAR Follow me not: stay here.   *Exit*

GENTLEMAN Made you no more offence but what you
speak of?

KENT None. How chance the king comes with so small a
number?

260   FOOL An thou had'st been set i'th'stocks for that
question, thou'dst well deserved it.

KENT Why, fool?

FOOL We'll set thee to school to an ant to teach thee
there's no labouring i'th'winter. All that follow their
265   noses are led by their eyes but blind men, and there's
not a nose among twenty but can smell him that's
stinking. Let go thy hold when a great wheel runs
down a hill lest it break thy neck with following: but
the great one that goes upward, let him draw thee

---

237 Displayed ... against openly behaved so impudently towards   **238 man than wit** courage than
sense   **drew** drew my sword   **242 Winter's ... way** i.e. there is more stormy weather (trouble) on the
way   **244 blind** i.e. to their father's needs   **245 bags** moneybags   **247 arrant** downright/notorious
248 turns the key opens the door/provides sexual favours   **249 dolours** griefs (puns on 'dollar', a silver
coin)   **250 tell** relate/count   **251 mother** i.e. hysteria (frequently a female affliction thought to arise from
the womb or, in men, the abdomen; characterized by breathlessness and agitation)   **252 *Hysterica passio***
the Latin term for hysteria   **253 element** rightful environment   **below** i.e. in the womb   **263 to school
to** i.e. to learn from   **ant ... i'th'winter** i.e. the ant gathers food only in the summer when it is abundant;
similarly, men work only when there is profit to be gained from a patron who is at the height of his
fortunes   **267 stinking** i.e. with the stench of decaying fortunes

270 after. When a wise man gives thee better counsel,
give me mine again: I would have none but knaves
follow it, since a fool gives it.
    That sir which serves and seeks for gain,   *Sings*
    And follows but for form,
275   Will pack when it begins to rain,
    And leave thee in the storm.
    But I will tarry, the fool will stay,
    And let the wise man fly:
    The knave turns fool that runs away,
280   The fool no knave, perdy.

Enter Lear and Gloucester

KENT Where learned you this, fool?

FOOL Not i'th'stocks, fool.

LEAR Deny to speak with me? They are sick, they are
    weary,
They have travelled all the night? Mere fetches,
285 The images of revolt and flying off.
Fetch me a better answer.

GLOUCESTER My dear lord,
You know the fiery quality of the duke,
How unremovable and fixed he is
290 In his own course.

LEAR Vengeance, plague, death, confusion!
Fiery? What quality? Why, Gloucester, Gloucester,
I'd speak with the Duke of Cornwall and his wife.

GLOUCESTER Well, my good lord, I have informed them
    so.

295 **LEAR** Informed them? Dost thou understand me, man?

GLOUCESTER Ay, my good lord.

LEAR The king would speak with Cornwall: the dear
    father
Would with his daughter speak, commands, tends,
    service.
Are they informed of this? My breath and blood!
300 Fiery? The fiery duke? Tell the hot duke that —
No, but not yet: maybe he is not well.
Infirmity doth still neglect all office

---

271 again back again   **273 sir** man   **274 form** appearances, outward show   **275 pack** pack up, be off
280 perdy by God (from the French *par dieu*)   **283 Deny** refuse   **284 fetches** tricks, stratagems (Lear goes
on to employ the sense of 'bring')   **285 flying off** desertion   **291 confusion** destruction, overthrow
298 tends attends, awaits   **302 Infirmity . . . bound** illness always makes us neglect the duties which, when
healthy, we are bound to carry out

Whereto our health is bound: we are not ourselves
When nature, being oppressed, commands the mind
305   To suffer with the body. I'll forbear,
And am fallen out with my more headier will,
To take the indisposed and sickly fit
For the sound man. Death on my state! Wherefore   *Sees Kent*
Should he sit here? This act persuades me
310   That this remotion of the duke and her
Is practice only. Give me my servant forth.
Go tell the duke and's wife I'd speak with them,
Now, presently: bid them come forth and hear me,
Or at their chamber-door I'll beat the drum
315   Till it cry sleep to death.
GLOUCESTER I would have all well betwixt you.   *Exit*
LEAR O me, my heart, my rising heart! But, down!
FOOL Cry to it, nuncle, as the cockney did to the eels
when she put 'em i'th'paste alive: she knapped 'em
320   o'th'coxcombs with a stick and cried 'Down,
wantons, down!' 'Twas her brother that, in pure
kindness to his horse, buttered his hay.
Enter Cornwall, Regan, Gloucester, Servants
LEAR Good morrow to you both.
CORNWALL Hail to your grace!
Kent here set at liberty
325   **REGAN** I am glad to see your highness.
LEAR Regan, I think you are. I know what reason
I have to think so: if thou shouldst not be glad,
I would divorce me from thy mother's tomb,
Sepulch'ring an adult'ress.— O, are you free?   *To Kent*
330   Some other time for that.— Belovèd Regan,
Thy sister's naught: O Regan, she hath tied
Sharp-toothed unkindness, like a vulture, here.   *Points to his heart*
I can scarce speak to thee. Thou'lt not believe
With how depraved a quality — O Regan!

---

304 **oppressed** overwhelmed/afflicted   306 **fallen . . . will** angry with my more headstrong impulse
308 **sound** healthy   **my state** royal state   310 **remotion** removal   311 **practice** deceit, cunning
Give . . . forth release my servant   312 **and's** and his   318 **cockney** squeamish or affected woman/town-
dweller not used to hardier country ways   319 **i'th'paste alive** alive into the pie (being too squeamish to kill
them first)   **knapped** hit   320 **o'th'coxcombs** on the heads   321 **wantons** frisky creatures
322 **buttered his hay** another example of misguided kindness (horses dislike grease)   329 **Sepulch'ring**
entombing   **adult'ress** i.e. as you could not possibly be my daughter if you were not glad to see me
331 **naught** wicked/worthless   332 **vulture** recalls the Greek legend of Prometheus, who was punished for
stealing fire from the gods by having his liver perpetually gnawed by vultures

335 REGAN I pray you, sir, take patience: I have hope
You less know how to value her desert
Than she to scant her duty.
LEAR Say? How is that?
REGAN I cannot think my sister in the least
340 Would fail her obligation: if, sir, perchance
She have restrained the riots of your followers,
'Tis on such ground and to such wholesome end
As clears her from all blame.
LEAR My curses on her!
345 REGAN O, sir, you are old:
Nature in you stands on the very verge
Of her confine: you should be ruled and led
By some discretion that discerns your state
Better than you yourself. Therefore, I pray you,
350 That to our sister you do make return:
Say you have wronged her.
LEAR Ask her forgiveness?
Do you but mark how this becomes the house:
Dear daughter, I confess that I am old;   *Kneels*
355 Age is unnecessary. On my knees I beg
That you'll vouchsafe me raiment, bed and food.
REGAN Good sir, no more: these are unsightly tricks:
Return you to my sister.
LEAR Never, Regan: *Rises*
360 She hath abated me of half my train,
Looked black upon me, struck me with her tongue
Most serpent-like upon the very heart.
All the stored vengeances of heaven fall
On her ingrateful top! Strike her young bones,
365 You taking airs, with lameness—
CORNWALL Fie, sir, fie!
LEAR You nimble lightnings, dart your blinding flames
Into her scornful eyes! Infect her beauty,
You fen-sucked fogs drawn by the powerful sun
370 To fall and blister!
REGAN O the blest gods! So will you wish on me
When the rash mood is on.

336 **You . . . duty** you are more likely to undervalue her worth than she is to neglect her duty
346 **verge . . . confine** limit of her domain (i.e. you are near death)   348 **discretion** (person of) good
judgement   **state** personal condition (imaged as a country; ironic glance at the sense of 'kingship')
353 **becomes the house** befits the royal line or family   355 **unnecessary** superfluous, useless
356 **vouchsafe** permit   **raiment** clothing   360 **abated** deprived   364 **top** head   365 **taking** infectious
369 **fen-sucked . . . blister** noxious vapours produced by sunshine on swampy ground were considered to be
infectious and so to cause blistering

LEAR No, Regan, thou shalt never have my curse:
    Thy tender-hafted nature shall not give
375   Thee o'er to harshness. Her eyes are fierce, but thine
    Do comfort and not burn. 'Tis not in thee
    To grudge my pleasures, to cut off my train,
    To bandy hasty words, to scant my sizes,
    And, in conclusion, to oppose the bolt
380   Against my coming in: thou better know'st
    The offices of nature, bond of childhood,
    Effects of courtesy, dues of gratitude:
    Thy half o'th'kingdom hast thou not forgot,
    Wherein I thee endowed.

385 REGAN Good sir, to th'purpose.   *Tucket within*

LEAR Who put my man i'th'stocks?

Enter Steward [Oswald]

CORNWALL What trumpet's that?

REGAN I know't my sister's: this approves her letter,
    That she would soon be here.— Is your lady come?   *To Oswald*

390 LEAR This is a slave, whose easy-borrowed pride
    Dwells in the sickly grace of her he follows.—
    Out, varlet, from my sight!

CORNWALL What means your grace?

Enter Goneril

LEAR Who stocked my servant? Regan, I have good hope
395   Thou didst not know on't. Who comes here? O
      heavens,
    If you do love old men, if your sweet sway
    Allow obedience, if you yourselves are old,
    Make it your cause, send down, and take my part!—
    Art not ashamed to look upon this beard?—   *To Goneril*
400   O Regan, will you take her by the hand?   *Regan and Goneril*

GONERIL Why not by th'hand, sir? How have I offended?   *join hands*
    All's not offence that indiscretion finds
    And dotage terms so.

LEAR O sides, you are too tough!
405   Will you yet hold?— How came my man i'th'stocks?

CORNWALL I set him there, sir: but his own disorders
    Deserved much less advancement.

---

374 tender-hafted delicately-framed, gently disposed   **378 scant my sizes** reduce my allowances (of food and drink etc.)   **379 oppose the bolt** lock the door   **381 offices of nature** natural filial duties
382 Effects outward marks   **385 to th'purpose** get to the point   **388 approves** confirms, bears out
390 easy-borrowed easily assumed   **391 sickly** diseased, corrupt   **grace** favour/royalty   **395 on't** of it
396 sway authority, rule   **397 Allow** sanctions, approves   **399 beard** grey beard, symbol of his age
402 indiscretion poor judgement   **404 sides** bodily frame, ribcage   **406 disorders** misconduct
407 much less advancement less favourable treatment

LEAR You? Did you?

REGAN I pray you, father, being weak, seem so.
410   If till the expiration of your month,
       You will return and sojourn with my sister,
       Dismissing half your train, come then to me:
       I am now from home, and out of that provision
       Which shall be needful for your entertainment.
415 LEAR Return to her? And fifty men dismissed?
       No, rather I abjure all roofs, and choose
       To wage against the enmity o'th'air,
       To be a comrade with the wolf and owl,
       Necessity's sharp pinch! Return with her?
420   Why, the hot-blooded France, that dowerless took
       Our youngest born, I could as well be brought
       To knee his throne and, squire-like, pension beg
       To keep base life afoot. Return with her?
       Persuade me rather to be slave and sumpter
425   To this detested groom.   *Points at Oswald*
     GONERIL At your choice, sir.
     LEAR I prithee, daughter, do not make me mad.
       I will not trouble thee, my child, farewell:
       We'll no more meet, no more see one another.
430   But yet thou art my flesh, my blood, my daughter —
       Or rather a disease that's in my flesh,
       Which I must needs call mine: thou art a boil,
       A plague-sore, or embossèd carbuncle,
       In my corrupted blood. But I'll not chide thee:
435   Let shame come when it will, I do not call it:
       I do not bid the thunder-bearer shoot,
       Nor tell tales of thee to high-judging Jove.
       Mend when thou canst, be better at thy leisure:
       I can be patient, I can stay with Regan,
440   I and my hundred knights.
     REGAN Not altogether so:
       I looked not for you yet, nor am provided
       For your fit welcome. Give ear, sir, to my sister,
       For those that mingle reason with your passion

---

414 **entertainment** hospitable reception   416 **abjure** renounce   417 **wage...o'th'air** battle against the hostility of the open air   419 **Necessity's** need's, deprivation's   422 **knee** kneel before   **squire-like** like a servant or follower   **pension** financial allowance   423 **afoot** going   424 **sumpter** packhorse, beast of burden   425 **groom** manservant   433 **embossèd carbuncle** swollen tumour   434 **corrupted blood** diseased lineage   438 **Mend** improve   442 **looked not for** did not expect   444 **mingle...passion** apply rational judgement to your impulsive behaviour

445   Must be content to think you old, and so —
            But she knows what she does.

LEAR Is this well spoken?

REGAN I dare avouch it, sir: what, fifty followers?
            Is it not well? What should you need of more?
450   Yea, or so many, sith that both charge and danger
            Speak gainst so great a number? How in one house
            Should many people under two commands
            Hold amity? 'Tis hard, almost impossible.

GONERIL Why might not you, my lord, receive attendance
455   From those that she calls servants, or from mine?

REGAN Why not, my lord? If then they chanced to slack ye,
            We could control them. If you will come to me —
            For now I spy a danger — I entreat you
            To bring but five-and-twenty: to no more
460   Will I give place or notice.

LEAR I gave you all—

REGAN And in good time you gave it.

LEAR Made you my guardians, my depositaries,
            But kept a reservation to be followed
465   With such a number. What, must I come to you
            With five-and-twenty? Regan, said you so?

REGAN And speak't again, my lord: no more with me.

LEAR Those wicked creatures yet do look well-favoured
            When others are more wicked: not being the worst
470   Stands in some rank of praise.— I'll go with thee: *To Goneril*
            Thy fifty yet doth double five-and-twenty,
            And thou art twice her love.

GONERIL Hear me, my lord:
            What need you five-and-twenty, ten, or five,
475   To follow in a house where twice so many
            Have a command to tend you?

REGAN What need one?

LEAR O, reason not the need! Our basest beggars
            Are in the poorest thing superfluous:
480   Allow not nature more than nature needs,

---

448 avouch declare, affirm   **450 sith that** since   **charge and danger** expense and the risk of riotous behaviour   **456 slack ye** treat you negligently   **457 control** discipline   **460 place or notice** room or acknowledgement   **462 in...it** it was about time you did so   **463 guardians, my depositaries** trustees   **464 kept a reservation** reserved the right   **468 well-favoured** good-looking   **470 Stands...praise** is, in relative terms, worthy of some praise   **478 Our...superfluous** even our most wretched beggars have something, however poor, that is more than they absolutely need   **480 Allow not** if you do not allow

Man's life is cheap as beast's. Thou art a lady;
If only to go warm were gorgeous,
Why, nature needs not what thou gorgeous wear'st,
Which scarcely keeps thee warm. But for true
 need —
485 You heavens, give me that patience, patience I need!
You see me here, you gods, a poor old man,
As full of grief as age, wretched in both.
If it be you that stirs these daughters' hearts
Against their father, fool me not so much
490 To bear it tamely: touch me with noble anger,
And let not women's weapons, water drops,
Stain my man's cheeks! No, you unnatural hags,
I will have such revenges on you both,
That all the world shall — I will do such things —
495 What they are yet I know not, but they shall be
The terrors of the earth! You think I'll weep:
No, I'll not weep: I have full cause of weeping,
Storm and tempest
 But this heart shall break into a hundred thousand
  flaws,
 Or ere I'll weep. O fool, I shall go mad!
     Exeunt [Lear, Gloucester, Kent and Fool]
500 **CORNWALL** Let us withdraw: 'twill be a storm.
REGAN This house is little: the old man and's people
 Cannot be well bestowed.
GONERIL 'Tis his own blame hath put himself from rest
 And must needs taste his folly.
505 **REGAN** For his particular, I'll receive him gladly,
 But not one follower.
GONERIL So am I purposed.
 Where is my lord of Gloucester?
Enter Gloucester
CORNWALL Followed the old man forth: he is returned.
510 **GLOUCESTER** The king is in high rage.
CORNWALL Whither is he going?
GLOUCESTER He calls to horse, but will I know not
 whither.
CORNWALL 'Tis best to give him way: he leads himself.

---

482 **If . . . gorgeous** if being sumptuously dressed simply entailed wearing sufficiently warm clothes
483 **what . . . wear'st** your magnificent clothes   489 **fool . . . much** don't make me such a fool as
498 **flaws** fragments   499 **Or ere** before   501 **and's** and his   502 **bestowed** lodged, accommodated
503 **blame** fault (that he)   **put . . . rest** turned himself away from repose/deprived himself of peace of
mind   505 **his particular** him individually   512 **will** will go   513 **give him way** let him go, give him scope

GONERIL My lord, entreat him by no means to stay.

515 GLOUCESTER Alack, the night comes on, and the high
winds
Do sorely ruffle, for many miles about
There's scarce a bush.

REGAN O, sir, to wilful men
The injuries that they themselves procure
520 Must be their schoolmasters. Shut up your doors:
He is attended with a desperate train,
And what they may incense him to, being apt
To have his ear abused, wisdom bids fear.

CORNWALL Shut up your doors, my lord, 'tis a wild
night.
525 My Regan counsels well: come out o'th'storm. *Exeunt*

Act 3 Scene 1   *running scene 6*

Storm still. Enter Kent and a Gentleman, severally

KENT Who's there, besides foul weather?

GENTLEMAN One minded like the weather, most
unquietly.

KENT I know you. Where's the king?

GENTLEMAN Contending with the fretful elements;
5 Bids the wind blow the earth into the sea
Or swell the curlèd waters 'bove the main,
That things might change or cease.

KENT But who is with him?

GENTLEMAN None but the fool, who labours to out-jest
10 His heart-struck injuries.

KENT Sir, I do know you,
And dare, upon the warrant of my note
Commend a dear thing to you. There is division —
Although as yet the face of it is covered
15 With mutual cunning — 'twixt Albany and
Cornwall,
Who have — as who have not, that their great stars

---

516 **ruffle** rage, bluster 519 **themselves procure** bring on themselves 521 **desperate train** retinue of dangerous men 523 **have...abused** be misled by what he is told 3.1 *Location: somewhere out in the open, not far from the Earl of Gloucester's residence* **severally** separately 2 **minded...unquietly** in the same restless and disturbed mood as the storm 4 **Contending** battling against/competing with 6 **main** mainland 9 **out-jest** drive out with jokes 10 **heart- struck injuries** injuries that strike to the heart 12 **warrant...note** basis of what I have observed (about you) 13 **Commend...you** entrust you with an important matter 16 **as...high** i.e. like anyone to whom fortune has given power and royal authority

Throned and set high? — servants, who seem no less,
Which are to France the spies and speculations
Intelligent of our state. What hath been seen,
20   Either in snuffs and packings of the dukes,
Or the hard rein which both of them hath borne
Against the old kind king, or something deeper,
Whereof perchance these are but furnishings.

GENTLEMAN I will talk further with you.

25   **KENT** No, do not.
For confirmation that I am much more
Than my out-wall, open this purse and take   *Gives a purse*
What it contains. If you shall see Cordelia —
As fear not but you shall — show her this ring,   *Gives a ring*
30   And she will tell you who that fellow is
That yet you do not know. Fie on this storm!
I will go seek the king.

GENTLEMAN Give me your hand. Have you no more to
say?

KENT Few words, but, to effect, more than all yet:
35   That when we have found the king — in which your
pain
That way, I'll this — he that first lights on him
Holla the other.   *Exeunt [separately]*

Act 3 Scene 2   *running scene 6 continues*

Storm still. Enter Lear and Fool

LEAR Blow winds and crack your cheeks! Rage, blow,
You cataracts and hurricanoes, spout
Till you have drenched our steeples, drown the cocks!
You sulphurous and thought-executing fires,
5   Vaunt-couriers of oak-cleaving thunderbolts,
Singe my white head! And thou, all-shaking thunder,
Strike flat the thick rotundity o'th'world!
Crack nature's moulds, all germens spill at once
That makes ingrateful man!

17 seem no less seem to be only servants (but are really spies)   **18 France** the King of France
speculations observers   **19 Intelligent of** bearing information about   **20 snuffs** resentments   **packings**
plots   **21 hard rein** harsh curbing (equestrian metaphor; puns on 'reign')   **borne** maintained
23 furnishings superficial trappings   **27 out-wall** outward appearance   **30 that fellow** i.e. Kent   **34 to**
effect in importance   **35 in…this** to which end you employ your efforts that way while I go this way
37 Holla shout to   **3.2   2 cataracts** floods/waterspouts   **hurricanoes** waterspouts   **3 cocks** weathercocks
4 thought-executing fires i.e. lightning (as swift as thought/thought-destroying)   **5 Vaunt-couriers**
forerunners   **8 nature's moulds** the moulds in which nature makes living creatures   **germens** seeds

10 **FOOL** O, nuncle, court holy-water in a dry house is better
        than this rain-water out o'door. Good nuncle, in, ask
        thy daughters' blessing: here's a night pities neither
        wise men nor fools.
    LEAR Rumble thy bellyful! Spit fire! Spout rain!
15   Nor rain, wind, thunder, fire, are my daughters.
        I tax not you, you elements, with unkindness:
        I never gave you kingdom, called you children;
        You owe me no subscription. Then let fall
        Your horrible pleasure: here I stand, your slave,
20   A poor, infirm, weak and despised old man:
        But yet I call you servile ministers,
        That will with two pernicious daughters join
        Your high-engendered battles gainst a head
        So old and white as this. O, ho, 'tis foul!
25 **FOOL** He that has a house to put's head in has a good
        head-piece:
                The codpiece that will house   *Sings*
                Before the head has any,
                The head and he shall louse,
30   So beggars marry many.
                The man that makes his toe
                What he his heart should make
                Shall of a corn cry woe,
                And turn his sleep to wake.
35   For there was never yet fair woman, but she made
        mouths in a glass.
    Enter Kent   *Disguised as Caius*
    LEAR No, I will be the pattern of all patience:
        I will say nothing.
    KENT Who's there?
40 **FOOL** Marry, here's grace and a codpiece: that's a wise
        man and a fool.

---

10 court holy-water courtly flattery **16 tax...with** accuse...of **18 subscription** allegiance
21 ministers agents **22 pernicious** destructive/wicked **23 high-engendered battles** battalions created
in the heavens **head** plays on the sense of 'army' **24 foul** wicked/bad (weather) **25 put's** put his
26 head-piece helmet/brain **27 codpiece** penis (literally, appendage worn on the front of a man's
breeches to cover and emphasise the genitals) **house** find a house for itself, i.e. have sex **28 any** i.e. any
shelter **29 louse** get lice (in pubic and head hair) **30 So...many** in this way beggars end up with a
string of mistresses (or 'end up not only with a woman but a quantity of lice') **31 makes...make** values
most what he should value least/considers his penis (sex) more important than his heart (love/moral
integrity) **33 corn** may suggest a syphilitic sore **35 made...glass** practised smiling or pouting in a
mirror **40 grace...codpiece** royalty and a fool (fools sometimes wore exaggerated codpieces and were
proverbially well-endowed)

KENT   Alas, sir, are you here? Things that love night
    Love not such nights as these: the wrathful skies
    Gallow the very wanderers of the dark
45   And make them keep their caves. Since I was man,
    Such sheets of fire, such bursts of horrid thunder,
    Such groans of roaring wind and rain, I never
    Remember to have heard: man's nature cannot carry
    Th'affliction nor the fear.
50   LEAR   Let the great gods,
    That keep this dreadful pudder o'er our heads,
    Find out their enemies now. Tremble, thou wretch,
    That hast within thee undivulgèd crimes
    Unwhipped of justice: hide thee, thou bloody hand,
55   Thou perjured, and thou simular of virtue
    That art incestuous: caitiff, to pieces shake,
    That under covert and convenient seeming
    Has practised on man's life: close pent-up guilts,
    Rive your concealing continents and cry
60   These dreadful summoners grace. I am a man
    More sinned against than sinning.
KENT   Alack, bare-headed?
    Gracious my lord, hard by here is a hovel:
    Some friendship will it lend you gainst the tempest.
65   Repose you there while I to this hard house —
    More harder than the stones whereof 'tis raised,
    Which even but now, demanding after you,
    Denied me to come in — return and force
    Their scanted courtesy.
70   LEAR   My wits begin to turn.
    Come on, my boy: how dost, my boy? Art cold?
    I am cold myself.— Where is this straw, my fellow?
    The art of our necessities is strange,
    And can make vile things precious. Come, your
      hovel.—

---

44 **Gallow** gally, i.e. frighten   **wanderers**...**dark** nocturnal animals   51 **pudder** pother, tumult
54 **Unwhipped of** unpunished by   55 **simular** faker, pretender   56 **caitiff** villain, wretch   57 **seeming**
false appearances, deception   58 **practised on** plotted against   59 **Rive** split open   **continents**
containers   **cry**...**grace** beg for mercy from these terrifying **summoners** (officers who summoned the
accused to court)   63 **hard** near   65 **hard house** pitiless household (Gloucester's house, under the
authority of Cornwall and Regan)   67 **demanding** (when I was) asking urgently   69 **scanted** withheld
72 **fellow** servant (but with connotations of 'companion')   73 **The**...**strange** necessity has a strange skill

75   Poor fool and knave, I have one part in my heart
        That's sorry yet for thee.

FOOL   He that has and a little tiny wit,   *Sings*
        With hey, ho, the wind and the rain,
        Must make content with his fortunes fit,
80   Though the rain it raineth every day.

LEAR True, boy.— Come, bring us to this hovel.

                      Exeunt [Lear and Kent]

FOOL This is a brave night to cool a courtesan.
        I'll speak a prophecy ere I go:
        When priests are more in word than matter;
85   When brewers mar their malt with water;
        When nobles are their tailors' tutors;
        No heretics burned, but wenches' suitors;
        When every case in law is right;
        No squire in debt, nor no poor knight;
90   When slanders do not live in tongues;
        Nor cutpurses come not to throngs;
        When usurers tell their gold i'th'field,
        And bawds and whores do churches build,
        Then shall the realm of Albion
95   Come to great confusion:
        Then comes the time, who lives to see't,
        That going shall be used with feet.
        This prophecy Merlin shall make, for I live before his
        time.   *Exit*

---

77 He . . . day adapted from Feste's song at the end of *Twelfth Night*   **and a** a very   **wit** possibly plays on the sense of 'penis'   **79 make . . . fit** make his happiness fit his fortunes/be content with the fortune that he deserves   **82 brave** fine   **cool** i.e. cool the lust of   **courtesan** courtier's mistress, high-class prostitute **84 in . . . matter** more concerned with words than substance (i.e. do not practise what they preach)   **85 mar** spoil (i.e. water down for their own profit)   **86 are . . . tutors** i.e. teach their tailors about fashion **87 heretics** religious dissenters, conventionally punished with burning at the stake   **wenches' suitors** i.e. who are afflicted with the burning effects of syphilis   **88 right** just   **91 cutpurses** thieves who cut the strings of moneybags hanging at their victims' waists   **throngs** crowds   **92 usurers** moneylenders, notorious for charging excessively high interest   **tell . . . i'th'field** count their money openly   **93 bawds** pimps   **94 Albion** ancient name for Britain   **95 confusion** destruction, overthrow   **96 who** whoever **97 going . . . feet** walking will be done on foot (perhaps simply meaning 'things will return to normal') **98 Merlin** in the legendary history of Britain, the reign of Lear precedes that of Arthur by centuries

Act 3 Scene 3

Enter Gloucester and Edmund   **Carrying torches**

GLOUCESTER Alack, alack, Edmund, I like not this
unnatural dealing. When I desired their leave that I
might pity him, they took from me the use of mine
own house, charged me on pain of perpetual
5 displeasure neither to speak of him, entreat for him,
or any way sustain him.

EDMUND Most savage and unnatural.

GLOUCESTER Go to; say you nothing. There is division
between the dukes, and a worse matter than that. I
10 have received a letter this night — 'tis dangerous to
be spoken — I have locked the letter in my closet. These
injuries the king now bears will be revenged home; there
is part of a power already footed. We must incline to
the king: I will look him and privily relieve him. Go you
15 and maintain talk with the duke, that my charity be not
of him perceived: if he ask for me, I am ill and gone to bed:
if I die for it — as no less is threatened me — the king my
old master must be relieved. There is strange things
toward, Edmund: pray you be careful.

Exit

20 **EDMUND** This courtesy forbid thee shall the duke
Instantly know, and of that letter too:
This seems a fair deserving and must draw me
That which my father loses: no less than all.
The younger rises when the old doth fall.   *Exit*

Act 3 Scene 4

Enter Lear, Kent and Fool   **Kent disguised as Caius**

KENT Here is the place, my lord. Good my lord, enter:
The tyranny of the open night's too rough
For nature to endure.

3.3 *Location: the Earl of Gloucester's residence* **2 leave . . . pity** permission to help, take pity on
8 Go to expression of impatient dismissal **11 closet** private room/cabinet **12 home** thoroughly
13 power army **footed** ashore **incline to** support, side with **14 look** look for **privily relieve** secretly
help **15 that** so that **16 of** by **19 toward** imminent **20 courtesy forbid thee** forbidden kindness (to
Lear) **22 This . . . deserving** i.e. my action should be worth a good reward **3.4** *Location: outside a
hovel somewhere out in the open, not far from the Earl of Gloucester's residence* **3 nature** human
nature

Storm still

LEAR Let me alone.

5 **KENT** Good my lord, enter here.

LEAR Will't break my heart?

KENT I had rather break mine own. Good my lord, enter.

LEAR Thou think'st 'tis much that this contentious storm
    Invades us to the skin so: 'tis to thee,
10   But where the greater malady is fixed
    The lesser is scarce felt. Thou'dst shun a bear,
    But if thy flight lay toward the roaring sea
    Thou'dst meet the bear i'th'mouth. When the mind's free,
    The body's delicate: the tempest in my mind
15   Doth from my senses take all feeling else
    Save what beats there. Filial ingratitude!
    Is it not as this mouth should tear this hand
    For lifting food to't? But I will punish home.
    No, I will weep no more. In such a night
20   To shut me out? Pour on, I will endure.
    In such a night as this? O Regan, Goneril,
    Your old kind father, whose frank heart gave all —
    O, that way madness lies: let me shun that:
    No more of that.

25 **KENT** Good my lord, enter here.

LEAR Prithee go in thyself: seek thine own ease:
    This tempest will not give me leave to ponder
    On things would hurt me more. But I'll go in.—
    In, boy, go first.—   *To the Fool*
              You houseless poverty—
30   Nay, get thee in.— I'll pray, and then I'll sleep.
                         Exit [Fool]

    Poor naked wretches, wheresoe'er you are,   *Kneels*
    That bide the pelting of this pitiless storm,
    How shall your houseless heads and unfed sides,
    Your lopped and windowed raggedness, defend you
35   From seasons such as these? O, I have ta'en
    Too little care of this! Take physic, pomp,
    Expose thyself to feel what wretches feel,
    That thou mayst shake the superflux to them
    And show the heavens more just.

---

10 greater malady i.e. mental suffering   **13 i'th'mouth** face to face   **free** free of worry, untroubled
14 delicate sensitive   **17 as** as if   **18 home** soundly   **22 frank** generous   **32 bide** endure   **33 sides**
bodies (with visible ribs)   **34 lopped and windowed** full of holes   **36 physic** medicine (often a
purgative)   **pomp** splendour, ostentatious display (i.e. rich and powerful people)   **38 superflux** superfluity,
excess (**flux** was used for a discharge of excrement from the bowels, the result of a purgative)

Enter Edgar and Fool   *Within the hovel*

40   **EDGAR** Fathom and half, fathom and half! Poor Tom!

FOOL Come not in here, nuncle, here's a spirit. Help me,
help me!

KENT Give me thy hand. Who's there?

FOOL A spirit, a spirit: he says his name's poor Tom.

45   **KENT** What art thou that dost grumble there i'th'straw?
Come forth.

Edgar comes out, disguised as a mad beggar

EDGAR Away! The foul fiend follows me! Through the
sharp hawthorn blow the winds. Hum! Go to thy bed
and warm thee.

50   **LEAR** Did'st thou give all to thy daughters? And art thou
come to this?

EDGAR Who gives anything to poor Tom? Whom the
foul fiend hath led through fire and through flame,
through ford and whirlpool, o'er bog and quagmire,

55   that hath laid knives under his pillow, and halters in
his pew, set ratsbane by his porridge, made him
proud of heart, to ride on a bay trotting-horse over
four-inched bridges, to course his own shadow for a
traitor. Bless thy five wits! Tom's a-cold. O, do de, do

60   de, do de. Bless thee from whirlwinds, star-blasting
and taking! Do poor Tom some charity, whom the
foul fiend vexes: there could I have him now — and
there — and there again, and there.

Storm still

LEAR Has his daughters brought him to this pass?

65   Couldst thou save nothing? Wouldst thou give 'em
all?

FOOL Nay, he reserved a blanket, else we had been all
shamed.

LEAR Now, all the plagues that in the pendulous air

70   Hang fated o'er men's faults light on thy daughters!

40 Fathom and half Edgar calls as though he is measuring the depth of the water in the hovel, as a sailor might in a leaking ship **Fathom** about six feet **41 spirit** evil spirit, demon **45 grumble** mutter, mumble **53 foul** wicked **55 knives . . . pew** the devil was believed to tempt men to damnation by leaving them the means of committing suicide (even in church) **56 ratsbane** rat poison **porridge** vegetable or meat soup **57 bay** reddish-brown **58 four-inched** four inches wide (the devil gives one the arrogance to try and perform extremely difficult feats) **course** hunt **for** as **59 five wits** five mental faculties (common wit, imagination, fantasy, estimation and memory) **do . . . de** the sound of chattering teeth? **60 star-blasting** being afflicted by the malign influence of the stars **61 taking** being infected with disease/ malign influence of the stars **62 vexes** torments **there . . . there** perhaps Edgar snatches at parts of his body as he tries to catch lice or the devil; or he may grab or point at the air around him **64 pass** state, predicament **67 reserved a blanket** kept a blanket (to cover himself) **69 pendulous** overhanging **70 fated . . . faults** destined to punish men's faults

KENT He hath no daughters, sir.

LEAR Death, traitor! Nothing could have subdued nature
To such a lowness but his unkind daughters.
Is it the fashion that discarded fathers
75   Should have thus little mercy on their flesh?
Judicious punishment! 'Twas this flesh begot
Those pelican daughters.

EDGAR Pillicock sat on Pillicock-hill: alow, alow, loo, loo!

FOOL This cold night will turn us all to fools and mad-
80   men.

EDGAR Take heed o'th'foul fiend: obey thy parents, keep
thy word's justice, swear not, commit not with man's
sworn spouse, set not thy sweetheart on proud array.
Tom's a-cold.

85   **LEAR** What hast thou been?

EDGAR A servingman, proud in heart and mind, that
curled my hair, wore gloves in my cap, served the
lust of my mistress' heart, and did the act of darkness
with her: swore as many oaths as I spake words, and
90   broke them in the sweet face of heaven: one that
slept in the contriving of lust, and waked to do it:
wine loved I dearly, dice dearly, and in woman out-
paramoured the Turk: false of heart, light of ear,
bloody of hand: hog in sloth, fox in stealth, wolf in
95   greediness, dog in madness, lion in prey. Let not the
creaking of shoes nor the rustling of silks betray thy
poor heart to woman: keep thy foot out of brothels,
thy hand out of plackets, thy pen from lenders' books,
and defy the foul fiend. Still through the hawthorn
100   blows the cold wind, says suum, mun, nonny,
Dolphin my boy, boy sessa! Let him trot by.

---

72 subdued nature reduced human nature   **75 thus . . . flesh** refers to Edgar's self-mutilation   **77 pelican**
young pelicans supposedly fed on their mother's blood; they were proverbial for filial cruelty
78 Pillicock . . . Pillicock-hill possibly part of an old nursery rhyme, but **Pillicock** is slang for penis and
Pillycock-hill the female genitals   **alow . . . loo** possibly from 'halloo' (cry to incite dogs in a hunt), perhaps
an imitation of a cock's crow, or simply a nonsensical sound   **81 obey** Edgar begins a paraphrased version
of five of the Ten Commandments   **82 commit not** i.e. do not commit adultery   **83 on proud array** in
overly fine clothes   **87 gloves** i.e. a mistress' gift, displayed by being worn in one's **cap   91 slept in** i.e.
dreamed of   **92 dice** i.e. gambling   **out-paramoured the Turk** had more lovers than the Turkish Sultan,
famous for his harem   **93 light of ear** eager to listen to gossip   **96 creaking . . . silks** i.e. the sounds of a
fashionable woman walking   **98 plackets** openings in skirts/vaginas   **pen . . . books** i.e. do not sign a loan
agreement   **100 suum, mun** presumably Edgar imitates the sounds of the wind   **nonny** often used as part
of a refrain in popular songs   **101 Dolphin . . . by** perhaps Edgar addresses an imaginary horse; **sessa** is a cry
of encouragement used in hunting or may derive from the French *cessez* ('stop')

Storm still

LEAR Thou wert better in a grave than to answer with
thy uncovered body this extremity of the skies. Is
man no more than this? Consider him well. Thou
105   ow'st the worm no silk, the beast no hide, the sheep
no wool, the cat no perfume. Ha? Here's three on's
are sophisticated. Thou art the thing itself:
unaccommodated man is no more but such a poor
bare, forked animal as thou art. Off, off, you lendings!
110   Come, unbutton here.   *Tears off his clothes*
Enter Gloucester with a torch

FOOL Prithee, nuncle, be contented: 'tis a naughty night
to swim in. Now a little fire in a wild field were like an
old lecher's heart, a small spark, all the rest on's body
cold. Look, here comes a walking fire.
115   **EDGAR** This is the foul Flibbertigibbet: he begins at
curfew and walks till the first cock: he gives the web
and the pin, squints the eye and makes the hare-lip,
mildews the white wheat, and hurts the poor
creature of earth.
120   Swithold footed thrice the old,   *Chants?*
He met the nightmare and her nine-fold:
Bid her alight,
And her troth plight,
And, aroint thee, witch, aroint thee!
125   **KENT** How fares your grace?
LEAR What's he?
KENT Who's there? What is't you seek?
GLOUCESTER What are you there? Your names?
EDGAR Poor Tom, that eats the swimming frog, the toad,
130   the tadpole, the wall-newt and the water, that in the
fury of his heart, when the foul fiend rages, eats cow-
dung for salads, swallows the old rat and the ditch-

---

102 **answer** face, encounter   106 **cat no perfume** the secretions of the anal glands of the civet cat are used
to make perfume   **on's** of us   107 **sophisticated** not simple or natural   108 **unaccommodated**
unprovided for (i.e. not wearing clothes)   109 **lendings** clothes that are 'lent' only, not part of him
111 **naughty** nasty, wicked   114 **walking fire** i.e. Gloucester and his torch   115 **Flibbertigibbet** the name
of a devil (all of the devils Edgar mentions are to be found in Samuel Harsnett's 1603 *Declaration of Egregious
Popish Impostures*)   116 **curfew** i.e. nightfall   **cock** cockcrow   **web . . . pin** cataract of the eye
117 **squints** causes to squint   120 **Swithold** probably Saint Withold, apparently a protector from harm
footed thrice walked three times   **old** wold, downs   121 **nightmare** evil female spirit supposed to settle
upon a sleeper's chest, inducing bad dreams and feelings of suffocation   **nine-fold** perhaps the imps who
attend her   123 **her troth plight** give a solemn promise (to do no more harm)   124 **aroint** begone (used to
witches and demons)   126 **What's** who's   130 **wall-newt** i.e. lizard on the wall   **water** i.e. water newt
132 **ditch-dog** i.e. dead dog in a ditch

dog, drinks the green mantle of the standing pool,
who is whipped from tithing to tithing, and stocked,
135   punished and imprisoned, who hath had three suits
to his back, six shirts to his body:

> Horse to ride, and weapon to wear,
> But mice and rats and such small deer
> Have been Tom's food for seven long year.

140   Beware my follower. Peace, Smulkin, peace, thou
fiend!

GLOUCESTER What, hath your grace no better
company?

EDGAR The prince of darkness is a gentleman: Modo he's
called, and Mahu.

145   **GLOUCESTER** Our flesh and blood, my lord, is grown so   *To Lear*
vile,
That it doth hate what gets it.

EDGAR Poor Tom's a-cold.

GLOUCESTER Go in with me: my duty cannot suffer
T'obey in all your daughters' hard commands:
150   Though their injunction be to bar my doors
And let this tyrannous night take hold upon you,
Yet have I ventured to come seek you out
And bring you where both fire and food is ready.

LEAR First let me talk with this philosopher.—
155   What is the cause of thunder?   *To Edgar*

KENT Good my lord, take his offer: go into th'house.

LEAR I'll talk a word with this same learnèd Theban.—
What is your study?   *To Edgar*

EDGAR How to prevent the fiend and to kill vermin.

160   **LEAR** Let me ask you one word in private.   *They talk apart*

KENT Importune him once more to go, my lord: *To Gloucester*
His wits begin t'unsettle.

GLOUCESTER Canst thou blame him?

Storm still
His daughters seek his death. Ah, that good Kent!
165   He said it would be thus, poor banished man!
Thou sayest the king grows mad: I'll tell thee, friend,
I am almost mad myself. I had a son,

---

133 mantle scum **standing** stagnant **134 whipped** the standard punishment for vagabonds **tithing** parish **135 three . . . shirts** the clothing allowance of a servant **138 deer** animals **140 Smulkin** the name of a devil (that, according to Harsnett, took the form of a mouse) **143 The . . . darkness** the devil **Modo . . . Mahu** the names of two devils **145 flesh and blood** i.e. children (Gloucester is thinking of Edgar, Goneril and Regan) **vile** debased, corrupted **146 gets** begets, conceives **157 Theban** i.e. Greek philosopher (from Thebes) **159 prevent** forestall, thwart **161 Importune** urge **162 t'unsettle** to be disturbed

Now outlawed from my blood: he sought my life
But lately, very late. I loved him, friend:
170   No father his son dearer. True to tell thee,
The grief hath crazed my wits. What a night's this!—
I do beseech your grace—   *To Lear*
LEAR O, cry you mercy, sir.—
Noble philosopher, your company.   *To Edgar*
175   **EDGAR** Tom's a-cold.
GLOUCESTER In, fellow, there, into th'hovel: keep thee   *To Edgar*
    warm.
LEAR Come let's in all.
KENT This way, my lord.
LEAR With him;
180   I will keep still with my philosopher.
KENT Good my lord, soothe him: let him take the fellow.   *To Gloucester*
GLOUCESTER Take him you on.   *To Kent*
KENT Sirrah, come on: go along with us.   *To Edgar*
LEAR Come, good Athenian.
185   **GLOUCESTER** No words, no words: hush.
EDGAR Child Rowland to the dark tower came,
    His word was still: fie, foh and fum,
    I smell the blood of a British man.   *Exeunt*

Act 3 Scene 5   *running scene 9*

Enter Cornwall and Edmund

CORNWALL I will have my revenge ere I depart his
    house.
EDMUND How, my lord, I may be censured, that nature
    thus gives way to loyalty, something fears me to
5   think of.
CORNWALL I now perceive it was not altogether your
    brother's evil disposition made him seek his death,
    but a provoking merit set a-work by a reprovable
    badness in himself.

---

168 **blood** lineage, family   173 **cry you mercy** excuse me   180 **keep still** remain   181 **soothe** indulge,
humour   182 **him you on** him along with you   184 **Athenian** i.e. Greek philosopher (from Athens)
186 **Child...came** perhaps a line from a lost ballad about the legendary French hero Roland (**Child** was the
title for a young man seeking knighthood)   187 **word** password/customary saying   **still** always   **fie...**
man the cry of the giant in the children's tale of Jack the giant-killer   **3.5** *Location: the Earl of*
Gloucester's residence   1 **his** i.e. Gloucester's   3 **nature** natural familial affection   4 **something fears**
somewhat frightens   7 **his** i.e. Gloucester's   8 **provoking...himself** Edgar's sense of his own worth,
provoked into action by Gloucester's reprehensible badness/a provoking quality in Gloucester, which incited
Edgar's reprehensible wickedness

10 EDMUND How malicious is my fortune — that I must
        repent to be just! This is the letter which he spoke of   *Shows a letter*
        which approves him an intelligent party to the
        advantages of France. O heavens! That this treason
        were not, or not I the detector!
15 CORNWALL Go with me to the duchess.
    EDMUND If the matter of this paper be certain, you have
        mighty business in hand.
    CORNWALL True or false, it hath made thee Earl of
        Gloucester. Seek out where thy father is, that he may
20   be ready for our apprehension.
    EDMUND If I find him comforting the king, it will stuff his   *Aside*
        suspicion more fully.— I will persevere in my course
        of loyalty, though the conflict be sore between that
        and my blood.
25 CORNWALL I will lay trust upon thee, and thou shalt find
        a dear father in my love.

                                                    Exeunt

Act 3 Scene 6   *running scene 10*

Enter Kent and Gloucester

    GLOUCESTER Here is better than the open air, take it
        thankfully. I will piece out the comfort with what
        addition I can: I will not be long from you.   *Exit*
    KENT All the power of his wits have given way to his
5   impatience: the gods reward your kindness!
        Enter Lear, Edgar and Fool   *Edgar disguised as Poor Tom*
    EDGAR Frateretto calls me, and tells me Nero is an angler
        in the lake of darkness. Pray, innocent, and beware
        the foul fiend.
    FOOL Prithee, nuncle, tell me whether a madman be a
10   gentleman or a yeoman?
    LEAR A king, a king!

---

11 to be of being   **12 approves** proves   **an intelligent party** a spy, an informer   **20 apprehension**
arrest   **21 his suspicion** suspicion of Gloucester   **3.6** *Location: unspecified; presumably an
outbuilding on the Earl of Gloucester's estate*   **2 piece out** supplement   **5 impatience** anger/inability to
bear suffering   **6 Frateretto** the name of a devil; in Harsnett he is associated with a 'fiddler', which perhaps
suggests **Nero**, the first-century Roman emperor who famously played the fiddle while Rome burned   **angler**
fisherman/thief   **7 lake of darkness** presumably the Stygian lake of the classical underworld, but a phallic
fishing rod and vaginal dark lake may also be implied; perhaps Nero's murder of his own mother is glanced
at – she reportedly asked to be stabbed in the womb as this was where her son had grown   **10 yeoman** land
owner below the rank of gentleman

FOOL No, he's a yeoman that has a gentleman to his son,
for he's a mad yeoman that sees his son a gentleman
before him.

15 LEAR To have a thousand with red burning spits
Come hizzing in upon 'em—

EDGAR Bless thy five wits!

KENT O pity! Sir, where is the patience now
That you so oft have boasted to retain?

20 EDGAR My tears begin to take his part so much   *Aside*
They mar my counterfeiting.

LEAR The little dogs and all,
Trey, Blanch and Sweetheart, see, they bark at me.

EDGAR Tom will throw his head at them. Avaunt, you
25   curs!
Be thy mouth or black or white,
Tooth that poisons if it bite,
Mastiff, greyhound, mongrel grim,
Hound or spaniel, brach or him,
30   Or bobtail tyke or trundle-tail,
Tom will make him weep and wail:
For, with throwing thus my head,
Dogs leapt the hatch, and all are fled.
Do de, de, de. Sessa! Come, march to wakes and fairs
35   and market towns. Poor Tom, thy horn is dry.

LEAR Then let them anatomize Regan: see what breeds
about her heart. Is there any cause in nature that
make these hard hearts?— You, sir, I entertain for   *To Edgar*
one of my hundred; only I do not like the fashion of
40   your garments: you will say they are Persian; but let
them be changed.

Enter Gloucester   *At a distance*

KENT Now, good my lord, lie here and rest awhile.

---

12 to as   **13 mad** sense now shifts to 'angry'   **15 a thousand** i.e. a thousand devils   **16 hizzing** hissing   **'em** i.e. Goneril and Regan; the Quarto text continues at this point with an imaginary 'arraignment' of Goneril (see 'Quarto passages that do not appear in the Folio', p. 134)   **21 mar my counterfeiting** spoil my pretence   **23 Trey…Sweetheart** names for bitches – even his female dogs, he imagines, have turned against him; their names may suggest Lear's daughters ('tray' can mean 'pain, affliction', 'blanch' can mean 'to deceive', 'to flatter')   **24 throw his head** unclear; presumably a threatening gesture of some sort   **Avaunt** begone   **26 or black or** either black or   **27 poisons** i.e. with rabies   **28 grim** fierce   **29 brach** bitch   **him** male   **30 bobtail tyke** small dog with a tail that has been bobbed (cut short)   **trundle-tail** dog with a long, curling tail   **33 hatch** lower half of a divided door **34 Do…de** apparently the sound of chattering teeth again   **Sessa!** cry of encouragement used in hunting or may derive from the French *cessez* ('stop')   **wakes** annual parish fairs (frequented by beggars)   **35 horn** beggars carried drinking horns on strings round their necks   **36 anatomize** dissect   **38 entertain** employ   **40 Persian** i.e. gorgeous, luxurious

LEAR Make no noise, make no noise: draw the curtains.
So, so, we'll go to supper i'th'morning.   *Sleeps*

45 **FOOL** And I'll go to bed at noon.

GLOUCESTER Come hither, friend: where is the king my
    master?   *To Kent*

KENT Here, sir, but trouble him not: his wits are gone.

GLOUCESTER Good friend, I prithee take him in thy
    arms;
I have o'erheard a plot of death upon him:

50 There is a litter ready, lay him in't
And drive toward Dover, friend, where thou shalt
    meet
Both welcome and protection. Take up thy master:
If thou shouldst dally half an hour, his life,
With thine and all that offer to defend him,

55 Stand in assurèd loss. Take up, take up,
And follow me, that will to some provision   *They carry Lear*
Give thee quick conduct. Come, come, away.   *Exeunt*

Act 3 Scene 7   *running scene 11*

*Enter Cornwall, Regan, Goneril, Bastard [Edmund] and
Servants*

CORNWALL Post speedily to my lord your husband; show   *To Goneril*
    him this letter: the army of France is landed.— Seek   *Gives a letter*
    out the traitor Gloucester.   [*Exeunt some Servants*]

REGAN Hang him instantly.

5 **GONERIL** Pluck out his eyes.

CORNWALL Leave him to my displeasure. Edmund, keep
    you our sister company: the revenges we are bound
    to take upon your traitorous father are not fit for
    your beholding. Advise the duke where you are

10 going, to a most festinate preparation: we are bound
    to the like. Our posts shall be swift and intelligent
    betwixt us. Farewell, dear sister: farewell, my lord of
    Gloucester.

---

43 **curtains** Lear imagines that he is in a curtained bed   50 **litter** vehicle containing a bed, here apparently
drawn by horses   51 **Dover** port on the south coast   56 **to . . . conduct** i.e. hastily guide you to the
necessary supplies for your journey   **3.7** *Location: the Earl of Gloucester's residence*   1 **Post** travel
swiftly   7 **sister** sister-in-law, i.e. Goneril   9 **Advise** counsel, urge   **duke** i.e. the Duke of Albany
10 **festinate preparation** hasty preparation of troops   11 **posts** messengers   **intelligent** possessed of
information   12 **lord of Gloucester** Edmund's new title (though when Oswald uses it, he refers to
Edmund's father)

Enter Oswald
How now? Where's the king?

15   **OSWALD** My lord of Gloucester hath conveyed him
             hence:
      Some five- or six-and-thirty of his knights,
      Hot questrists after him, met him at gate,
      Who, with some other of the lord's dependants,
      Are gone with him toward Dover, where they boast
20   To have well-armèd friends.
      CORNWALL Get horses for your mistress.
      GONERIL Farewell, sweet lord, and sister.
                        Exeunt [Goneril, Edmund and Oswald]
      CORNWALL Edmund, farewell.—
      Go seek the traitor Gloucester,
25   Pinion him like a thief, bring him before us.
                        [Exeunt other Servants]
      Though well we may not pass upon his life
      Without the form of justice, yet our power
      Shall do a court'sy to our wrath, which men
      May blame but not control.
      Enter Gloucester and Servants
                              Who's there? The traitor?
30   **REGAN** Ingrateful fox! 'Tis he.
      CORNWALL Bind fast his corky arms.
      GLOUCESTER What means your graces?
      Good my friends, consider you are my guests:
      Do me no foul play, friends.
35   **CORNWALL** Bind him, I say.   *Servants bind him*
      REGAN Hard, hard. O, filthy traitor!
      GLOUCESTER Unmerciful lady as you are, I'm none.
      CORNWALL To this chair bind him.— Villain, thou shalt
             find—   *Regan plucks his beard*
      GLOUCESTER By the kind gods, 'tis most ignobly done
40   To pluck me by the beard.
      REGAN So white, and such a traitor?
      GLOUCESTER Naughty lady,
      These hairs which thou dost ravish from my chin
      Will quicken and accuse thee. I am your host:
45   With robbers' hands my hospitable favours
      You should not ruffle thus. What will you do?

17 **questrists** seekers   18 **the lord's** i.e. Gloucester's   25 **Pinion him** bind his arms   26 **pass…justice**
issue a death sentence without a formal trial   28 **do a court'sy** bow, yield   31 **corky** withered, dry
plucks his beard a highly insulting gesture   41 **white** i.e. old, dignified   42 **Naughty** wicked   43 **ravish**
seize forcibly, pluck   44 **quicken** come to life   45 **hospitable favours** welcoming (facial) features
46 **ruffle** treat roughly/snatch

CORNWALL Come, sir, what letters had you late from
    France?

REGAN Be simple answered, for we know the truth.

CORNWALL And what confederacy have you with the
    traitors

50   Late footed in the kingdom?

REGAN To whose hands you have sent the lunatic king?
    Speak.

GLOUCESTER I have a letter guessingly set down,
    Which came from one that's of a neutral heart,
    And not from one opposed.

55 CORNWALL Cunning.

REGAN And false.

CORNWALL Where hast thou sent the king?

GLOUCESTER To Dover.

REGAN Wherefore to Dover? Wast thou not charged at
    peril—

60 CORNWALL Wherefore to Dover? Let him answer that.

GLOUCESTER I am tied to th'stake and I must stand the
    course.

REGAN Wherefore to Dover?

GLOUCESTER Because I would not see thy cruel nails
    Pluck out his poor old eyes, nor thy fierce sister

65   In his anointed flesh stick boarish fangs.
    The sea, with such a storm as his bare head
    In hell-black night endured, would have buoyed up
    And quenched the stellèd fires:
    Yet, poor old heart, he holp the heavens to rain.

70   If wolves had at thy gate howled that stern time,
    Thou shouldst have said 'Good porter, turn the key.'
    All cruels else subscribe: but I shall see
    The wingèd vengeance overtake such children.

CORNWALL See't shalt thou never. Fellows, hold the
    chair.—

75   Upon these eyes of thine I'll set my foot.

GLOUCESTER He that will think to live till he be old,
    Give me some help! O cruel! O you gods!   *Cornwall grinds out his eye*

---

48 Be simple answered answer straightforwardly   **50 Late footed** recently landed   **52 guessingly**
without certain knowledge   **54 opposed** i.e. to the dukes   **59 charged at peril** commanded on peril of
your life   **61 tied to th'stake** like a bear in the popular sport of bear-baiting   **stand** endure   **course**
designated bout, during which the bear was attacked by dogs   **65 anointed** i.e. holy (having been anointed
with holy oil at the coronation)   **67 buoyed** swelled, risen   **68 stellèd** starry   **69 holp...rain** i.e. by
weeping   **holp** helped   **70 stern** cruel, unyielding   **71 turn the key** i.e. to let them in   **72 All...**
subscribe i.e. in such circumstances, all other cruel people would sanction a kind action   **73 wingèd**
vengeance i.e. vengeance of the gods   **74 Fellows** servants

REGAN One side will mock another: th'other too.
CORNWALL If you see vengeance—
80   SERVANT Hold your hand, my lord:
        I have served you ever since I was a child,
        But better service have I never done you
        Than now to bid you hold.
     REGAN How now, you dog?
85   SERVANT If you did wear a beard upon your chin,   *To Regan*
        I'd shake it on this quarrel.— What do you mean?
     CORNWALL My villain?   *They draw and fight*
     SERVANT Nay, then, come on, and take the chance of
          anger.
     REGAN Give me thy sword. A peasant stand up thus?   *To a Servant*
     Kills him
90   SERVANT O, I am slain! My lord, you have one eye left
        To see some mischief on him. O!   *Dies*
     CORNWALL Lest it see more, prevent it. Out, vile jelly!   *Puts out*
        Where is thy lustre now?   *Gloucester's other eye*
     GLOUCESTER All dark and comfortless. Where's my son
          Edmund?
95   Edmund, enkindle all the sparks of nature
        To quit this horrid act.
     REGAN Out, treacherous villain!
        Thou call'st on him that hates thee: it was he
        That made the overture of thy treasons to us,
100   Who is too good to pity thee.
     GLOUCESTER O, my follies! Then Edgar was abused.
        Kind gods, forgive me that, and prosper him!
     REGAN Go thrust him out at gates, and let him smell
        His way to Dover.   *Exit [a Servant] with Gloucester*
105   How is't, my lord? How look you?
     CORNWALL I have received a hurt: follow me, lady.—
        Turn out that eyeless villain: throw this slave
        Upon the dunghill.— Regan, I bleed apace:
        Untimely comes this hurt. Give me your arm. *Exeunt*

---

86 shake . . . quarrel i.e. defy you (or 'challenge you to a fight') over this cause   **What . . . mean?** What do
you think you are doing?   **87 villain** servant   **88 chance of anger** risk of what anger may bring (in a
fight)   **91 mischief on him** injury done to him   **95 sparks of nature** warmth of natural filial affection
96 quit requite, avenge   **97 Out** expression of impatience and disgust   **99 overture** disclosure
101 abused wronged, maligned   **105 How look you?** How are you?   **108 apace** rapidly
109 Untimely at the wrong time (with war imminent)   ***Exeunt*** here the Quarto text has an additional
sequence in which loyal servants apply a palliative to Gloucester's eye sockets (see 'Quarto passages that do
not appear in the Folio', p. 135)

Act 4 Scene 1

Enter Edgar   *Disguised as Poor Tom*

    EDGAR Yet better thus, and known to be contemned,
       Than still contemned and flattered. To be worst,
       The lowest and most dejected thing of fortune,
       Stands still in esperance, lives not in fear:
5   The lamentable change is from the best,
       The worst returns to laughter. Welcome, then,
       Thou unsubstantial air that I embrace!
       The wretch that thou hast blown unto the worst
       Owes nothing to thy blasts.

Enter Gloucester and an Old Man

10   But who comes here? My father, poorly led?
       World, world, O world!
       But that thy strange mutations make us hate thee,
       Life would not yield to age.

    OLD MAN O, my good lord, I have been your tenant and
15   your father's tenant these fourscore years.

    GLOUCESTER Away, get thee away! Good friend, be
       gone:
       Thy comforts can do me no good at all,
       Thee they may hurt.

    OLD MAN You cannot see your way.

20   **GLOUCESTER** I have no way and therefore want no eyes:
       I stumbled when I saw. Full oft 'tis seen
       Our means secure us, and our mere defects
       Prove our commodities. O dear son Edgar,
       The food of thy abusèd father's wrath!
25   Might I but live to see thee in my touch,
       I'd say I had eyes again!

    OLD MAN How now? Who's there?

    EDGAR O gods! Who is't can say, 'I am at the worst'?   *Aside*
       I am worse than e'er I was.

30   **OLD MAN** 'Tis poor mad Tom.

4.1 *Location: somewhere out in the open, not far from the Earl of Gloucester's residence* **1 thus** i.e. a beggar **contemned** despised **2 contemned and flattered** despised secretly though flattered to your face **4 esperance** hope **5 The…laughter** the most miserable kind of change is a decline in fortunes; when things are at their worst they can only get better **10 poorly led** led by a poor man/led in a way unsuitable to his status **12 But** were it not **mutations** changes/fickleness **13 Life…age** we would not accept old age **15 fourscore** eighty **18 Thee…hurt** i.e. you may be punished for helping me **22 means secure us** wealth gives us false security, overconfidence **mere defects** sheer deficiencies **23 Prove our commodities** turn out to be benefits **24 abusèd** deceived

EDGAR And worse I may be yet: the worst is not   *Aside*
    So long as we can say 'This is the worst.'
OLD MAN Fellow, where goest?
GLOUCESTER Is it a beggar-man?
35 OLD MAN Madman and beggar too.
GLOUCESTER He has some reason, else he could not beg.
    I'th'last night's storm I such a fellow saw,
    Which made me think a man a worm: my son
    Came then into my mind and yet my mind
40   Was then scarce friends with him. I have heard more
      since.
    As flies to wanton boys are we to th'gods:
    They kill us for their sport.
EDGAR How should this be?   *Aside*
    Bad is the trade that must play fool to sorrow,
45   Ang'ring itself and others.— Bless thee, master!
GLOUCESTER Is that the naked fellow?
OLD MAN Ay, my lord.
GLOUCESTER Get thee away: if for my sake
    Thou wilt o'ertake us hence a mile or twain
50   I'th'way toward Dover, do it for ancient love,
    And bring some covering for this naked soul,
    Which I'll entreat to lead me.
OLD MAN Alack, sir, he is mad.
GLOUCESTER 'Tis the time's plague, when madmen lead
    the blind.
55 Do as I bid thee, or rather do thy pleasure:
    Above the rest, be gone.
OLD MAN I'll bring him the best 'pparel that I have,
    Come on't what will.   *Exit*
GLOUCESTER Sirrah, naked fellow—
60 EDGAR Poor Tom's a-cold.— I cannot daub it further.   *Aside*
GLOUCESTER Come hither, fellow.
EDGAR And yet I must.— Bless thy sweet eyes, they   *Aside*
    bleed.
GLOUCESTER Know'st thou the way to Dover?
EDGAR Both stile and gate, horseway and footpath. Poor
65   Tom hath been scared out of his good wits: bless thee,
    good man's son, from the foul fiend!

---

31 **is not** has not yet arrived   36 **reason** rationality, sanity   41 **wanton** unruly/cruelly mischievous
44 **trade** course of action/practice   50 **ancient love** old affection   54 **plague** affliction   56 **the rest**
all   57 **'pparel** apparel, clothing   58 **Come…will** whatever may come of it   60 **daub it** put on a false
face, pretend

GLOUCESTER Here, take this purse, thou whom the
    heav'ns' plagues   *Gives a purse*
    Have humbled to all strokes: that I am wretched
    Makes thee the happier: heavens, deal so still.
70   Let the superfluous and lust-dieted man,
    That slaves your ordinance, that will not see
    Because he does not feel, feel your pow'r quickly,
    So distribution should undo excess,
    And each man have enough. Dost thou know Dover?
75 EDGAR Ay, master.
GLOUCESTER There is a cliff, whose high and bending
    head
    Looks fearfully in the confinèd deep:
    Bring me but to the very brim of it
    And I'll repair the misery thou dost bear
80   With something rich about me: from that place
    I shall no leading need.
EDGAR Give me thy arm:
    Poor Tom shall lead thee.   *Exeunt*

Act 4 Scene 2   *running scene 13*

Enter Goneril, Bastard [Edmund] and Steward [Oswald]

GONERIL Welcome, my lord: I marvel our mild husband
    Not met us on the way.— Now, where's your
    master?
OSWALD Madam, within, but never man so changed.
    I told him of the army that was landed,
5   He smiled at it: I told him you were coming,
    His answer was 'The worse': of Gloucester's
    treachery
    And of the loyal service of his son
    When I informed him, then he called me 'sot'
    And told me I had turned the wrong side out.
10   What most he should dislike seems pleasant to him;
    What like, offensive.

---

68 strokes blows, afflictions   **69 happier** more fortunate   **70 superfluous** immoderate, extravagant, overindulgent   **lust-dieted** fed solely by pleasure   **71 slaves your ordinance** subjects your laws to his desires   **72 feel** empathize, feel compassion (sense then shifts to 'experience')   **quickly** soon/while he is alive/sharply   **76 bending** overhanging   **77 confinèd** channelled (between England and France) **78 brim** edge   **80 about me** that I have on my person   **4.2** *Location: outside Goneril and the Duke of Albany's residence*   **1 my lord** i.e. Edmund   **4 army** i.e. French army   **8 'sot'** fool   **9 turned ... out** turned inside out, got things the wrong way round (clothing metaphor)

GONERIL Then shall you go no further.   *To Edmund*
It is the cowish terror of his spirit,
That dares not undertake: he'll not feel wrongs
15 Which tie him to an answer. Our wishes on the way
May prove effects. Back, Edmund, to my brother:
Hasten his musters and conduct his powers.
I must change names at home and give the distaff
Into my husband's hands. This trusty servant
20 Shall pass between us: ere long you are like to
      hear —
If you dare venture in your own behalf —
A mistress's command. Wear this; spare speech.   *Gives a favour*
Decline your head: this kiss, if it durst speak,   *Kisses him*
Would stretch thy spirits up into the air.
25 Conceive, and fare thee well.
EDMUND Yours in the ranks of death.   *Exit*
GONERIL My most dear Gloucester!
      O, the difference of man and man!
      To thee a woman's services are due:
30   My fool usurps my body.
OSWALD Madam, here comes my lord.   *Exit*
Enter Albany
GONERIL I have been worth the whistle.
ALBANY O Goneril,
      You are not worth the dust which the rude wind
35   Blows in your face.
GONERIL   Milk-livered man,
      That bear'st a cheek for blows, a head for wrongs,
      Who hast not in thy brows an eye discerning
      Thine honour from thy suffering.

---

13 cowish cowardly   **14 undertake** take action   **15 tie…answer** oblige him to respond   **on the way** i.e. that we expressed during the journey here   **16 prove effects** be fulfilled   **brother** brother-in-law, i.e. Cornwall   **17 musters** gathering of troops   **conduct his powers** escort his forces   **18 change** exchange   **distaff** spindle for weaving, common symbol of womanhood or wifeliness   **20 like** likely   **22 mistress** ruler/lover   *favour* love token   **24 thy** Goneril starts to use the more intimate pronoun to Edmund   **spirits** plays on sense of 'penis'   **25 conceive** understand/imagine (with procreative connotations)   **26 death** plays on sense of 'orgasm'   **29 services** sexual services   **30 fool** i.e. Albany **usurps** wrongfully possesses   **32 worth the whistle** worth looking for (from the proverb 'it is a poor dog that is not worth the whistling')   **33 Goneril…face** the Quarto text has a longer dialogue in which Albany berates Goneril (see 'Quarto passages that do not appear in the Folio', p. 136)   **34 rude** rough   **36 Milk-livered** pale-livered, cowardly (cowardice was associated with lack of blood in the liver and milk with women)   **38 discerning…suffering** that can distinguish between what may be honourably tolerated from what must not be endured

40   **ALBANY** See thyself, devil!
        Proper deformity seems not in the fiend
        So horrid as in woman.
    GONERIL O vain fool!

Enter a Messenger

    MESSENGER O, my good lord, the Duke of Cornwall's
        dead,
45   Slain by his servant, going to put out
        The other eye of Gloucester.
    ALBANY Gloucester's eyes?
    MESSENGER A servant that he bred, thrilled with
        remorse,
        Opposed against the act, bending his sword
50   To his great master, who, threat-enraged,
        Flew on him and amongst them felled him dead,
        But not without that harmful stroke which since
        Hath plucked him after.
    ALBANY This shows you are above,
55   You justices, that these our nether crimes
        So speedily can venge. But, O, poor Gloucester!
        Lost he his other eye?
    MESSENGER Both, both, my lord.—
        This letter, madam, craves a speedy answer: *Gives a letter*
60   'Tis from your sister.
    GONERIL One way I like this well: *Aside*
        But being widow, and my Gloucester with her,
        May all the building in my fancy pluck
        Upon my hateful life: another way,
65   The news is not so tart.— I'll read, and answer. [*Exit*]
    ALBANY Where was his son when they did take his eyes?
    MESSENGER Come with my lady hither.
    ALBANY He is not here.
    MESSENGER No, my good lord, I met him back again.
70   **ALBANY** Knows he the wickedness?
    MESSENGER Ay, my good lord: 'twas he informed
        against him,
        And quit the house on purpose that their punishment
        Might have the freer course.

---

41 Proper . . . woman deformity does not seem as abhorrent in a devil (to whom it is appropriate) as it does in a woman   **43 vain** stupid/worthless   **48 bred** brought up in his household   **thrilled** pierced, moved   **remorse** pity (for Gloucester)   **49 Opposed** opposed himself   **bending** aiming, directing   **50 threat-enraged** enraged by the threat   **53 after** i.e. to death   **55 justices** (divine) judges   **nether** earthly   **56 venge** avenge, punish   **63 all . . . life** demolish the dream (of having Edmund) that I have constructed, leaving me with the life I hate   **65 tart** sour   **69 back** going back

ALBANY Gloucester, I live
75   To thank thee for the love thou showed'st the king
        And to revenge thine eyes.— Come hither, friend:
        Tell me what more thou know'st.   *Exeunt*

Act 4 Scene 3   *running scene 14*

*Enter with Drum and Colours Cordelia, Gentleman and
Soldiers*

CORDELIA Alack, 'tis he: why, he was met even now
        As mad as the vexed sea, singing aloud,
        Crowned with rank fumiter and furrow weeds,
        With burdocks, hemlock, nettles, cuckoo-flowers,
5   Darnel, and all the idle weeds that grow
        In our sustaining corn. A sentry send forth;
        Search every acre in the high-grown field
        And bring him to our eye.—   [*Exit a Soldier*]
                                What can man's wisdom
        In the restoring his bereavèd sense?
10   He that helps him take all my outward worth.
GENTLEMAN There is means, madam:
        Our foster-nurse of nature is repose,
        The which he lacks: that to provoke in him
        Are many simples operative, whose power
15   Will close the eye of anguish.
CORDELIA All blest secrets,
        All you unpublished virtues of the earth,
        Spring with my tears! Be aidant and remediate
        In the good man's distress! Seek, seek for him,
20   Lest his ungoverned rage dissolve the life
        That wants the means to lead it.

4.3 *Location: the French camp, near Dover. The Quarto text precedes this scene with another one in
which Kent and a Gentleman discuss the French king's return to France and Cordelia's concern for her
father (see 'Quarto passages that do not appear in the Folio', pp. 137–8)* **Colours** military banners
Gentleman perhaps the same man that Kent gave instructions to in Act 3 scene 1   **2 vexed** angry,
turbulent   **3 rank fumiter** abundant fumitory (a vigorously growing weed)   **furrow weeds** weeds that
grow in the furrows of ploughed fields   **4 burdocks** weeds with prickly flower-heads or burs   **hemlock**
plant producing a potentially lethal sedative   **cuckoo-flowers** name given to various wild flowers growing
when the cuckoo calls (i.e. May/June)   **5 Darnel** type of grass that grows as a weed amongst corn   **idle**
useless   **8 What…wisdom** what can human knowledge do   **9 bereavèd** stolen, lost   **10 outward**
worth worldly goods   **12 repose** rest, sleep   **13 that…operative** there are many effective medicinal
herbs that can induce that in him   **17 unpublished virtues** secret powers (of herbs)   **18 aidant** helpful
remediate remedial, healing   **20 rage** frenzy   **21 wants the means** i.e. lacks the sanity

Enter Messenger

MESSENGER News, madam:
>The British powers are marching hitherward.

CORDELIA 'Tis known before: our preparation stands
25 >In expectation of them. O dear father,
>It is thy business that I go about:
>Therefore great France
>My mourning and importuned tears hath pitied.
>No blown ambition doth our arms incite,
30 >But love, dear love, and our aged father's right:
>Soon may I hear and see him!   *Exeunt*

Act 4 Scene 4   *running scene 15*

Enter Regan and Steward [Oswald]

REGAN But are my brother's powers set forth?
OSWALD Ay, madam.
REGAN Himself in person there?
OSWALD Madam, with much ado:
5 >Your sister is the better soldier.
REGAN Lord Edmund spake not with your lord at home?
OSWALD No, madam.
REGAN What might import my sister's letter to him?
OSWALD I know not, lady.
10 **REGAN** Faith, he is posted hence on serious matter.
>It was great ignorance, Gloucester's eyes being out,
>To let him live: where he arrives he moves
>All hearts against us. Edmund, I think, is gone,
>In pity of his misery, to dispatch
15 >His nighted life: moreover, to descry
>The strength o'th'enemy.
OSWALD I must needs after him, madam, with my letter.
REGAN Our troops set forth tomorrow. Stay with us:
>The ways are dangerous.
20 **OSWALD** I may not, madam:
>My lady charged my duty in this business.
REGAN Why should she write to Edmund? Might not you
>Transport her purposes by word? Belike,

---

24 preparation equipped military force   **27 France** i.e. the King of France   **28 importuned** importunate, pressing   **29 blown** swollen with pride/corrupt   **4.4** *Location: the Earl of Gloucester's residence*   **4 ado** fuss   **8 import** mean, contain   **10 posted** hurried   **11 ignorance** folly   **15 nighted** darkened (literally, and in terms of his fortunes)   **descry** discover   **17 after** go after   **19 ways** roads   **21 charged my duty** swore me to obedience   **23 Belike** perhaps/probably

Some things I know not what. I'll love thee much,
25   Let me unseal the letter.

OSWALD Madam, I had rather—

REGAN I know your lady does not love her husband,
I am sure of that: and at her late being here
She gave strange oeillades and most speaking looks
30   To noble Edmund. I know you are of her bosom.

OSWALD I, madam?

REGAN I speak in understanding. Y'are, I know't.
Therefore I do advise you, take this note.
My lord is dead: Edmund and I have talked,
35   And more convenient is he for my hand
Than for your lady's: you may gather more.
If you do find him, pray you give him this,   *Gives a token or a letter*
And when your mistress hears thus much from you,
I pray desire her call her wisdom to her.
40   So, fare you well.
If you do chance to hear of that blind traitor,
Preferment falls on him that cuts him off.

OSWALD Would I could meet, madam, I should show
What party I do follow.

45 **REGAN** Fare thee well.   *Exeunt*

Act 4 Scene 5

running scene 16

Enter Gloucester and Edgar   *Edgar dressed like a peasant*

GLOUCESTER When shall I come to th'top of that same
hill?

EDGAR You do climb up it now: look how we labour.

GLOUCESTER Methinks the ground is even.

EDGAR Horrible steep.
5   Hark, do you hear the sea?

GLOUCESTER No, truly.

EDGAR Why, then, your other senses grow imperfect
By your eyes' anguish.

GLOUCESTER So may it be, indeed:
10   Methinks thy voice is altered and thou speak'st
In better phrase and matter than thou didst.

---

24 **I'll love thee** Regan switches to the familiar **thee** to cajole him – **love** implies the promise of favours, sexual or otherwise **29 oeillades** amorous glances **speaking** eloquent **30 of her bosom** in her confidence/sexually intimate **32 Y'are** ye (you) are **33 take this note** note this well **35 convenient** fitting **36 gather more** infer the rest **39 call . . . her** have more sense **43 meet** i.e. meet him **4.5** *Location: somewhere out in the open, near Dover* **1 that same hill** the hill I mentioned (i.e. the cliff Gloucester described at the end of Act 4 scene 1) **11 phrase and matter** style and sense

EDGAR You're much deceived: in nothing am I changed
But in my garments.

GLOUCESTER Methinks you're better spoken.

15 **EDGAR** Come on, sir, here's the place: stand still. How
fearful
And dizzy 'tis to cast one's eyes so low!
The crows and choughs that wing the midway air
Show scarce so gross as beetles: halfway down
Hangs one that gathers samphire, dreadful trade!

20 Methinks he seems no bigger than his head.
The fishermen that walk upon the beach
Appear like mice, and yond tall anchoring bark
Diminished to her cock, her cock, a buoy
Almost too small for sight. The murmuring surge,

25 That on th'unnumbered idle pebble chafes,
Cannot be heard so high. I'll look no more,
Lest my brain turn and the deficient sight
Topple down headlong.

GLOUCESTER Set me where you stand.

30 **EDGAR** Give me your hand: you are now within a foot
Of th'extreme verge: for all beneath the moon
Would I not leap upright.

GLOUCESTER Let go my hand.
Here, friend's another purse: in it a jewel   *Gives a purse*

35 Well worth a poor man's taking: fairies and gods
Prosper it with thee! Go thou further off:
Bid me farewell, and let me hear thee going.

EDGAR Now fare ye well, good sir.

GLOUCESTER With all my heart.

40 **EDGAR** Why I do trifle thus with his despair   *Aside*
Is done to cure it.

GLOUCESTER O you mighty gods!   *Kneels*
This world I do renounce, and in your sights
Shake patiently my great affliction off:

45 If I could bear it longer, and not fall
To quarrel with your great opposeless wills,
My snuff and loathèd part of nature should

17 **choughs** jackdaws or other birds of the crow family   **wing** fly across   **midway** i.e. middle regions
of 18 **gross** large   19 **samphire** aromatic plant used in pickling; it was picked from cliffs by men
suspended on ropes   22 **yond** yonder, that   **bark** small ship   23 **her cock** (the size of) her cock-boat, a
small boat towed behind a ship   25 **th'unnumbered idle pebble** countless insignificant pebbles   27 **the
deficient** my defective   28 **Topple** topple me   32 **leap upright** jump up in the air   34 **Here, friend's**
here, friend, is   36 **Prosper it** cause it to prosper   40 **trifle** play   46 **opposeless** irresistible
47 **My . . . nature** the smouldering wick and hated remains of my life

Burn itself out. If Edgar live, O, bless him!—
Now, fellow, fare thee well.   *He falls forward*

50 EDGAR Gone, sir: farewell.—
And yet I know not how conceit may rob   *Aside*
The treasury of life, when life itself
Yields to the theft: had he been where he thought,
By this had thought been past. Alive or dead?—

55 Ho, you sir! Friend! Hear you, sir! Speak!—
Thus might he pass indeed: yet he revives.—   *Aside*
What are you, sir?

GLOUCESTER Away, and let me die.

EDGAR Hadst thou been aught but gossamer, feathers,
      air —

60 So many fathom down precipitating —
Thou'dst shivered like an egg: but thou dost breathe,
Hast heavy substance, bleed'st not, speak'st, art
      sound.
Ten masts at each make not the altitude
Which thou hast perpendicularly fell:

65 Thy life's a miracle. Speak yet again.

GLOUCESTER But have I fall'n or no?

EDGAR From the dread summit of this chalky bourn.
Look up a-height: the shrill-gorged lark so far
Cannot be seen or heard: do but look up.

70 GLOUCESTER Alack, I have no eyes.
Is wretchedness deprived that benefit,
To end itself by death? 'Twas yet some comfort
When misery could beguile the tyrant's rage
And frustrate his proud will.

75 EDGAR Give me your arm.   *Helps him up*
Up, so. How is't? Feel you your legs? You stand.

GLOUCESTER Too well, too well.

EDGAR This is above all strangeness.
Upon the crown o'th'cliff what thing was that

80 Which parted from you?

GLOUCESTER A poor unfortunate beggar.

EDGAR As I stood here below, methought his eyes
Were two full moons: he had a thousand noses,
Horns whelked and waved like the engèd sea.

---

51 **conceit** imagination   53 **Yields** submits willingly   54 **this** this time, now   56 **pass** die
57 **What** who (Edgar adopts another persona)   59 **aught** anything   60 **precipitating** falling headlong
61 **shivered** shattered   63 **at each** end to end   67 **bourn** boundary (between land and sea)
68 **a-height** on high   **shrill-gorged** shrill-throated   73 **beguile** cheat   84 **whelked** twisted

85   It was some fiend: therefore, thou happy father,
        Think that the clearest gods, who make them
            honours
        Of men's impossibilities, have preserved thee.
        GLOUCESTER I do remember now: henceforth I'll bear
        Affliction till it do cry out itself
90   'Enough, enough' and die. That thing you speak of,
        I took it for a man: often 'twould say
        'The fiend, the fiend': he led me to that place.
        EDGAR Bear free and patient thoughts.
        Enter Lear   *Dressed with weeds*
                                But who comes here?
        The safer sense will ne'er accommodate
95   His master thus.
        LEAR No, they cannot touch me for crying: I am the king
        himself.
        EDGAR O thou side-piercing sight!
        LEAR Nature's above art in that respect. There's your
100   press-money. That fellow handles his bow like a
        crow-keeper. Draw me a clothier's yard. Look, look, a
        mouse! Peace, peace, this piece of toasted cheese will
        do't. There's my gauntlet: I'll prove it on a giant.
        Bring up the brown bills. O, well flown, bird!
105   I'th'clout, i'th'clout: hewgh! Give the word.
        EDGAR Sweet marjoram.
        LEAR Pass.
        GLOUCESTER I know that voice.
        LEAR Ha? Goneril with a white beard? They flattered me
110   like a dog and told me I had the white hairs in my
        beard ere the black ones were there. To say 'Ay' and

---

85 fiend i.e. tempting him to the sin of suicide   **happy father** fortunate old man (**father** was a form of address for an elderly man, though Edgar plays with the literal sense)   **86 clearest** brightest, purest   **make...impossibilities** acquire honour for themselves by performing things that are impossible in the human world   **93 free** untroubled   **94 The...thus** were he (Lear) in his right mind, he would never permit himself to dress like this (or possibly 'Gloucester's senses will not be able to withstand seeing his master like this')   **96 touch** accuse, blame/lay hands on   **100 press-money** money paid to military recruits when they were conscripted (Lear seems to imagine he is recruiting an army)   **101 crow-keeper** scarecrow/person employed to scare crows from the crops   **Draw...yard** draw your bow to its fullest extent (the length of a longbow's arrow, which, at about thirty-six inches, was the same as the length of a cloth-seller's measuring rod)   **103 gauntlet** armoured glove thrown down as a challenge to a duel   **prove it on** make good my cause against   **104 brown bills** long-handled weapons, painted or varnished brown and topped with axe-like blades; or soldiers carrying such weapons   **well flown, bird** the language of falconry, here used to describe an arrow's flight   **105 I'th'clout** cloth at the centre of an archer's target   **hewgh** perhaps Lear imitates the sound of the arrow as it flies through the air or hits the target   **word** password (continues Lear's military fantasy)   **106 Sweet marjoram** Edgar invents a password that relates to Lear's headgear and to the plant's alleged medicinal properties in treating brain disorders   **110 like a dog** i.e. as if they were fawning dogs   **had...there** i.e. was wise even while I was still a child

'No' to everything that I said 'Ay' and 'No' to was no
good divinity. When the rain came to wet me once
and the wind to make me chatter, when the thunder
115 would not peace at my bidding, there I found 'em,
there I smelt 'em out. Go to, they are not men o'their
words: they told me I was everything: 'tis a lie, I am
not ague-proof.

GLOUCESTER The trick of that voice I do well remember:
120 Is't not the king?

LEAR Ay, every inch a king.
When I do stare, see how the subject quakes.
I pardon that man's life. What was thy cause?
Adultery?
125 Thou shalt not die: die for adultery? No.
The wren goes to't and the small gilded fly
Does lecher in my sight. Let copulation thrive,
For Gloucester's bastard son was kinder to his father
Than were my daughters got 'tween the lawful
sheets.
130 To't, luxury, pell-mell, for I lack soldiers.
Behold yond simp'ring dame,
Whose face between her forks presages snow,
That minces virtue and does shake the head
To hear of pleasure's name:
135 The fitchew nor the soilèd horse goes to't
With a more riotous appetite. Down from the waist
They are centaurs, though women all above:
But to the girdle do the gods inherit,
Beneath is all the fiends':
140 There's hell, there's darkness, there is the sulphurous
pit: burning, scalding, stench, consumption. Fie, fie,
fie! Pah, pah! Give me an ounce of civet, good
apothecary, sweeten my imagination: there's money
for thee.

145 GLOUCESTER O, let me kiss that hand!

---

113 **divinity** theology   114 **me** i.e. my teeth   115 **peace** be still   118 **ague-proof** immune to fever and
shivering   119 **trick** characteristic, individual quality   123 **cause** charge, offence   126 **goes to't** does it,
has sex   127 **lecher** fornicate   129 **got** begot, conceived   130 **luxury** lechery, lust   **for...soldiers** i.e.
more sex means more children to man his army   132 **between...snow** forecasts frigidity between her
legs   133 **minces virtue** affects chastity   **shake the head** i.e. in disapproval   135 **fitchew** polecat/
prostitute   **soilèd** fed with green fodder, so lively, skittish   136 **riotous** unrestrained, lustful
137 **centaurs** mythical creatures that were human above the waist and horse below; reputed to be lustful
138 **But...girdle** only as far as the waist   **inherit** possess, have power over   140 **hell** slang term for the
vagina   **sulphurous** suggests both hell and syphilis   141 **burning...consumption** alludes to painful
syphilitic burning, odour and decay (**consumption**)   142 **civet** perfume   **apothecary** person who prepared
and sold drugs, spices, perfumes etc.

LEAR Let me wipe it first: it smells of mortality.

GLOUCESTER O, ruined piece of nature! This great world
    Shall so wear out to nought. Dost thou know me?

LEAR I remember thine eyes well enough. Dost thou
150   squinny at me? No, do thy worst, blind Cupid: I'll not
    love. Read thou this challenge, mark but the penning
    of it.

GLOUCESTER Were all thy letters suns, I could not see.

EDGAR I would not take this from report: it is,   *Aside*
155   And my heart breaks at it.

LEAR Read.

GLOUCESTER What, with the case of eyes?

LEAR O, ho, are you there with me? No eyes in your
    head, nor no money in your purse? Your eyes are in a
160   heavy case, your purse in a light, yet you see how
    this world goes.

GLOUCESTER I see it feelingly.

LEAR What, art mad? A man may see how this world
    goes with no eyes. Look with thine ears: see how
165   yond justice rails upon yond simple thief. Hark, in
    thine ear: change places, and handy-dandy, which is
    the justice, which is the thief? Thou hast seen a
    farmer's dog bark at a beggar?

GLOUCESTER Ay, sir.

170 **LEAR** And the creature run from the cur? There thou
    mightst behold the great image of authority: a dog's
    obeyed in office.
    Thou rascal beadle, hold thy bloody hand!
    Why dost thou lash that whore? Strip thy own back:
175   Thou hotly lusts to use her in that kind
    For which thou whip'st her. The usurer hangs the
        cozener.
    Through tattered clothes great vices do appear:
    Robes and furred gowns hide all. Place sins with gold,
    And the strong lance of justice hurtless breaks:

---

146 mortality being human/death   **148 so** similarly   **150 squinny** squint   **Cupid** Roman god of love, traditionally depicted as **blind** or blindfolded   **151 challenge** written challenge to a duel   **penning** style/handwriting   **154 take...report** believe it if I heard it reported   **157 case** sockets   **160 heavy case** sorrowful predicament   **162 feelingly** literally, through touch/with great emotion   **165 justice** judge   **simple** humble   **166 handy-dandy** take your pick (from the child's game of guessing which clenched hand contains something)   **171 a...office** given authority, even a dog will be obeyed   **173 beadle** parish officer, responsible for punishing thieves, prostitutes and vagabonds   **175 use** employ sexually   **kind** manner   **176 usurer** moneylender, notorious for charging excessively high interest   **cozener** cheat   **178 Place...gold** i.e. when sins are committed by the rich   **179 hurtless** harmlessly

180   Arm it in rags, a pigmy's straw does pierce it.
      None does offend, none, I say, none: I'll able 'em.
      Take that of me, my friend, who have the power
      To seal th'accuser's lips. Get thee glass eyes,
      And like a scurvy politician seem
185   To see the things thou dost not. Now, now, now,
            now.
      Pull off my boots: harder, harder: so.

EDGAR O, matter and impertinency mixed! Reason in   *Aside*
      madness!

LEAR If thou wilt weep my fortunes, take my eyes.
      I know thee well enough: thy name is Gloucester.
190   Thou must be patient; we came crying hither.
      Thou know'st the first time that we smell the air
      We wail and cry. I will preach to thee: mark.

GLOUCESTER Alack, alack the day!

LEAR When we are born, we cry that we are come
195   To this great stage of fools. This a good block:
      It were a delicate stratagem to shoe
      A troop of horse with felt: I'll put't in proof,
      And when I have stol'n upon these son-in-laws,
      Then kill, kill, kill, kill, kill, kill!

Enter a Gentleman [with Attendants]

200   **GENTLEMAN** O, here he is: lay hand upon him.— Sir,
      Your most dear daughter—

LEAR No rescue? What, a prisoner? I am even
      The natural fool of fortune. Use me well,
      You shall have ransom. Let me have surgeons:
205   I am cut to th'brains.

GENTLEMAN You shall have anything.

LEAR No seconds? All myself?
      Why, this would make a man a man of salt
      To use his eyes for garden water-pots,
210   I will die bravely, like a smug bridegroom. What?
      I will be jovial. Come, come, I am a king,
      Masters, know you that?

GENTLEMAN You are a royal one, and we obey you.

---

180 **it** i.e. sin   181 **able 'em** authorize them   184 **scurvy politician** despicable schemer   185 **Now...
now** perhaps comforting Gloucester, perhaps distracted by his boots   187 **matter and impertinency** sense
and nonsense   190 **hither** i.e. into this world   195 **block** style of hat or mould for hats (perhaps Lear
removes his headgear)/block from which to mount a horse/tree stump (**stage** may even give rise to a sense of
'scaffold and executioner's block')   196 **delicate** ingenious   197 **put't in proof** try it out   203 **natural
fool** born fool (as opposed to a professional jester)   207 **seconds** supporters (as for a duel)   208 **salt** i.e.
tears   210 **die** plays on the sense of 'orgasm'   **bravely** handsomely   211 **jovial** cheerful/majestic (like
Jove, king of the gods)   212 **Masters** sirs

LEAR Then there's life in't. Come, an you get it, you shall
215   get it by running. Sa, sa, sa, sa.   *Exit*   *Running,*
GENTLEMAN A sight most pitiful in the meanest wretch,   *Attendants follow*
       Past speaking of in a king! Thou hast a daughter
       Who redeems nature from the general curse
       Which twain have brought her to.
220 EDGAR Hail, gentle sir.
GENTLEMAN Sir, speed you: what's your will?
EDGAR Do you hear aught, sir, of a battle toward?
GENTLEMAN Most sure and vulgar: everyone hears that
       Which can distinguish sound.
225 EDGAR But, by your favour,
       How near's the other army?
GENTLEMAN Near and on speedy foot: the main descry
       Stands on the hourly thought.
EDGAR I thank you, sir: that's all.
230 GENTLEMAN Though that the queen on special cause is
       here,
       Her army is moved on.   *Exit*
EDGAR I thank you, sir.
GLOUCESTER You ever-gentle gods, take my breath from
       me:
       Let not my worser spirit tempt me again
235   To die before you please!
EDGAR Well pray you, father.
GLOUCESTER Now, good sir, what are you?
EDGAR A most poor man, made tame to fortune's blows,
       Who, by the art of known and feeling sorrows,
240   Am pregnant to good pity. Give me your hand:
       I'll lead you to some biding.   *Takes his arm*
GLOUCESTER Hearty thanks:
       The bounty and the benison of heaven
       To boot, and boot.

---

215 Sa . . . sa hunting cry, from French Óa ('that's it', 'it's there')   218 nature i.e. human nature   **general curse** curse of original sin   219 twain Adam and Eve (but also suggests Goneril and Regan)   220 gentle noble   221 speed you (may God) prosper you   222 toward impending   223 vulgar widely-known   225 by your favour if you would be so good   227 main . . . thought sight of the main army is expected hourly   230 Though that though   on special cause for a special reason (i.e. to find Lear)   234 worser spirit evil angel/bad side of my nature   239 known . . . sorrows deeply felt sorrows I have experienced   240 pregnant . . . pity disposed to compassion   241 biding dwelling   243 benison blessing   244 To . . . boot in addition, and may it benefit you

Enter Steward [Oswald]

245 OSWALD A proclaimed prize! Most happy!
That eyeless head of thine was first framed flesh
To raise my fortunes. Thou old unhappy traitor,   *Draws*
Briefly thyself remember: the sword is out
That must destroy thee.
250 GLOUCESTER Now let thy friendly hand
Put strength enough to't.   *Edgar interposes*
OSWALD Wherefore, bold peasant,
Darest thou support a published traitor? Hence,
Lest that th'infection of his fortune take
255 Like hold on thee. Let go his arm.
EDGAR 'Chill not let go, zir, without vurther 'casion.
OSWALD Let go, slave, or thou diest!
EDGAR Good gentleman, go your gait, and let poor volk
pass. An 'chud ha' bin zwaggered out of my life,
260 'twould not ha' bin zo long as 'tis by a vortnight.
Nay, come not near th'old man: keep out, che vor ye,
or I'se try whether your costard or my ballow be the
harder. 'Chill be plain with you.
OSWALD Out, dunghill!
265 EDGAR 'Chill pick your teeth, zir: come, no matter vor   *They fight*
your foins.
OSWALD Slave, thou hast slain me. Villain, take my
purse:
If ever thou wilt thrive, bury my body
And give the letters which thou find'st about me
To Edmund, Earl of Gloucester: seek him out
270 Upon the English party. O, untimely death! Death!   *He dies*
EDGAR I know thee well: a serviceable villain,
As duteous to the vices of thy mistress
As badness would desire.
GLOUCESTER What, is he dead?
275 EDGAR Sit you down, father: rest you.
Let's see these pockets: the letters that he speaks of

---

245 **proclaimed prize** i.e. a man with a price on his head   **happy** fortunate   246 **framed flesh** conceived and born   248 **thyself remember** recall your sins (i.e. prepare to die)   253 **published** proclaimed 256 **'Chill . . . 'casion** I shall not let go, sir, without further occasion (cause); for his new persona, Edgar adopts a West Country accent in which he substitutes 'v' for 'f' and 'z' for 's'   **'Chill** I shall   258 **your gait** on your way   259 **An . . . vortnight** if I could have been killed by boasting, I would not have lasted a fortnight (or 'it would have been shorter by a fortnight')   261 **che vor ye** I warrant you, I promise you   262 **I'se** I shall   **costard** head (literally, a large apple)   **ballow** cudgel   265 **pick** knock out with the cudgel   **foins** sword-thrusts   270 **party** side   271 **serviceable** eager to serve, ready to do anything

May be my friends. He's dead: I am only sorry
He had no other deathsman. Let us see.   *Opens the letter*
Leave, gentle wax, and manners, blame us not:
280   To know our enemies' minds we rip their hearts:
Their papers is more lawful.
Reads the letter
'Let our reciprocal vows be remembered. You have
many opportunities to cut him off: if your will want
not, time and place will be fruitfully offered. There is
285   nothing done if he return the conqueror: then am I
the prisoner, and his bed my jail, from the loathed
warmth whereof deliver me, and supply the place for
your labour. Your — wife, so I would say —
affectionate servant, Goneril.'
290   O, undistinguished space of woman's will!
A plot upon her virtuous husband's life,
And the exchange my brother! Here in the sands
Thee I'll rake up, the post unsanctified
Of murderous lechers: and in the mature time
295   With this ungracious paper strike the sight
Of the death-practised duke: for him 'tis well
That of thy death and business I can tell.
GLOUCESTER The king is mad: how stiff is my vile sense,
That I stand up and have ingenious feeling
300   Of my huge sorrows. Better I were distract,
So should my thoughts be severed from my griefs,
                                             Drum afar off
And woes by wrong imaginations lose
The knowledge of themselves.
EDGAR Give me your hand:
305   Far off, methinks, I hear the beaten drum.
Come, father, I'll bestow you with a friend.   *Exeunt*

---

278 **deathsman** executioner   279 **Leave** give me leave, permit me   283 **will** desire/lust   **want not** is not
lacking   285 **done** achieved   287 **for your labour** as a reward for your efforts/as a place for sexual
activity   289 **servant** lover   290 **undistinguished space** limitless scope   **will** lust   293 **Thee...up** I
will bury you (Oswald)   **post unsanctified** unholy messenger   294 **in...time** when the time is ripe
295 **ungracious** wicked, sinful   **strike** blast/afflict   296 **death-practised** whose death is plotted
298 **stiff** stubborn   299 **ingenious** sensitive, intelligent   300 **distract** mad   302 **wrong imaginations**
illusions

Act 4 Scene 6

Enter Cordelia, Kent and Gentleman   **Kent still disguised**

CORDELIA O thou good Kent, how shall I live and work
To match thy goodness? My life will be too short,
And every measure fail me.
KENT To be acknowledged, madam, is o'erpaid.
5   All my reports go with the modest truth,
Nor more nor clipped, but so.
CORDELIA Be better suited:
These weeds are memories of those worser hours,
I prithee put them off.
10   **KENT** Pardon, dear madam,
Yet to be known shortens my made intent:
My boon I make it, that you know me not
Till time and I think meet.
CORDELIA Then be't so, my good lord.— How does the
king?
15   **GENTLEMAN** Madam, sleeps still.
CORDELIA O you kind gods,
Cure this great breach in his abusèd nature!
Th'untuned and jarring senses, O, wind up
Of this child-changèd father!
20   **GENTLEMAN** So please your majesty
That we may wake the king: he hath slept long.
CORDELIA Be governed by your knowledge, and proceed
I'th'sway of your own will. Is he arrayed?
Enter Lear in a chair carried by Servants
GENTLEMAN Ay, madam: in the heaviness of sleep
25   We put fresh garments on him.
Be by, good madam, when we do awake him:
I doubt of his temperance.
CORDELIA O my dear father! Restoration hang   **Kisses him**
Thy medicine on my lips and let this kiss

4.6 *Location: the French camp, near Dover* **3 every** . . . **me** all my efforts will be inadequate
4 o'erpaid i.e. already more than enough **5 All** . . . **truth** everything I have told you is the simple truth (or
possibly 'may all reports of me be unexaggerated and accurate') **6 No** . . . **clipped** neither overstated nor
abbreviated **7 suited** dressed **8 weeds** clothes **11 Yet** . . . **intent** to have my identity known now would
spoil the plan I have devised **12 My** . . . **it** the favour I ask is **know me not** do not acknowledge me
13 meet suitable **18 wind up** put in tune (by tightening the pegs on a stringed instrument) **19 child-
changèd** changed by his children **23 I'th'sway** . . . **will** as you see fit, under your own authority **arrayed**
dressed (appropriately) **27 doubt of** fear for **temperance** self-control

30 Repair those violent harms that my two sisters
Have in thy reverence made!

KENT Kind and dear princess!

CORDELIA Had you not been their father, these white
flakes
Did challenge pity of them. Was this a face
35 To be opposed against the jarring winds?
Mine enemy's dog though he had bit me
Should have stood that night against my fire,
And wast thou fain, poor father,
To hovel thee with swine and rogues forlorn
40 In short and musty straw? Alack, alack!
'Tis wonder that thy life and wits at once
Had not concluded all.— He wakes: speak to him.

GENTLEMAN Madam, do you: 'tis fittest.

CORDELIA How does my royal lord? How fares your
majesty?

45 **LEAR** You do me wrong to take me out o'th'grave:
Thou art a soul in bliss, but I am bound
Upon a wheel of fire, that mine own tears
Do scald like molten lead.

CORDELIA Sir, do you know me?

50 **LEAR** You are a spirit, I know: where did you die?

CORDELIA Still, still, far wide!

GENTLEMAN He's scarce awake: let him alone awhile.

LEAR Where have I been? Where am I? Fair daylight?
I am mightily abused. I should ev'n die with pity
55 To see another thus. I know not what to say.
I will not swear these are my hands. Let's see:
I feel this pinprick. Would I were assured
Of my condition!

CORDELIA O, look upon me, sir,   *Kneels?*
60 And hold your hand in benediction o'er me:
You must not kneel.   *Stops him from kneeling?*

LEAR Pray, do not mock me:
I am a very foolish fond old man,
Fourscore and upward, not an hour more nor less,
65 And to deal plainly,

---

31 reverence i.e. position deserving respect, venerable state   **33 Had you** even if you had   **flakes** locks of
hair   **34 Did challenge** would have demanded   **of** from   **38 fain** obliged   **39 rogues forlorn** destitute
vagabonds   **40 short** i.e. broken up (and hence less comfortable)   **41 at once** at the same time
42 concluded all come entirely to an end   **46 bliss** i.e. heaven   **47 wheel of fire** i.e. one of hell's tortures
of the damned; recalls Ixion, who, in Greek mythology, was bound to a wheel of fire for attempting to seduce
the queen of the gods   **that** so that   **51 wide** wide of the mark, confused   **54 abused** wronged, ill-treated/
deluded   **57 Would ... condition!** I wish I could be sure of what state I am in!   **63 fond** silly

I fear I am not in my perfect mind.
Methinks I should know you and know this man,
Yet I am doubtful, for I am mainly ignorant
What place this is, and all the skill I have
70   Remembers not these garments, nor I know not
Where I did lodge last night. Do not laugh at me,
For, as I am a man, I think this lady
To be my child Cordelia.

CORDELIA And so I am, I am.   *Weeps*

75   LEAR Be your tears wet? Yes, faith. I pray, weep not:
If you have poison for me, I will drink it.
I know you do not love me, for your sisters
Have, as I do remember, done me wrong:
You have some cause, they have not.

80   CORDELIA No cause, no cause.

LEAR Am I in France?

KENT In your own kingdom, sir.

LEAR Do not abuse me.

GENTLEMAN Be comforted, good madam: the great rage,
85   You see, is killed in him. Desire him to go in:
Trouble him no more till further settling.

CORDELIA Will't please your highness walk?

LEAR You must bear with me. Pray you now, forget and
forgive:
I am old and foolish.   *Exeunt*

Act 5 Scene 1   *running scene 18*

*Enter with Drum and Colours Edmund, Regan, Gentlemen
and Soldiers*

EDMUND Know of the duke if his last purpose hold,   *To a Gentleman*
Or whether since he is advised by aught
To change the course: he's full of alteration
And self-reproving: bring his constant pleasure.
                                              [*Exit Gentleman*]
5   REGAN Our sister's man is certainly miscarried.

EDMUND 'Tis to be doubted, madam.

REGAN Now, sweet lord,
You know the goodness I intend upon you:

84 rage frenzy   86 further settling his mind is more settled   5.1 *Location: the British camp, near Dover   Drum and Colours* soldiers with military flags and a drum beating   1 Know of find out from   last purpose most recent intention   2 since subsequently   advised persuaded/warned   aught anything, i.e. any news   4 self-reproving self-reproach   constant pleasure fixed wishes   5 miscarried come to harm   6 doubted feared

Tell me but truly — but then speak the truth —
10   Do you not love my sister?
EDMUND In honoured love.
REGAN But have you never found my brother's way
    To the forfended place?
EDMUND No, by mine honour, madam.
15 **REGAN** I never shall endure her: dear my lord,
    Be not familiar with her.
EDMUND Fear not. She and the duke her husband!
Enter with Drum and Colours Albany, Goneril, Soldiers
ALBANY Our very loving sister, well be-met.
    Sir, this I heard: the king is come to his daughter,
20   With others whom the rigour of our state
    Forced to cry out.
REGAN Why is this reasoned?
GONERIL Combine together gainst the enemy,
    For these domestic and particular broils
25   Are not the question here.
ALBANY Let's then determine
    With th'ancient of war on our proceeding.
REGAN Sister, you'll go with us?
GONERIL No.
30 **REGAN** 'Tis most convenient: pray, go with us.
GONERIL O, ho, I know the riddle.— I will go.   *Aside*
    Exeunt both the armies. [Albany remains]
Enter Edgar   *Disguised*
EDGAR If e'er your grace had speech with man so poor,
    Hear me one word.
ALBANY I'll overtake you.— Speak.
35 **EDGAR** Before you fight the battle, ope this letter: *Gives a letter*
    If you have victory, let the trumpet sound
    For him that brought it. Wretched though I seem,
    I can produce a champion that will prove
    What is avouchèd there. If you miscarry,

---

11 honoured honourable   **13 forfended place** forbidden place, i.e. Goneril's vagina   **15 I...her** I cannot stand her   **16 familiar** too friendly/sexually intimate   **20 rigour...state** harshness of our government   **21 cry out** i.e. protest in pain   **22 Why...reasoned?** Why are we discussing this?   **23 Combine together** i.e. let us combine our two armies   **24 domestic...broils** private internal squabbles   **27 th'ancient of war** experienced senior officers   **30 convenient** suitable, seemly   **31 know the riddle** understand your enigmatic request, see your trick (Regan wants to keep a suspicious eye on Goneril)   **34 I'll overtake you** presumably Albany calls after those who have or are in the process of departing   **35 ope** open   **letter** i.e. the letter Oswald was carrying from Goneril to Edmund   **36 sound** i.e. sound a summons   **38 champion** one who fights in single combat   **39 avouchèd** declared, affirmed   **miscarry** lose the battle and die

40   Your business of the world hath so an end,
      And machination ceases. Fortune loves you.
      ALBANY Stay till I have read the letter.
      EDGAR I was forbid it.
      When time shall serve, let but the herald cry
45   And I'll appear again.   *Exit*
      ALBANY Why, fare thee well: I will o'erlook thy paper.
Enter Edmund
      EDMUND The enemy's in view: draw up your powers.
      Here is the guess of their true strength and forces   *Offers a paper*
      By diligent discovery, but your haste
50   Is now urged on you.
      ALBANY We will greet the time.   *Exit*
      EDMUND To both these sisters have I sworn my love,
      Each jealous of the other, as the stung
      Are of the adder. Which of them shall I take?
55   Both? One? Or neither? Neither can be enjoyed
      If both remain alive. To take the widow
      Exasperates, makes mad her sister Goneril,
      And hardly shall I carry out my side,
      Her husband being alive. Now then, we'll use
60   His countenance for the battle, which being done,
      Let her who would be rid of him devise
      His speedy taking off. As for the mercy
      Which he intends to Lear and to Cordelia,
      The battle done and they within our power,
65   Shall never see his pardon, for my state
      Stands on me to defend, not to debate.   *Exit*

Act 5 Scene 2   *running scene 19*

*Alarum within. Enter, with Drum and Colours, Lear,
Cordelia and Soldiers over the stage and exeunt. Enter Edgar
and Gloucester*

      EDGAR Here, father, take the shadow of this tree
      For your good host. Pray that the right may thrive.

41 **machination** plotting 44 **cry** make the proclamation 46 **o'erlook** read over 47 **powers** troops
49 **discovery** intelligence-gathering, reconnaissance 51 **greet the time** be ready when the time comes
53 **jealous** suspicious, mistrustful 58 **hardly** with difficulty **carry . . . side** fulfil my side of the agreement
(with Goneril)/achieve my own (power-seeking) ends 60 **countenance** authority 62 **taking off** murder
65 **Shall** i.e. they shall **my . . . debate** my position relies on action not discussion **5.2** *Location: not far
from the battlefield, near Dover* **Alarum** trumpet call to arms 1 **father** form of address for an old
man 2 **host** i.e. shelter

If ever I return to you again,
I'll bring you comfort.

5   **GLOUCESTER** Grace go with you, sir!   *Exit [Edgar]*
Alarum and retreat within
Enter Edgar

EDGAR Away, old man! Give me thy hand, away!
King Lear hath lost, he and his daughter ta'en:
Give me thy hand, come on.

GLOUCESTER No further, sir: a man may rot even here.

10   **EDGAR** What, in ill thoughts again? Men must endure
Their going hence, even as their coming hither:
Ripeness is all: come on.

GLOUCESTER And that's true too.   *Exeunt*

Act 5 Scene 3   *running scene 20*

Enter in conquest, with Drum and Colours, Edmund, Lear
and Cordelia as prisoners, Soldiers, Captain

EDMUND Some officers take them away: good guard,
Until their greater pleasures first be known
That are to censure them.

CORDELIA We are not the first   *To Lear*

5   Who with best meaning have incurred the worst.
For thee, oppressèd king, I am cast down:
Myself could else out-frown false fortune's frown.
Shall we not see these daughters and these sisters?

LEAR No, no, no, no! Come, let's away to prison.

10   We two alone will sing like birds i'th'cage:
When thou dost ask me blessing, I'll kneel down
And ask of thee forgiveness: so we'll live,
And pray, and sing, and tell old tales, and laugh
At gilded butterflies, and hear poor rogues

15   Talk of court news, and we'll talk with them too —
Who loses and who wins, who's in, who's out —
And take upon's the mystery of things,
As if we were God's spies: and we'll wear out

---

5 *retreat* trumpet call signalling retreat   **7 ta'en** (are) captured   **12 Ripeness** readiness/the right time
5.3   *Location: the British camp, near Dover*   good guard guard them carefully   **2 greater pleasures** the
wishes of more important people (i.e. Goneril, Regan, Albany)   **3 censure** judge, sentence
5 meaning intentions   **6 cast down** humbled by fortune/defeated in battle/dejected   **14 gilded
butterflies** actual butterflies/lavishly dressed courtiers   **poor rogues** wretched fellows   **17 take ... things**
understand the secret inner workings of the world   **18 God's spies** spying on the world on God's behalf/
looking at the world from a lofty vantage point, like God   **wear out** outlive

In a walled prison packs and sects of great ones
20   That ebb and flow by th'moon.

EDMUND Take them away.

LEAR Upon such sacrifices, my Cordelia,
        The gods themselves throw incense. Have I caught
            thee?
        He that parts us shall bring a brand from heaven
25   And fire us hence like foxes. Wipe thine eyes:
        The good years shall devour them, flesh and fell,
        Ere they shall make us weep: We'll see 'em starved
            first. Come.

                    Exeunt [Lear and Cordelia, guarded]

EDMUND Come hither, captain, hark.
        Take thou this note, go follow them to prison.   *Gives a paper*
30   One step I have advanced thee: if thou dost
        As this instructs thee, thou dost make thy way
        To noble fortunes. Know thou this: that men
        Are as the time is; to be tender-minded
        Does not become a sword. Thy great employment
35   Will not bear question: either say thou'lt do't
        Or thrive by other means.

CAPTAIN I'll do't, my lord.

EDMUND About it, and write happy when th'hast done.
        Mark, I say, instantly, and carry it so
40   As I have set it down.   *Exit Captain*

Flourish. Enter Albany, Goneril, Regan, Soldiers

ALBANY Sir, you have showed today your valiant strain,
        And fortune led you well. You have the captives
        Who were the opposites of this day's strife:
        I do require them of you, so to use them
45   As we shall find their merits and our safety
        May equally determine.

EDMUND   Sir, I thought it fit
        To send the old and miserable king to some retention
        Whose age had charms in it, whose title more,
50   To pluck the common bosom on his side

19 **packs and sects** cliques and factions   20 **That . . . th'moon** i.e. whose fortunes ebb and flow like the tides   22 **sacrifices** refers either Cordelia's sacrifice for Lear or their joint loss of freedom   23 **throw incense** i.e. like priests performing the sacrifice   24 **brand . . . foxes** alludes to the practice of smoking foxes out of their holes   26 **flesh and fell** flesh and skin (i.e. entirely)   27 **starved** dead   33 **tender-minded** sensitive, soft-hearted   34 **become** befit, suit   35 **bear question** permit discussion   38 **write happy** count yourself fortunate   39 **carry** manage   41 **strain** lineage   43 **opposites** opponents   44 **use** treat   48 **retention** detention, confinement   49 **Whose** refers to the **king   charms** bewitching spells   **title** name of king/legal entitlement (to land and power)   50 **pluck . . . bosom** draw the sympathies of the common people

And turn our impressed lances in our eyes
Which do command them. With him I sent the
    queen,
My reason all the same, and they are ready
Tomorrow, or at further space, t'appear
55   Where you shall hold your session.
ALBANY Sir, by your patience,
    I hold you but a subject of this war,
    Not as a brother.
REGAN That's as we list to grace him.
60   Methinks our pleasure might have been demanded
    Ere you had spoke so far. He led our powers,
    Bore the commission of my place and person,
    The which immediacy may well stand up
    And call itself your brother.
65 **GONERIL** Not so hot:
    In his own grace he doth exalt himself
    More than in your addition.
REGAN In my rights,
    By me invested, he compeers the best.
70 **ALBANY** That were the most if he should husband you.
REGAN Jesters do oft prove prophets.
GONERIL Holla, holla!
    That eye that told you so looked but asquint.
REGAN Lady, I am not well, else I should answer
75   From a full-flowing stomach.— General,   *To Edmund*
    Take thou my soldiers, prisoners, patrimony:
    Dispose of them, of me: the walls is thine:
    Witness the world that I create thee here
    My lord and master.
80 **GONERIL** Mean you to enjoy him?
ALBANY The let-alone lies not in your good will.
EDMUND Nor in thine, lord.
ALBANY Half-blooded fellow, yes.
REGAN Let the drum strike and prove my title thine.   *To Edmund*

---

51 turn...them i.e. turn our conscripted soldiers' weapons against ourselves **52 queen** i.e. Cordelia
55 session hearing in a court of justice **56 by your patience** if you'll excuse me **57 subject of**
subordinate in **59 list** please **60 pleasure... demanded** wishes might have been asked
62 commission authority **63 immediacy** closeness, connection **66 grace** merit **67 your addition** the
honours or titles you bestow on him **69 compeers** equals **70 That...most** i.e. he would be most fully
invested with your rights **72 Holla** whoa, stop **73 asquint** crookedly, distortedly **75 full-flowing**
stomach a stomach full of anger (where **stomach** is used like 'heart' for the seat of the passions)
76 patrimony inheritance **77 Dispose of** use, deal with **walls** Regan images herself as a fortress
surrendering **78 Witness the world** let the world witness **80 enjoy** i.e. have sex with him as your
husband **81 let-alone** permission or refusal to give it **83 Half-blooded** illegitimate (**fellow** is
contemptuous)

85   **ALBANY** Stay yet, hear reason. Edmund, I arrest thee
      On capital treason, and, in thy arrest,
      This gilded serpent. For your claim, fair sister,
      I bar it in the interest of my wife:
      'Tis she is subcontracted to this lord,
90   And I, her husband, contradict your banns.
      If you will marry, make your loves to me,
      My lady is bespoke.
  GONERIL An interlude!
  ALBANY Thou art armed, Gloucester: let the trumpet
        sound:
95   If none appear to prove upon thy person
      Thy heinous, manifest, and many treasons,
      There is my pledge: I'll make it on thy heart,   *Throws down a glove*
      Ere I taste bread, thou art in nothing less
      Than I have here proclaimed thee.
100   **REGAN** Sick, O, sick!
  GONERIL If not, I'll ne'er trust medicine.   *Aside*
  EDMUND There's my exchange: what in the world he's
      That names me traitor, villain-like he lies.   *Throws down a glove*
      Call by the trumpet: he that dares approach,
105   On him, on you — who not? — I will maintain
      My truth and honour firmly.
  Enter a Herald
  ALBANY A herald, ho!
      Trust to thy single virtue, for thy soldiers,   *To Edmund*
      All levied in my name, have in my name
110   Took their discharge.
  REGAN My sickness grows upon me.
  ALBANY She is not well: convey her to my tent.—
                           [Exit Regan, led]
      Come hither, herald. Let the trumpet sound
      And read out this.
  A trumpet sounds
115   **HERALD** *Reads* 'If any man of quality or degree within
      the lists of the army will maintain upon Edmund,
      supposed Earl of Gloucester, that he is a manifold

---

86 in i.e. along with   **87 gilded serpent** i.e. Goneril   **For** as for   **88 bar it** prevent its advancement (legal term)   **89 subcontracted** engaged for a second time, entered into a contract that is subsidiary to her marriage contract with Albany   **90 banns** proclamation of marriage (spelled 'banes' in Folio, perhaps playing on 'evil-doings')   **91 make...to** woo, make advances to   **92 bespoke** spoken for   **93 interlude** brief comic play (i.e. 'What a farce!')   **97 pledge** challenge/pledge to fight   **make it** i.e. make it good **98 nothing** no way   **101 medicine** drugs (i.e. poison)   **102 what** whoever   **108 single virtue** unaided courage or strength   **115 quality or degree** noble birth or high rank   **116 lists** catalogue of soldiers

traitor, let him appear by the third sound of the
trumpet: he is bold in his defence.'

First trumpet

120 **HERALD** Again!

Second trumpet

HERALD Again!

Third trumpet

Trumpet answers within

Enter Edgar armed   *His helmet visor down*

ALBANY Ask him his purposes, why he appears
Upon this call o'th'trumpet.

HERALD What are you?

125   Your name, your quality, and why you answer
This present summons?

EDGAR Know, my name is lost
By treason's tooth bare-gnawn and canker-bit:
Yet am I noble as the adversary

130   I come to cope.

ALBANY Which is that adversary?

EDGAR What's he that speaks for Edmund Earl of
Gloucester?

EDMUND Himself: what say'st thou to him?

EDGAR Draw thy sword,

135   That, if my speech offend a noble heart,
Thy arm may do thee justice: here is mine.   *Draws*
Behold, it is my privilege —
The privilege of mine honours —
My oath and my profession. I protest,

140   Maugre thy strength, place, youth and eminence,
Despise thy victor sword and fire-new fortune,
Thy valour and thy heart, thou art a traitor:
False to thy gods, thy brother and thy father,
Conspirant gainst this high illustrious prince,

145   And from th'extremest upward of thy head
To the descent and dust below thy foot
A most toad-spotted traitor. Say thou no,
This sword, this arm and my best spirits are bent
To prove upon thy heart whereto I speak,

150   Thou liest.

---

128 canker-bit eaten away by canker-worms (grubs that feed on plants)   **130 cope** encounter, fight
with   **138 honours...profession** i.e. as a knight   **139 protest** declare   **140 Maugre** despite   **place**
position, rank   **141 fire-new** i.e. brand new, freshly minted   **144 Conspirant** a conspirator   **145 upward**
top, crown   **146 descent** lowest part, sole   **147 toad-spotted** toads' spots were believed to contain
venom   **148 bent** resolved/tensed for action

EDMUND In wisdom I should ask thy name,
  But since thy outside looks so fair and warlike,
  And that thy tongue some say of breeding breathes,
  What safe and nicely I might well delay
155 By rule of knighthood, I disdain and spurn.
  Back do I toss these treasons to thy head,
  With the hell-hated lie o'erwhelm thy heart,
  Which, for they yet glance by and scarcely bruise,
  This sword of mine shall give them instant way,
160 Where they shall rest forever. Trumpets, speak!   *Draws*
  Alarums. Fights   *Edmund falls*
ALBANY Save him, save him!
GONERIL This is practice, Gloucester:
  By th'law of war thou wast not bound to answer
  An unknown opposite: thou art not vanquished,
165 But cozened and beguiled.
ALBANY Shut your mouth, dame,
  Or with this paper shall I stop it.— Hold, sir.—
  Thou worse than any name, read thine own evil. *To Goneril*
  No tearing, lady: I perceive you know it. *Shows her the letter*
170 GONERIL Say, if I do, the laws are mine, not thine:
  Who can arraign me for't.   *Exit*
ALBANY Most monstrous! O, know'st thou this paper?
EDMUND Ask me not what I know.
ALBANY Go after her: she's desperate: govern her.
            [*Exit a soldier*]
175 EDMUND What you have charged me with, that have I
   done,
  And more, much more: the time will bring it out:
  'Tis past and so am I.— But what art thou *To Edgar*
  That hast this fortune on me? If thou'rt noble,
  I do forgive thee.
180 EDGAR Let's exchange charity.
  I am no less in blood than thou art, Edmund:
  If more, the more th'hast wronged me.
  My name is Edgar, and thy father's son. *Removes his helmet*
  The gods are just, and of our pleasant vices
185 Make instruments to plague us:

---

153 **say** assay, evidence 154 **nicely** in strict keeping with the rules 157 **hell-hated lie** the lie I hate as much as hell 158 **for they** since they (the treasons) **by** off 159 **instant way** an immediate passage (to your heart) 161 **him** probably a call to Edgar to spare Edmund's life so that a confession can be obtained from him 162 **practice** trickery 165 **cozened and beguiled** cheated and deceived 166 **dame** woman 169 **know** recognize 171 **arraign** indict, bring to trial 174 **govern** restrain 178 **fortune on** good fortune to defeat 180 **charity** forgiveness 182 **th'hast** thou hast (i.e. you have) 184 **pleasant** pleasurable (sexually so in this case)

The dark and vicious place where thee he got
Cost him his eyes.

EDMUND Th'hast spoken right: 'tis true,
The wheel is come full circle: I am here.

190 **ALBANY** Methought thy very gait did prophesy   *To Edgar*
A royal nobleness: I must embrace thee.
Let sorrow split my heart if ever I
Did hate thee or thy father!

EDGAR Worthy prince, I know't.

195 **ALBANY** Where have you hid yourself?
How have you known the miseries of your father?

EDGAR By nursing them, my lord. List a brief tale,
And when 'tis told, O, that my heart would burst!
The bloody proclamation to escape

200 That followed me so near — O, our lives' sweetness!
That we the pain of death would hourly die
Rather than die at once! — taught me to shift
Into a madman's rags, t'assume a semblance
That very dogs disdained: and in this habit

205 Met I my father with his bleeding rings,
Their precious stones new lost, became his guide,
Led him, begged for him, saved him from despair,
Never — O, fault! — revealed myself unto him
Until some half-hour past, when I was armed.

210 Not sure, though hoping, of this good success,
I asked his blessing, and from first to last
Told him our pilgrimage: but his flawed heart —
Alack, too weak the conflict to support —
'Twixt two extremes of passion, joy and grief,

215 Burst smilingly.

EDMUND This speech of yours hath moved me,
And shall perchance do good: but speak you on:
You look as you had something more to say.

ALBANY If there be more, more woeful, hold it in,

220 For I am almost ready to dissolve,
Hearing of this.

Enter a Gentleman   *With a bloody knife*

GENTLEMAN Help, help, O, help!

---

186 dark literally and metaphorically   **vicious** immoral   **got** begot, conceived   **189 wheel** wheel of
fortune   **190 prophesy** suggest, foretell   **197 List** listen (to)   **199 bloody proclamation** i.e. the sentence
of death pronounced on him   **201 the…die** would repeatedly suffer pain as bad as death
203 semblance outward appearance   **204 habit** clothing/guise, appearance   **205 rings** i.e. eye sockets
207 despair the spiritual hopelessness that precedes suicide   **210 success** outcome (in the duel with
Edmund)   **212 pilgrimage** course of events/period of exile/spiritual journey   **flawed** cracked
220 dissolve i.e. in tears

EDGAR What kind of help?

ALBANY Speak, man.

225   EDGAR What means this bloody knife?

GENTLEMAN 'Tis hot, it smokes:
    It came even from the heart of — O, she's dead!

ALBANY Who dead? Speak, man.

GENTLEMAN Your lady, sir, your lady; and her sister
230   By her is poisoned: she confesses it.

EDMUND I was contracted to them both: all three
    Now marry in an instant.

EDGAR Here comes Kent.

Enter Kent

ALBANY Produce the bodies, be they alive or dead:

Goneril and Regan's bodies brought out

235   This judgement of the heavens, that makes us tremble,
    Touches us not with pity.— O, is this he?—   *Sees Kent*
    The time will not allow the compliment   *To Kent*
    Which very manners urges.

KENT I am come
240   To bid my king and master aye goodnight:
    Is he not here?

ALBANY Great thing of us forgot!
    Speak, Edmund, where's the king? And where's
       Cordelia?—
    See'st thou this object, Kent?   *Points to the bodies*

245   KENT Alack, why thus?

EDMUND Yet Edmund was beloved:
    The one the other poisoned for my sake
    And after slew herself.

ALBANY Even so. Cover their faces.

250   EDMUND I pant for life: some good I mean to do,
    Despite of mine own nature. Quickly send —
    Be brief in it — to th'castle, for my writ
    Is on the life of Lear and on Cordelia:
    Nay, send in time.

255   ALBANY Run, run, O, run!

EDGAR To who, my lord? Who has the office?
    Send thy token of reprieve.   *To Edmund*

EDMUND Well thought on: take my sword,
    Give it the captain.

---

226 smokes i.e. steams with **hot** blood   **237 compliment** etiquette (of greeting)   **240 aye** forever (Kent is aware he is dying)   **242 Great thing** vital matter   **244 object** sight   **249 Even** exactly   **252 writ** written order (for execution; a legal term)   **256 office** task, responsibility

260 **EDGAR** Haste thee, for thy life.   *To a Gentleman*

[*Exit Gentleman*]

EDMUND He hath commission from thy wife and me
   To hang Cordelia in the prison and
   To lay the blame upon her own despair,
   That she fordid herself.

265 **ALBANY** The gods defend her! Bear him hence awhile. *Edmund is borne off*
Enter Lear with Cordelia in his arms   *Gentleman and others following*

LEAR Howl, howl, howl! O, you are men of stones:
   Had I your tongues and eyes, I'd use them so
   That heaven's vault should crack. She's gone for
      ever!
   I know when one is dead and when one lives:
270   She's dead as earth. Lend me a looking-glass:
   If that her breath will mist or stain the stone,
   Why, then she lives.

KENT Is this the promised end?

EDGAR Or image of that horror?

275 **ALBANY** Fall and cease!

LEAR This feather stirs: she lives! If it be so,
   It is a chance which does redeem all sorrows
   That ever I have felt.

KENT O my good master!   *Kneels*

280 **LEAR** Prithee, away.

EDGAR 'Tis noble Kent, your friend.

LEAR A plague upon you, murderers, traitors all!
   I might have saved her: now she's gone for ever!—
   Cordelia, Cordelia! Stay a little. Ha?
285   What is't thou say'st?— Her voice was ever soft,
   Gentle and low, an excellent thing in woman.—
   I killed the slave that was a-hanging thee.

GENTLEMAN 'Tis true, my lords, he did.

LEAR Did I not, fellow?
290   I have seen the day, with my good biting falchion
   I would have made him skip: I am old now,
   And these same crosses spoil me.— Who are you?
   Mine eyes are not o'th'best: I'll tell you straight.

---

264 fordid killed   **271 stone** specular stone, a crystalline substance used to make mirrors   **273 promised end** the death Lear expected (when he divided the kingdom)/Judgement Day, the end of the world (the sense that Edgar understands)   **275 Fall and cease!** either Albany calls for the end of the world, or he wishes for Lear to die and be put out of his anguish   **287 slave** villain/wretched servant   **290 falchion** curved sword   **292 crosses** troubles, frustrations   **293 Mine . . . o'th'best** failing sight was believed to be a sign of approaching death   **straight** in a moment

KENT If fortune brag of two she loved and hated,
295   One of them we behold.

LEAR This is a dull sight. Are you not Kent?

KENT The same,
          Your servant Kent: where is your servant Caius?

LEAR He's a good fellow, I can tell you that:
300   He'll strike, and quickly too. He's dead and rotten.

KENT No, my good lord, I am the very man—

LEAR I'll see that straight.

KENT That from your first of difference and decay
          Have followed your sad steps.

305   **LEAR** You are welcome hither.

KENT Nor no man else: all's cheerless, dark and deadly.
          Your eldest daughters have fordone themselves,
          And desperately are dead.

LEAR Ay, so I think.

310   **ALBANY** He knows not what he says, and vain is it
          That we present us to him.

Enter a Messenger

EDGAR Very bootless.

MESSENGER Edmund is dead, my lord.

ALBANY That's but a trifle here.
315   You lords and noble friends, know our intent:
          What comfort to this great decay may come
          Shall be applied. For us, we will resign,
          During the life of this old majesty,
          To him our absolute power:— you, to your rights   *To Edgar and Kent*
320   With boot and such addition as your honours
          Have more than merited. All friends shall taste
          The wages of their virtue, and all foes
          The cup of their deservings.— O, see, see!

LEAR And my poor fool is hanged! No, no, no life?
325   Why should a dog, a horse, a rat have life,
          And thou no breath at all? Thou'lt come no more,

---

294 two . . . hated perhaps 'two people she first loved and then hated'; it is not entirely clear who the **one** Kent refers to is   **296 dull sight** refers either to Lear's dim eyesight or to the motionless Cordelia
298 Caius the only mention of the name Kent assumed when he was in disguise   **302 I'll . . . straight** I'll attend to that in a moment   **303 your . . . decay** the beginning of the change and decline in your fortunes (may also suggest mental decay)   **306 Nor . . . else** completes Kent's previous, unfinished sentence with 'and no one else' as well as beginning his current one with 'neither I nor anyone else (is welcome)'
307 fordone killed   **308 desperately** as a result of the spiritual despair that precedes suicide
310 vain . . . him it is useless for us to tell him who we are   **312 bootless** pointless   **316 this great decay** noble ruin, i.e. Lear   **317 For** as for   **resign** hand over   **320 boot** advantage, additions   **addition** titles, honours   **323 cup** painful experience (plays on the related sense of 'drinking vessel')   **see, see** something attracts Albany's attention, presumably to Lear   **324 fool** i.e. Cordelia (fool was a term of endearment), but recalls Lear's Fool as well

Never, never, never, never, never!
Pray you undo this button: thank you, sir.
Do you see this? Look on her, look, her lips,
330   Look there, look there!   *He dies*

EDGAR He faints! My lord, my lord!

KENT Break, heart, I prithee, break.

EDGAR Look up, my lord.

KENT Vex not his ghost: O, let him pass! He hates him
335   That would upon the rack of this tough world
Stretch him out longer.

EDGAR He is gone, indeed.

KENT The wonder is he hath endured so long:
He but usurped his life.

340 **ALBANY** Bear them from hence. Our present business
Is general woe.—
Friends of my soul, you twain   *To Kent and Edgar*
Rule in this realm, and the gored state sustain.

KENT I have a journey, sir, shortly to go:
345   My master calls me, I must not say no.

EDGAR The weight of this sad time we must obey:
Speak what we feel, not what we ought to say.
The oldest hath borne most: we that are young
Shall never see so much nor live so long.

                       Exeunt with a dead march

---

328 this button may refer to Cordelia's (hoping to help her breathe) or Lear's own (if he is once again afflicted by 'the mother', the hysteria that causes one to struggle for breath)   **sir** it is unclear whom Lear addresses here   **334 ghost** spirit   **335 rack** torture instrument that stretched the limbs   **336 longer** for a longer period of time/to longer physical dimensions   **339 usurped** stole, made illegal use of (beyond its rightful length)   **343 gored** wounded, bleeding   **sustain** support/keep alive   **344 journey** i.e. to death

TEXTUAL NOTES

Q = First Quarto text of 1608
F = First Folio text of 1623
F2 = a correction introduced in the Second Folio text of 1632
Ed = a correction introduced by a later editor
SD = stage direction
SH = speech heading (i.e. speaker's name)

List of parts = Ed

EDMUND *sometimes spelled* Edmond, *often referred to in directions and speech headings as* Bastard
1.1.33 SD one ... then = Q. *Not in* F **36 lord** = F. Q = Liege **39 fast** = F. Q = first **40 age** = F. Q = state **41 Conferring** = F. Q = Confirming **strengths** = F. Q = yeares **41–6 while ... now** = F. *Not in* Q **50–1 Since ... state** = F. *Not in* Q **60 found** = F. Q = friend **65–6 and ... rivers** = F. *Not in* Q **69 of Cornwall** = F. Q = to *Cornwell*, speake **80 ponderous** = F. Q = richer **84 conferred** = F. Q = confirm'd **85 our ... love** = F. Q = the last, not least in our deere loue **87 interessed** = Ed. F = interest **draw** = F. Q = win **90 SH LEAR Nothing? ... Nothing.** = F. *Not in* Q **106 sisters** = F. Q = sisters, to loue my father all. **113 mysteries** = F2. F = miseries. Q = mistresse **night** = F. Q = might **121 shall ... bosom** = F. Q = Shall **139 shall** = F. Q = still **154 falls** = F. Q = stoops **Reserve thy state** = F. Q = Reuerse thy doome **161 pawn** = F. Q = a pawne **162 ne'er** = F. Q = nor **167 SH LEAR** = Q. F = *Kear.* **168 SH KENT** = Q. F = *Lent.* **170 Miscreant** = F. Q = recreant **171 SH ALBANY ... forbear.** = F. *Not in* Q **SH CORDELIA** *some editors expand* F's *Cor. to Cornwall* **173 gift** = F. Q = doome **178 strained** = F. Q = straied **179 sentences** = F *corrected.* F *uncorrected,* Q = sentence **182 Five** = F. Q = Foure **183 disasters** = F. Q = diseases **184 sixth** = F. Q = fift **185 next** = Ed. F, Q = tenth **190 Freedom** = F. Q = Friendship **197 SH CORDELIA** = F *(corrected). Some editors expand to Cornwall.* Q = *Glost.* **216 Dowered** = F. Q = Couered **228 object** = F. Q = best obiect **237 Should** = F. Q = Could **240 will** = F. Q = well **241 make known** = F. Q = may know **251 but** = F. Q = no more but **255 regards** = F. Q = respects **258 king** = F. Q = *Leir* **266 respect and fortunes** = F. Q = respects / Of fourtune **274 my** = F. Q = thy **289 Love** = F. Q = vse **294 SH REGAN** = F *(Regn).* Q = Gonorill **295 SH GONERIL** = F. Q = *Regan* **298 want** = F. Q = worth **299 plighted** = F. Q = pleated **300 with shame derides** = F. Q = shame them derides **309 not been** = Q. F = beene **323 sit** = F. Q = hit
1.2.1 SH EDMUND = Ed. F, Q = *Bast. (throughout)* **13 tirèd** = F. Q = lyed **18 fine word, 'legitimate'** = F. *Not in* Q **21 to th'legitimate** = F. *Sometimes emended to* top the legitimate **24 Prescribed** = F. Q = subscribd **40 o'erlooking** = F. Q = liking **56 wake** = F. Q = wakt **59 you to this** = F. Q = this to you **75 declined** = F. Q = declining **88 that ... writ** = F. Q = he hath wrote **89 other** = F. Q = further **109–14 This ... graves** = F. *Not in* Q **117 honesty! 'Tis strange** = F. Q = honest, strange strange **122 stars** = F. Q = the starres **124 spherical** = F. Q = spirituall **129 a star** = F. Q = Starres **132 I should** = F. Q = Fut, I should. **133 maidenliest** *spelled* maidenlest *in* F *and* Q **134 bastardizing** = F. Q = bastardy **135 Pat** = F. Q = *Edgar*; and out **136–7 sigh ... o'Bedlam** = F. Q = sith like them of Bedlam **138 Fa ... mi.** = F. *Not in* Q **144 writes** = F. Q = writ **161–4 I ... brother?** = F. *Not in* Q **165 I am** = F. Q = go arm'd, I am

126

1.3.0 SD *Steward* = F. Q = *Gentleman* **3 SH OSWALD** = Ed. F = *Ste.* Q = *Gent.*
(throughout) **14 I'd** = F. Q = *I'll* **15 distaste** = F. Q = dislike **17 have
said** = F. Q = tell you **21 so.** = F. Q = so. I would breed from hence occasions, and I shall,
That I may speak: **course. Prepare** = F. Q = very course, goe prepare

1.4.1 will = _. F. Q = well **6 So . . . thy** = F. Q = thy **7 SD** *Horns . . . Attendants* = F. Q = *Enter
Lear* **43 SD** *Enter Steward appears one line later in* F **49 SH KNIGHT** = F *(spelled* Knigh
here and on two other occasions in Act 1 scene 4). Q = *Kent* **daughter** = Q. F = Daughters **52
SH KNIGHT** = F. Q = *seruant (throughout)* **58 of kindness appears** = F. Q = apeer's **68
purpose** = F. Q = purport **75 SD** *Enter Steward placed one line later in* F **80 these** = F. Q
= this **your pardon** = F. Q = you pardon me **83 strucken** = F. Q = struck **89
Have . . . So** = F. Q = you haue wisedome **95 SH LEAR Why, my boy?** = F. Q = *Kent.*
Why Fool? **105 all my** = F. Q = any **109 the Lady Brach** = F. Q = Ladie oth'e brach **111
gall** = F. Q = gull **114 nuncle** = F. Q = vncle **125 SH KENT** = F. Q = *Lear* **134 one** = F.
Q = foole **146 grace** = F. Q = wit **148 And** = F. Q = They **to** = F. Q = doe **157 fool** = F.
Q = fooles **169 You** = F. Q = Methinks you **171 frowning** = F. Q = frowne **177 nor
crust** = F. Q = neither crust **nor crumb** = Q. F = not crum **179 shelled** *spelled* sheal'd *in*
F, *sheald in* Q **194 know** = F. Q = trow **199 I** = F. Q = Come sir, I **your** = F. Q = that **201
transport** = F. Q = transforme **205 This** = F. Q = why this **207 weakens, his** = F. Q =
weaknes, or his **208 Ha! Waking?** = F. Q = sleeping or wakeing; ha! sure **210 SH FOOL
Lear's shadow.** = F. *Assigned to Lear in* Q **212 This admiration, sir** = F. Q = Come sir,
this admiration **221 graced** = F. Q = great **233 SD** *Albany* = F. Q = *Duke
(throughout)* **234 Woe** = F. Q = We **235 Speak . . . my** = F. Q = that wee prepare
any **239 SH ALBANY Pray . . . patient.** = F. *Not in* Q **240 liest** = F. Q = list **241 My** = F.
Q = list my **are** = F. Q = and **252 Of . . . you.** = F. *Not in* Q **264 cadent** = F. Q =
accent **268 Away, away!** = F. Q = goe, goe, my people? **270 more of it** = F. Q = the
cause **279 thee worth them** = F. Q = the worst **280 Th'untented** = F. Q *uncorrected* =
the vntender **281 Pierce** = F. Q *uncorrected* = peruse **thee! Old** = F. Q = the old **283
loose** = F. Q = make **284–5 Ha? . . . daughter** = F. Q = yea, i'st come to this? yet haue I
left a daughter **288 flay** *spelled* flea *in* F *and* Q **291 that** = F. Q = that my Lord **294–5
Pray . . . sir** = F. Q = Come sir no more, you **303–15 SH GONERIL This . . . SD** *Enter
Steward* = F. Q = *Gon.* What *Oswald*, ho. **315 How now, Oswald?** = F. Q = *Oswald.*
Here Madam. **316 What** = F. Q = *Gon.* What **324 condemn** = F. Q = dislike **325 at task**
= F. Q *uncorrected* = alapt. Q *corrected* = attaskt **328 better, oft** = F. Q = better ought

1.5.0 SD *Enter . . . Fool* = F. Q = *Enter Lear.* **19 tell** = F. Q = not tell **45–6 Keep . . . now,** =
F. Q = I would not be mad, keepe me in temper, I would not be mad, **47 SH GENTLEMAN**
= F. Q = *Seruant.*

2.1.2 you = Q. F = your **8 ear-kissing** = F. Q = eare-bussing **18 act . . . work** = F. Q = aske
breefnes . . . helpe **29–30 pardon . . . I** = F. Q = pardon me in crauing, I **37 SD**
Enter . . . torches = F. Q = *Enter Glost.* **40 Mumbling** = F. Q = warbling **41 stand** = F.
Q = stand's **49 revenging** = F. Q = reuengiue **50 the thunder** = F. Q = their thunders **56
latched** = F. Q = lancht **57 And** = F. Q = but **60 Full** = F. Q = but **67 coward** = F. Q =
caytife **73 would the reposal** = F. Q = could the reposure **75 should I** = F. Q = I
should **78 practice** = F. Q = pretence **81 spirits** = F. Q = spurres **83 O, strange** = F. Q =
Strong **84 said he?** = F. Q = I neuer got him, **85 where** = F. Q = why **91 SD**
Enter . . . Attendants = F. Q = *Enter the Duke of Cornwall* **93 strangeness** = F. Q = strange
newes **101 tended** = F. Q = tends **106 th'expense . . . of** = F. Q *uncorrected* = these—and
wast of this. Q *corrected* = the wast and spoyle of **115 bewray** = F. Q = betray **129
threading** = F. Q = threatning **130 prize** = F. Q *corrected* = poyse **133 differences** = F. Q
uncorrected = defences **best** = F. Q *corrected* = lest **thought** = Q. F = though **134 home** =
F. Q *uncorrected* = hand **137 businesses** = F. Q = busines

2.2.1 dawning = F. Q *corrected* = euen. Q *uncorrected* = deuen **15 worsted-stocking** = Q
corrected. F = woosted-stocking. Q *uncorrected* = wosted stocken **16 whoreson** = F. Q =

knaue, a whorson **super-serviceable finical** = F. Q = supersinicall **21 clamorous** *spelled* clamours *in* F **27 since** = F. Q = ago since **30 you** = F. Q = draw, you **43 if** = F. Q = and **57 they** = F. Q = hee **58 years o'th'trade** = F. Q = houres at the trade **59 SH CORNWALL** = F. Q = *Glost.* **67 know you** = F. Q = you haue **72 the holy** = F. Q = those **73 too intrinse** = Ed. F = t'intrince **75 fire** = F. Q = stir **the** = F. Q = their **76 Revenge** = F. Ed = Reneage **77 gall** = F. Q = gale **78 dogs** = F. Q = dayes **80 Smile** *spelled* Smoile *in* F, *smoyle in* Q **83 What** = F. Ed = Why **87 fault** = F. Q = offence **98 An...plain** = F. Q = he must be plaine **104 faith, in** = F. Q = sooth, or in **107 flickering** = Q *(flitkering).* F = flicking **118 compact** = F. Q = coniunct **123 fleshment** = F. Q = flechuent **dread** = Q. F = dead **128 ancient** = F. Q *corrected* = miscreant. Q *uncorrected* = ausrent **135 Stocking** = F. Q *corrected* = stopping. Q *uncorrected* = stobing. **146 he** = F. Q = hee's **152 duke's** = Q. F = Duke **155 travelled** *spelled* trauail'd *in* F *and* Q **160 saw** = F. Q *uncorrected* = say **165 miracles** = F. Q *corrected* = my wracke. Q *uncorrected* = my rackles **167 most** = F. Q *uncorrected* = not **171 Take** = F. Q *uncorrected* = Late **heavy** *spelled* heanie *in* F **177 unusual** *spelled* vnusall *in* F **183 hairs** = F. Q = haire **188 arms** = F. Q = bare arms **189 Pins** = F. Q *uncorrected* = Pies **190 farms** = F. Q = seruice **192 Sometimes** = F. Q = Sometime **194 SD** *Enter...Gentleman* = F. Q = *Enter King* **197 SH GENTLEMAN** = F. Q = *Knight (throughout)* **199 this** = F. Q = his **201 thy** = Q. F = ahy **204 heads** = F. Q = heeles **205 man's** = Q. F = man **215–16 By...ay** = F. Q = No no, they would not./ *Kent.* Yes they haue **221 impose** = F. Q = purpose **227 panting** = Q. F = painting **230 those** = F. Q = whose **231 meiny** = F. Q = men **242–50 SH FOOL Winter's...a year.** = F. *Not in* Q **252 Hysterica** *spelled Historica in* F *and* Q **258 the** = Q. F = the the **259 number** = F. Q = traine **266 twenty** = F. Q = a I00 **269 upward** = F. Q = vp the hill **271 have** = Q. F = hause **273 serves and seeks** = F. Q = serues **284 have...the** = F. Q = traueled hard to; **travelled** *spelled* travail'd *in* F **fetches** = F. Q = Iustice **294–5 SH GLOUCESTER Well...man?** = F. *Not in* Q **297 father** = F. Q *uncorrected* = fate **298 commands, tends,** = F. Q *corrected* = commands her. Q *uncorrected* = come and tends **299–300 Are...Fiery?** = F. *Not in* Q **319 knapped** = F. Q = rapt **326 you** = Q. F = your **328 mother's tomb** = Q *corrected.* F = Mother Tombe. Q *uncorrected* = mothers fruit **338–43 SH LEAR Say?...blame.** = F. *Not in* Q **347 her** = Q. F = his **370 blister** = F. Q = blast her pride **394 SH LEAR** = F. Q = *Gon.* **stocked** = F. Q = struck **420 hot-blooded** = F *uncorrected.* F *corrected* = hot-bloodied. Q = hot bloud in **432 boil** *spelled* Byle *in* F **478 need** = F. Q = deed **481 is** = F. Q = as. *Sometimes emended to* is as **490 tamely** = F. Q = lamely **498 flaws** = F. Q = flowes **507 SH GONERIL** = F. Q = *Duke* **509 SH CORNWALL** = F. Q = *Reg.* **511–12 SH CORNWALL Wither...horse** = F. *Not in* Q **513 SH CORNWALL** = F. Q = *Re.* **515 high** = F. Q = bleak

3.1.1 Who's there, besides = F. Q = Whats here beside **12 note** = F. Q = Arte **16–23 Who...furnishings** = F. *See 'Quarto passages that do not appear in the Folio', pp. 133–4, for alternative lines in* Q **30 that** = F. Q = your **35–6 in...this** = F. Q = Ile this way, you that

3.2.8 all = F. Ed = an **germens** *spelled* germaines *in* F **13 wise...fools** = F. Q = wise man nor foole **16 tax** = F. Q = taske **22 will...join** = F. Q = haue...ioin'd **42 are** = F. Q = sit **49 fear** = F. Q = force **55 of** = F. Q = man of **59 concealing continents** = F. Q = concealed centers **67 you** = F. Q = me **76 That's sorry** = F. Q = That sorrowes **77 little tiny** = Ed. F = little-tyne. Q = little tine **80 Though** = F. Q = for **81 True, boy** = F. Q = True my good boy **82–99 SH FOOL This...time.** = F. *Not in* Q

3.3.0 SD *Edmund* = F. Q = *the Bastard with lights.* **4 perpetual** = F. Q = their **13 footed** = F. Q = landed **16 if** = F. Q = though **18 strange things** = F. Q = some strange thing

3.4.8 contentious = F. Q *corrected* = tempestious. Q *uncorrected* = crulentious **9 skin so:** = F *corrected.* F *uncorrected* = skin: so: **12 thy** = Q. F = they **roaring** = F. Q *uncorrected* = raging **18 home** = F. Q = sure **19–20 In...endure** = F. *Not in* Q **22 all** = F. Q = you all 29–30 In . . . sleep = F. *Not in* Q 32 storm = F. Q = night 34 lopped = F. Q = loopt 40 SH EDGAR Fathom . . . Tom! = F. *Not in* Q 48 blow the winds = F. Q = blowes the cold wind Hum! . . . bed = F. Q = goe to thy cold bed 50 Did'st . . . thy = F. Q = Hast thou giuen all to thy two 53 through fire = Q. F = though Fire and through flame = F. *Not in* Q 54 ford = Q. F = Sword 59 Bless = Q. F = Blisse 59–60 O . . . de. = F. *Not in* Q 60 Bless = Q. F = blisse 64 Has = F. Q = What. Ed = What, have 65 Wouldst = F. Q = didst 70 light = F. Q = fall 82 word's justice = F. Q = words justly 92 I dearly = F. Q = I deeply 100 says . . . nonny = F. Q = hay no on ny 101 boy, boy = F. Q = boy, my boy, sessa = Ed. F = *Sesey.* Q = cease 102 a = F. Q = thy 109–10 lendings! . . . here = F. Q *corrected* = lendings, come on. Q *uncorrected* = leadings, come on bee true 113 on's = F. Q = in 115 foul = F. Q = foul fiend 116 till the = Q. F = at 117 squints = F. Q *corrected* = squemes. Q *uncorrected* = queues 122 alight = F. Q = O light 134–5 stocked, punished = F. Q = stock-punisht 135 hath had three = Q. F = hath three 140 Smulkin = F. Q = snulbug 145 my . . . vile = F. Q = is growne so vild my Lord 157 same = F. Q = most 173 you = F. Ed = your 186 tower came = F. Q = towne come

3.5.14 were not = F. Q = were

3.6.12–14 SH FOOL No . . . him. = F. *Not in* Q 21 They = F. Q = Theile 28–9 mongrel grim, Hound = Ed. F = Mongrill,Grim, / Hound. Q = mungril, grim-hound 29 him = F *(Hym). Sometimes emended to* lym 30 tyke = Q (tike). F = tight 34 Do . . . Sessa! = F. Q = loudla doodla 38 these hard hearts = F. Q = this hardnes 40 Persian = F. Q = Persian attire 42 and rest awhile = F. Q = awhile 44 So, so, we'll = F. Q = so, so, so, / Weele i'th'morning = F. Q = i'th'morning so, so, so 45 SH FOOL And . . . noon = F. *Not in* Q 55 Take up, take up = F. Q *corrected* = Take vp the King. Q *uncorrected* = Take vp to keepe

3.7.3 traitor = F. Q = vilaine 9 Advise = Q. F = Aduice 10 festinate *spelled* festiuate in F *and* festuant *in* Q 37 none = F. Q = true 48 answered = F. Q = answerer 60 answer = F. Q = first answere 62 Dover? = F. Q = Dover, sir? 65 stick = F. Q = rash 66 as his bare = F. Q *corrected* = on his lowd. Q *uncorrected* = of his lou'd 67 buoyed = F. Q *corrected* = bod. Q *uncorrected* = layd 69 rain = F. Q = rage 70 howled that stern = F. Q = heard that dearne 95 enkindle = F. Q = vnbridle

4.1.6–10 Welcome . . . comes = F. Q = Who's 10 poorly led = F. Q *corrected* = parti,eyd 15 these fourscore years = F. Q = this forescore 19 You = F. Q = Alack sir, you 42 kill = F. Q = bitt 48 Get thee away = F. Q = Then, prethee, get thee gon 49 hence = F. Q = here 60 daub = F. Q = dance 62 And . . . Bless = F. Q = Blesse 65–6 thee . . . son = F. Q = the good man 71 slaves = F. Q = stands 73 undo = F. Q = under 77 fearfully = F. Q = firmely

4.2.10 most . . . dislike = F. Q = hee should most desire 13 terror = F. Q *uncorrected* = curre 16 Edmund = F. Q = *Edgar* 18 names = F. Q = armes 28 O . . . man! = F. *Not in* Q 30 My fool = F. Q *corrected* = A Foole. Q *uncorrected* = My foote body = F. Q *corrected* = bed 32 whistle = F. Q *corrected* = whistling 41 seems = F. Q *corrected* = shewes 44 SH MESSENGER = F. Q = *Gent.* 48 thrilled = F. Q = thrald 50 threat-enraged = F. Q = thereat inraged 55 justices = F. Q *corrected* = Iustisers. Q *uncorrected* = your Iustices 65 tart = F. Q = tooke

4.3.0 SD *Gentleman* = Ed. F = *Gentlemen.* Q = *Doctor* 2 vexed = F. Q = vent 3 fumiter = Ed. F = Fenitar. Q = femiter 4 burdocks = Ed. F = Hardokes. Q = hor-docks 6 sentry *spelled* Centery *in* F, centurie *in* Q send = F. Q = sent 10 helps = F. Q = can help 19 distress = Q. F = desires 28 importuned = F. Q = important 29 incite = F. Q = in sight

4.4.6 lord = F. Q = lady 13 Edmund = F. Q = and now 16 o'th'enemy = F. Q = at'h army 17 madam . . . letter = F. Q = with my letters 18 troops set = F. Q = troope sets 24 Some things = F. Q = Some thing 29 oeillades *spelled* Eliads *in* F, aliads *in* Q 43 meet = F. Q = meet him should = F. Q = would

4.5.0 SD *Edgar* = F. Q = *Edmund* **1 I** = F. Q = we **21 walk** = Q. F = walk'd **48 bless him** = F. Q = blesse **67 summit** = F. Q = summons **76 How is't? Feel** = F. Q = how feele **84 whelked** *spelled* wealk'd *in* F **enragèd** = F. Q = enridged **86 make them** = F. Q = made their **96 crying** = F. Q = coyning **102 piece of toasted** = F. Q = tosted **105 I'th'clout, i'th'clout: hewgh** = F. Q = in the ayre, hagh **109 Goneril . . . beard?** = F. Q = *Gonorill*, ha *Regan*, **118 ague-proof** = F. Q = argue-proofe **129 were** = Ed. *Not in* F, Q **141 consumption** = F. Q = consumation **142–3 civet . . . sweeten** = F. Q = Ciuet, good Apothecarie, to sweeten **146 Let me** = F. Q = Here **151 this** = F. Q = that **153 thy** = F. Q = the **see** = F. Q = see one **166 change places, and** = F. *Not in* Q **171 dog's obeyed** = F. Q = dogge, so bade **177 tattered clothes great** = F. Q = tottered raggs, smal **178–83 Place . . . lips** = F. *Not in* Q; **175 Place sins** = F. Ed. = Plate sin **185 Now . . . now.** = F. Q = no now **192 wail** *spelled* wawle *in* F, wayl *in* Q **196 shoe** = F. Q = shoot **197 felt** = F. Q = fell **I'll . . . proof** = F. *Not in* Q **200 hand . . . Sir** = F. Q = hands upon him sirs **204 surgeons** = F. Q = a churgion **209 water-pots** = F. Q = water-pots, Ay, and laying autumn's dust. / *Gent.* Good sir— / *Lear.* **210 smug bridegroom** = F. Q = bridegroome **212 Masters** = F. Q = my maisters **214 Come** = F. Q = nay **215 Sa . . . sa.** = F. *Not in* Q **217 a daughter** = F. Q = one daughter **224 sound** = F. Q = sence **227 speedy foot** = F. Q = speed fort **238 tame to** = F. Q = lame by **243 bounty . . . benison** = F. Q *uncorrected* = bornet and beniz **244 To . . . boot** = F. Q *corrected* = to boot, to boot. Q *uncorrected* = to saue thee **247 old** = F. Q = most **262 I'se** *spelled* ice *in* F **ballow** = F. Q *corrected* = bat. Q *uncorrected* = battero **270 English** = F. Q = British **276 these** = F. Q = his **the** = F. Q = These **277 sorry** = F. Q = sorrow **289 affectionate servant, Goneril** = F. Q = your affectionate seruant and for your own *Venter, Gonorill* **290 will** = F. Q = wit **301 severed** = F. Q = fenced

Act 4 Scene 6 = Ed. F = *Scna Septima*

4.6.0 SD *Gentleman* = F. Q = *Doctor* **18 jarring** = F. Q = hurrying **24 SH GENTLEMAN** = F. Q *assigns this and the next line to the Doctor, and the following two lines to a Gentleman* **27 of** = F. Q = not of **temperance.** = F. Q = temperance. / *Cord.* Very well. / *Doct.* Please you draw neere, louder the musicke there, **35 opposed** = F. Q = exposd **jarring** = F. Q = warring **36 enemy's** = F. Q = iniurious **49 do . . . me?** = F. Q = know me. **64 not . . . less** = F. *Not in* Q **85 killed** = F. Q = cured **him.** = F. Q = him and yet it is danger to make him euen ore the time hee has lost

5.1.3 alteration = F. Q *uncorrected* = abdication **11 In** = F. Q = I. **17 not** = F. Q = me not **19 Sir . . . heard** = F. Q = For . . . heare **24 and particular broils** = F. Q = dore particulars **27 proceeding.** = F. Q = proceeding. / *Bast.* I shall attend you presently at your tent. **41 And machination ceases** = F. *Not in* Q **loves** = F. Q = loue **48 Here** = F. Q = Hard **guess** = F. Q = quesse **true** = F. Q = great

5.2.1 tree = F. Q = bush **13 SH GLOUCESTER And . . . too.** = F. *Not in* Q.

5.3.2 first = **F. Q** = best **26 good years** = F. Q = goode **40 down.** = F. Q = down. / *Cap.* I cannot draw a cart, nor eate dride oats, / If it bee mans worke ile do't. **48 send** = F. Q *uncorrected* = saue **retention** = F. Q *uncorrected* = retention and appointed guard **49 had** = F. Q = has **60 might** = F. Q = should **63 immediacy** = F. Q = imediate **67 addition** = F. Q = aduancement **70 SH ALBANY** = F. Q = *Gon.* **77 Dispose . . . thine:** = F. *Not in* Q **84 SH REGAN** = F. Q = *Bast.* **thine** = F. Q = good **86 thy arrest** = F. Q = thine attaint **87 sister** = Q. F = sister **88 bar** = Ed. F = bare **91 loves** = F. Q = loue **94 let . . . sound:** = F. *Not in* Q **95 person** = F. Q = head **97 make** = F. Q = proue **101 medicine** = F. Q = poyson **116 lists** = F. Q = hoast **118 by** = F. Q = at **120 SH HERALD** = F. Q = *Edmund* **129–30 Yet . . . cope** = F. Q = yet are I mou't / Where is the aduersarie I come to cope with all **137–8 my . . . honours** — = F. Q = the priuiledge of my tongue. **141 Despise** = F. Q = Despite **144 Conspirant** = F. Q = Conspicuate **146 below thy foot** = F. Q = beneath thy feet **148 are** = As **153 tongue** = F. Q = being **154 What . . . delay** = F. *Not in* Q **155 rule** = F. Q = right **156 Back** = F. Q = Heere

157 hell-hated lie o'erwhelm = F. Q = hell hatedly, oreturnd **158 scarcely** = Q. F = scarely **163 war** = F. Q = armes **wast** = F. Q = art **167 stop...sir** = F. Q = stople it **168 name** = F. Q = thing **173 SH EDMUND** = F. Q = *Gon.* **184 vices** = F. Q = vertues **185 plague** = F. Q = scourge **201 we** = F. Q = with **208 fault** = F. Q = Father **212 our** = F. Q = my **223 SH EDGAR** = F. Q = *Alb.* **224 SH ALBANY Speak, man.** = F. *Not in* Q **225 SH EDGAR** = F. Q *assigns line to Albany* **227 O, she's dead!** = F. *Not in* Q **228 Who...man.** = F. Q = Who man, speake? **230 confesses** = F. Q = hath confest **235 judgement** = F. Q = Iustice **236 is this** = F. Q = tis **266 you** = Q. F = your **282 you, murderers, traitors** = F. Q = your murderous traytors **288 SH GENTLEMAN** = F. Q = *Cap.* **291 him** = F. Q = them **296 This...sight.** = F. *Not in* Q **299 you that** = F. Q = that **303 first** = F. Q = life **310 says** = F. Q = sees **328 sir.** = F. Q = sir, O, o, o, o. **329–30 Do...there!** = F. *Not in* Q **332 SH KENT** = F. Q = *Lear* **343 realm** = F. Q = kingdome **346 SH EDGAR** = F. Q = *Duke*

QUARTO PASSAGES THAT DO NOT APPEAR IN THE FOLIO

Lines are numbered continuously, for ease of reference.

Following 1.2.96:

EDMUND Nor is not, sure.

GLOUCESTER To his father, that so tenderly and entirely loves him. Heaven and earth!

Following 1.2.144:

5   as of unnaturalness between the child and the parent, death, dearth, dissolutions of ancient amities, divisions in state, menaces and maledictions against king and nobles, needless diffidences, banishment of friends, dissipation of cohorts, nuptial breaches, and I know not what.

EDGAR How long have you been a sectary astronomical?

EDMUND Come, come,

Following 1.3.16:

10   Not to be overruled. Idle old man,
That still would manage those authorities
That he hath given away! Now by my life
Old fools are babes again, and must be used
With checks as flatteries, when they are seen abused.

Following 1.4.135:

15   **FOOL** That lord that counselled thee to give away thy land,
Come place him here by me, do thou for him stand,
The sweet and bitter fool will presently appear:
The one in motley here, the other found out there.

LEAR Dost thou call me fool, boy?

---

1 Nor…sure and I am sure he is not   **4 unnaturalness** lack of natural family feeling   **dearth** famine   **5 ancient amities** long-standing friendships   **divisions** breaches, disagreements   **maledictions** curses   **6 diffidences** doubts, mistrust   **7 dissipation of cohorts** dispersal of troops   **nuptial breaches** breaking of marriage vows   **8 sectary astronomical** devotee of astrology (in the period, astronomy and astrology were often indistinguishable from one another)   **10 Not** i.e. we are not   **Idle** foolish/useless   **13 used** handled, dealt with   **14 checks as flatteries** rebukes instead of flattery   **seen abused** seen to be misguided   **16 stand** i.e. stand in   **17 presently** immediately   **18 motley** the traditional multicoloured costume of the fool

20 **FOOL** All thy other titles thou hast given away, that thou wast born with.

KENT This is not altogether fool my lord.

FOOL No, faith, lords and great men will not let me, if I had a monopoly out,
they would have part on't: and ladies too, they will not let me have all the
fool to myself, they'll be snatching.

Following 1.4.210:

25 I would learn that, for by the marks of sovereignty, knowledge, and
reason, I should be false persuaded I had daughters.

FOOL Which they will make an obedient father.

Following 2.2.144:

His fault is much, and the good king, his master,
Will check him for't: your purposed low correction
30 Is such as basest and 'temnest wretches
For pilf'rings and most common trespasses
Are punished with.

Following 3.1.7:

tears his white hair,
Which the impetuous blasts with eyeless rage
35 Catch in their fury, and make nothing of,
Strives in his little world of man to out-scorn,
The to-and-fro-conflicting wind and rain:
This night wherein the cubdrawn bear would couch,
The lion and the belly-pinchèd wolf
40 Keep their fur dry, unbonneted he runs,
And bids what will take all.

Replaces 3.1.16–23:

But true it is, from France there comes a power
Into this scattered kingdom, who already
Wise in our negligence, have secret feet
45 In some of our best ports, and are at point
To show their open banner.
Now to you:
If on my credit you dare build so far
To make your speed to Dover, you shall find
50 Some that will thank you, making just report
Of how unnatural and bemadding sorrow
The king hath cause to 'plain.
I am a gentleman of blood and breeding,

---

21 altogether fool entirely foolish (the Fool replies to the sense of 'the only fool') **23 on't** of it **24 snatching** may imply snatching at the Fool's genitals or phallic baton (picking up on and shifting the sense of **part**; fools were proverbially well-endowed) **25 marks** outward signs **26 false** falsely **29 check** rebuke **low correction** base punishment **30 'temnest** most despised (contemnest) **31 pilf'rings** petty thefts **trespasses** crimes **34 eyeless** blind **35 Catch** seize **38 cubdrawn** drained of milk by her cubs, ravenous **couch** take cover, lie in its lair **39 belly-pinchèd** starving **40 unbonneted** bare-headed **41 bids...all** invites anyone who wishes to do so to take everything **42 power** army **43 scattered** divided **44 Wise in** aware of/taking advantage of **feet** footholds **45 at...show** on the point of displaying **48 on...far** i.e. if you trust me so far as **credit** trustworthiness **50 making just report** for making an accurate report **51 bemadding** madness-provoking **52 'plain** complain, lament **53 blood** noble family

And from some knowledge and assurance,
55   Offer this office to you.

Following 3.6.16:

EDGAR The foul fiend bites my back.

FOOL He's mad that trusts in the tameness of a wolf, a horse's health, a boy's
      love, or a whore's oath.

LEAR It shall be done, I will arraign them straight,
60   Come sit thou here most learnèd justice.—   *To Edgar*
      Thou, sapient sir sit here.   *To the Fool*
      No, you she foxes—

EDGAR Look where he stands and glares. Want'st thou eyes at trial, madam?
      Come o'er the bourn, Bessy, to me—

65   **FOOL** Her boat hath a leak,   *Sings*
          And she must not speak
          Why she dares not come over to thee.

EDGAR The foul fiend haunts poor Tom in the voice of a nightingale, Hopdance
      cries in Tom's belly for two white herring,
70   Croak not black angel, I have no food for thee.

KENT How do you sir? Stand you not so amazed,
      Will you lie down and rest upon the cushings?

LEAR I'll see their trial first, bring in their evidence.—
      Thou robèd man of justice, take thy place—   *To Edgar*
75   And thou, his yoke-fellow of equity,   *To the Fool*
      Bench by his side:— you are o'th'commission,   *To Kent*
      Sit you too.

EDGAR Let us deal justly.
      Sleepest or wakest thou, jolly shepherd?
80   Thy sheep be in the corn,
      And for one blast of thy minikin mouth,
      Thy sheep shall take no harm.
      Purr, the cat is grey.

LEAR Arraign her first, 'tis Goneril. I here take my oath before this honourable
85   assembly, she kicked the poor king her father.

FOOL Come hither, mistress. Is your name Goneril?

LEAR She cannot deny it.

FOOL Cry you mercy, I took you for a joint-stool.

LEAR And here's another whose warped looks proclaim
90   What store her heart is made on: stop her there!

---

54 **assurance** certainty   55 **office** task   59 **arraign** indict, put on trial   **straight** straight away   60 **justice** judge
61 **sapient** wise   63 **Want'st thou** do you lack   **eyes** may signify 'spectators'   64 **Come ... me** a snatch of popular
song   **bourn** stream   65 **Her ... leak** i.e. she is menstruating (or possibly 'she has gonorrhoea')   66 **speak** say   67 **come
over** i.e. for sex   68 **foul** possible pun on 'fool'   **Hopdance** a devil associated with music (like all of the fiends Edgar mentions,
taken from Samuel Harsnett's 1603 *Declaration of Egregious Popish Impostures*)   70 **black angel** i.e. the fiend in Tom's belly,
which is causing it to rumble   71 **do** are   **amazed** stunned, overwhelmed   72 **cushings** cushions   75 **yoke-fellow of
equity** partner in fairness   76 **Bench** sit on the bench   **o'th'commission** of the panel of judges   81 **for ... mouth** i.e. if the
shepherd summons his sheep back by playing his pipe   **minikin** dainty/shrill   83 **Purr** Harsnett mentions a devil called Purr,
though devils were popularly thought to assume the shape of cats   88 **Cry you mercy** I beg your pardon   **joint-stool** a
well-made stool   89 **another** i.e. Regan   **warped looks** contorted facial expression/warped wood   90 **store** material/
tradesman's stock   **on** of

Arms, arms, sword, fire! Corruption in the place!
False justicer, why hast thou let her scape?

Following 3.6.57:

KENT Oppressed nature sleeps:
This rest might yet have balmed thy broken sinews,
95   Which, if convenience will not allow,
Stand in hard cure.— Come help to bear thy master: **To Fool**
Thou must not stay behind.   *Exeunt. [Edgar remains]*

EDGAR When we our betters see bearing our woes,
We scarcely think our miseries our foes.
100   Who alone suffers, suffers most i'th'mind,
Leaving free things and happy shows behind,
But then the mind much sufferance doth o'erskip,
When grief hath mates, and bearing fellowship:
How light and portable my pain seems now,
105   When that which makes me bend, makes the king bow:
He childed as I fathered. Tom away!
Mark the high noises and thyself bewray
When false opinion, whose wrong thoughts defile thee,
In thy just proof repeals and reconciles thee.
110   What will hap more tonight, safe scape the king:
Lurk, lurk.   *Exit*

Following 3.7.109:

SERVANT I'll never care what wickedness I do,
If this man come to good.

SECOND SERVANT If she live long,
115   And in the end meet the old course of death,
Women will all turn monsters.

FIRST SERVANT Let's follow the old earl, and get the Bedlam
To lead him where he would: his madness
Allows itself to anything.

120   **SECOND SERVANT** Go thou: I'll fetch some flax and whites of eggs
To apply to his bleeding face. Now heaven help him!

---

92 **False justicer** corrupt judge **scape** escape 93 **Oppressed** overwhelmed/afflicted 94 **balmed . . . sinews** soothed
your shattered nerves 95 **convenience** opportunity 96 **Stand . . . cure** will be hard to heal 98 **bearing our woes**
enduring the same suffering as us 100 **Who . . . i'th'mind** mental anguish is worst for those who suffer alone 101 **free**
carefree **happy shows** displays of happiness/visions of good fortune 102 **sufferance** suffering **o'erskip** pass over, not
notice 103 **bearing** endurance (of affliction) 104 **portable** bearable 105 **bow** i.e. bow down under a truly heavy weight
(with suggestion of servile bowing, inappropriate to a king) 106 **He . . . fathered** his children have treated him as my father
has treated me 107 **high noises** important rumours/what is being said amongst the powerful **bewray** reveal
109 **In . . . proof** in proving you to be just 110 **What . . . king** whatever else happens tonight, may the king escape safely
111 **Lurk** i.e. stay out of sight 115 **old . . . death** i.e. die naturally, in old age 117 **Bedlam** Bedlam beggar, i.e. Poor
Tom 118 **where he would** wherever he wants to go 119 **Allows itself to** enables him to do 120 **flax . . . eggs** both were
conventionally used to soothe damaged eyes

Following 4.1.66:

> Five fiends have been in poor Tom at once: of lust, as Obidicut,
> Hobbididence, prince of dumbness, Mahu of stealing, Modo of murder,
> Flibbertigibbet of mopping and mowing, who since possesses
125 > chambermaids and waiting-women. So, bless thee, master

Following 4.2.35:

> I fear your disposition:
> That nature, which contemns i'th'origin
> Cannot be bordered certain in itself.
> She that herself will sliver and disbranch
130 > From her material sap perforce must wither
> And come to deadly use.

GONERIL No more, the text is foolish.

ALBANY Wisdom and goodness to the vile seem vile:
Filths savour but themselves. What have you done?
135 Tigers, not daughters, what have you performed?
A father, and a gracious agèd man,
Whose reverence even the head-lugged bear would lick,
Most barbarous, most degenerate, have you madded.
Could my good brother suffer you to do it?
140 A man, a prince, by him so benefited!
If that the heavens do not their visible spirits
Send quickly down to tame the vile offences, it will come,
Humanity must perforce prey on itself,
Like monsters of the deep.

Following 4.2.39:

145   that not know'st
Fools do those villains pity who are punished
Ere they have done their mischief. Where's thy drum?
France spreads his banners in our noiseless land,
With plumèd helm, thy state begins threat,
150 Whilst thou, a moral fool, sits still and cries
'Alack, why does he so?'

Following 4.2.43:

ALBANY Thou changèd and self-covered thing, for shame
Bemonster not thy feature. Were't my fitness
To let these hands obey my blood,

122 **Obidicut . . . Flibbertigibbet** more fiends mentioned by Samuel Harsnett; 'flibbertigibbet' can also mean 'a gossip' or 'a flighty, frivolous woman'   124 **mopping and mowing** grimacing, making faces   127 **contemns i'th'origin** despises its originator (father)   128 **bordered certain** safely contained   129 **sliver and disbranch** split and break off (like a branch from a tree)   130 **material** essential, substantial   **perforce** necessarily   131 **come . . . use** be destroyed (like firewood)   132 **text** sermon   134 **savour** but only enjoy, appreciate   136 **gracious** generous/good/(as a king) possessed of divine grace   137 **reverence** position deserving respect, venerable condition   **head-lugged** that has been pulled about by its head, i.e. enraged   138 **madded** sent mad   139 **brother** brother-in-law, i.e. Cornwall   **suffer** allow   141 **visible spirits** spirits in visible form, avenging angels   142 **tame** crush   146 **Fools . . . mischief** i.e. only fools pity villains (like Lear) who are punished as a preventative measure before they have done wrong   148 **France** the King of France   **noiseless** silent, inactive   149 **plumèd helm** (soldiers') helmets adorned with feathers   **thy . . . threat** begins to threaten the state   150 **moral** moralizing   152 **self-covered** self-concealing   153 **Bemonster . . . feature** do not make your beauty hideous by revealing your true fiend's face   **Were't my fitness** if it were proper for me   154 **blood** anger

155   They are apt enough to dislocate and tear
        Thy flesh and bones: howe'er thou art a fiend,
        A woman's shape doth shield thee.

GONERIL Marry, your manhood mew—

Enter a Gentleman

ALBANY What news?

Following 4.2.77:

Enter Kent and a Gentleman

160   **KENT** Why the King of France is so suddenly gone back, know you no reason?

        GENTLEMAN Something he left imperfect in the state, which since his coming
                forth is thought of, which imports to the kingdom so much fear and
                danger that his personal return was most required and necessary.

        KENT Who hath he left behind him general?

165   **GENTLEMAN** The Marshal of France, Monsieur La Far.

        KENT Did your letters pierce the queen to any demonstration of grief?

        GENTLEMAN Ay, sir, she took them, read them in my presence,
                And now and then an ample tear trilled down
                Her delicate cheek: it seemed she was a queen over
170   Her passion, who, most rebel-like,
                Sought to be king o'er her.

        KENT O, then it moved her.

        GENTLEMAN Not to a rage: patience and sorrow strove
                Who should express her goodliest. You have seen
175   Sunshine and rain at once: her smiles and tears
                Were like a better way: those happy smilets,
                That played on her ripe lip seem not to know
                What guests were in her eyes, which, parted thence,
                As pearls from diamonds dropped. In brief,
180   Sorrow would be a rarity most beloved,
                If all could so become it.

        KENT Made she no verbal question?

        GENTLEMAN Faith, once or twice she heaved the name of 'father'
                Pantingly forth, as if it pressed her heart:
185   Cried 'Sisters, sisters! Shame of ladies, sisters!
                Kent, father, sisters! What, i'th'storm, i'th'night?
                Let pity not be believed!' There she shook
                The holy water from her heavenly eyes,
                And clamour moistened her: then away she started
190   To deal with grief alone.

        KENT It is the stars,
                The stars above us, govern our conditions,
                Else one self mate and make could not beget
                Such different issues. You spoke not with her since?

---

156 howe'er however much, although **158 Marry** by the Virgin Mary   **mew** a contemptuous and belittling cat's miaow
160 back i.e. to France **161 imperfect** unfinished **162 imports** signifies, brings with it **168 trilled** trickled
170 passion strong emotion/grief **174 goodliest** best, most effectively **176 smilets** little smiles, half-smiles **181 so
become it** grace it so well, make it seem so attractive **187 Let … believed!** Put no trust in pity! **189 clamour moistened
her** the expression of her grief moistened her with tears   **started** hastened, went abruptly **193 mate and make** husband and
wife **194 issues** children

195 **GENTLEMAN** No.

KENT Was this before the king returned?

GENTLEMAN No, since.

KENT Well, sir, the poor distressèd Lear's i'th'town;
Who sometime, in his better tune, remembers
200 What we are come about, and by no means
Will yield to see his daughter.

GENTLEMAN Why, good sir?

KENT A sovereign shame so elbows him: his own unkindness,
That stripped her from his benediction, turned her
205 To foreign casualties, gave her dear rights
To his dog-hearted daughters: these things sting
His mind so venomously, that burning shame
Detains him from Cordelia.

GENTLEMAN Alack, poor gentleman!

210 **KENT** Of Albany's and Cornwall's powers you heard not?

GENTLEMAN 'Tis so, they are afoot.

KENT Well, sir, I'll bring you to our master Lear,
And leave you to attend him: some dear cause
Will in concealment wrap me up awhile.
215 When I am known aright, you shall not grieve
Lending me this acquaintance. I pray you go
Along with me.   *Exeunt*

Following 4.6.27:

CORDELIA Very well.

DOCTOR Please you, draw near.— Louder the music there!

Following 4.6.35:

220 To stand against the deep dread-bolted thunder,
In the most terrible and nimble stroke
Of quick cross lightning? To watch — poor *perdu!* —
With this thin helm?

Following 4.6.89:

GENTLEMAN Holds it true, sir, that the Duke of Cornwall was so slain?

225 **KENT** Most certain, sir.

GENTLEMAN Who is conductor of his people?

KENT As 'tis said, the bastard son of Gloucester.

GENTLEMAN They say Edgar, his banished son, is with the Earl of Kent in Germany.

230 **KENT** Report is changeable. 'Tis time to look about: the powers of the kingdom approach apace.

199 sometime sometimes **tune** i.e. frame of mind   **203 sovereign** overpowering (plays on the related literal sense of 'kingly')   **elbows** pushes, jostles   **205 casualties** chance, uncertainties   **211 afoot** on the move   **213 attend** wait on, look after   **dear cause** important reason   **215 aright** rightly, as myself   **grieve** regret   **220 deep** rumbling, deep-voiced **dread-bolted** hurling terrifying thunderbolts   **222 cross** forked   **watch** remain awake/be on guard   **perdu** 'lost one' (French), the name given to a guard placed in an extremely open, dangerous position   **223 helm** helmet/covering of hair   **226 conductor ... people** commander of his forces   **230 Report** rumour   **powers ... kingdom** British forces **apace** rapidly

GENTLEMAN The arbitrament is like to be bloody. Fare you well, sir.

KENT My point and period will be throughly wrought,
Or well or ill, as this day's battle's fought.   *Exit*

Following 5.1.13:

235 **EDMUND** That thought abuses you.

REGAN I am doubtful that you have been conjunct
And bosomed with her, as far as we call hers.

Following 5.1.17:

GONERIL I had rather lose the battle than that sister
Should loosen him and me.

Following 5.1.21:

240   Where I could not be honest,
I never yet was valiant. For this business,
It touches us as France invades our land,
Not bolds the king, with others whom I fear,
Most just and heavy causes make oppose.

245 **EDMUND** Sir, you speak nobly.

Following 5.3.55:

At this time
We sweat and bleed: the friend hath lost his friend;
And the best quarrels, in the heat, are cursed
By those that feel their sharpness:
250   The question of Cordelia and her father
Requires a fitter place.

Following 5.3.221:

EDGAR This would have seemed a period
To such as love not sorrow, but another,
To amplify too much, would make much more,
255   And top extremity.
Whilst I was big in clamour, came there in a man,
Who, having seen me in my worst estate,
Shunned my abhorred society, but then finding
Who 'twas that so endured, with his strong arms
260   He fastened on my neck and bellowed out
As he'd burst heaven, threw me on my father,
Told the most piteous tale of Lear and him
That ever ear received, which in recounting

232 **arbitrament** deciding of the dispute   233 **point . . . wrought** the conclusion of my aims will be thoroughly brought about   234 **Or** either   235 **abuses** dishonours, wrongs   236 **doubtful** fearful   **conjunct And bosomed** sexually intimate   237 **as . . . hers** to the fullest extent   240 **honest** honourable   241 **For** as for   242 **touches us as** i.e. affects our honour insofar as   243 **bolds** insofar as it emboldens   **with** (who) along with   244 **Most . . . oppose** has most just and weighty grounds for hostility   248 **the . . . sharpness** i.e. in the heat of emotion even the best grounds for hostility are cursed by those who have suffered the losses and afflictions of battle (Edmund pretends to be anxious that Lear and Cordelia receive a fair trial)   252 **period** limit, extreme point   253 **such . . . not** those who do not love   **another . . . extremity** to enlarge upon another sorrowful tale (that of Kent) would increase sorrow even further and exceed all limits   256 **big in clamour** loud in lamentation   257 **estate** condition   260 **fastened . . . neck** i.e. embraced me   261 **As** as if

His grief grew puissant and the strings of life
265   Began to crack: twice then the trumpets sounded,
And there I left him 'tranced.

ALBANY But who was this?

EDGAR Kent, sir, the banished Kent, who in disguise
Followed his enemy king and did him service
270   Improper for a slave.

TEXTUAL NOTES

Q = First Quarto text of 1608
Q2 = a correction introduced in the Second Quarto text of 1619
Ed = a correction introduced by a later editor
SH = Speech heading (i.e. speaker's name)

1 SH EDMUND = Ed. Q = *Bast. (throughout)* **23 on't** = Q. Q2 = an't **ladies** = Q *(corrected)*. Q *(uncorrected)* = lodes **30 bases** and **'temnest** = Q *(corrected)*. Q *(uncorrected)* = belest and contaned **63 Want'st** = Q2. Q = wanst **64 boum** = Ed. Q = broom **85 she kicked** = Ed. Q = kickt **88 joint-stool** = Q2. Q = ioyne stoole **90 on** = Ed. Q = an **118 madness** = Q *(corrected)*. Q *(uncorrected)* = rogish madnes **124 Flibbertigibbet** *spelled Stiberdigebit in* Q **mopping and mowing** = Ed. Q = Mobing, & *Mohing* **143 Humanity** = Q *(corrected)*. Q *(uncorrected)* = Humanly **149 threat** *spelled* thereat *in* Q *(corrected)* **state begin threat** = Q (corrected). Q *(uncorrected)* = slayer begin threats **158 mew** = Q *(corrected)*. Q *(uncorrected)* = now **167 Ay, sir,** = Ed. Q = I say **173 strove** = Ed. Q = streme

264 puissant powerful **strings of life** i.e. heartstrings **266 'tranced** absorbed by grief/in a faint, unconscious
269 enemy king i.e. the king who had treated him as an enemy **270 Improper for** unfitting even for

SCENE-BY-SCENE ANALYSIS

ACT 1 SCENE 1

Relationships between key characters are established. Several themes are introduced: power/authority, deception, nature, kinship, sanity and sight.

Lines 1–33: Kent and Gloucester discuss Lear. Edmund is introduced. Gloucester insists that Edmund is as dear to him as his older, legitimate, son Edgar and claims that 'the whoreson must be acknowledged'. The bawdy language used to describe Edmund's conception undermines the good intentions behind this.

Lines 34–196: A trumpet flourish emphasizes the ceremonial, public nature of events from this point. Instructing Gloucester to fetch France and Burgundy, Lear reveals his 'darker purpose' – to allocate a piece of kingdom to each of his three daughters, intending the 'largest bounty' to whoever 'doth love [him] most'. This reveals Lear's inability to separate public and domestic and highlights his perception of emotions as subject to pecuniary measurement. Tensions exist between his love of power and his portrayal of himself as an old man who wishes to 'Unburdened crawl toward death'.

Goneril's speech is effusive but ambiguous, as she declares that she loves her father 'more than word can wield the matter'. Regan is similarly flattering but ambiguous, telling Lear to 'prize' her at Goneril's 'worth', as she is 'made of that self-mettle' as her sister. Cordelia's asides show her dilemma – she is torn between genuine love for her father and reluctance or inability to voice this before the court. She is offered 'a third more opulent' than her sisters – unlike

Gloucester, Lear does not even suggest he values his daughters equally. In contrast to her sisters, Cordelia's response is simply 'Nothing'. Lear encourages her to say more, because 'Nothing will come of nothing', a concept that is explored throughout the play. Lear disinherits Cordelia and Kent's attempts to speak up for her fuel his anger.

Retaining a hundred knights, Lear divides his kingdom between Goneril and Regan, intending to live with each of them for alternate months. Kent intervenes, showing respect for Lear, but suggesting that he is not thinking clearly and urging him to 'check / This hideous rashness'. Lear banishes Kent.

Lines 197–284: Lear explains to the King of France and Duke of Burgundy that Cordelia's 'price is fallen'. She is no longer 'dear' to him, a word that highlights his belief that love is quantifiable. Burgundy cannot decide, so Lear offers his daughter to France, but says he would not want him to marry a 'wretch' that 'Nature is ashamed' of. France asks what Cordelia's 'monstrous' offence is and she asks Lear to make it clear that it is lack of the 'glib and oily art' of false speech. Burgundy says that he will take her with her original dowry. Echoing Cordelia, Lear declares that this is 'Nothing', so Burgundy declines. France sees Cordelia's virtues and comments that 'unprized precious' Cordelia is 'most rich, being poor', highlighting France and Lear's differing perceptions of 'worth', and challenging Lear's assertion that 'Nothing will come of nothing'.

Lines 285–302: Leaving with France, Cordelia says goodbye 'with washèd eyes', suggesting tears but also clear perception of her sisters' characters.

Lines 303–327: Goneril and Regan discuss Lear's 'poor judgement' and the 'changes' and 'infirmity' of his old age, but Regan observes that 'he hath ever but slenderly known himself'. Goneril expresses concern about Lear's desire for authority. Regan agrees that they must 'think' about this, but Goneril says that they 'must do something', highlighting a subtle difference between them.

ACT 1 SCENE 2

Lines 1–22: Edmund is angry that he will not inherit. He protests about the label 'base' and argues that he is as good as 'honest madam's issue' – better, even, because there was passion in his conception. He reveals his designs on Edgar's inheritance.

Lines 23–118: Edmund conceals a letter from Gloucester in a way that draws attention to it. He tells Gloucester it is 'Nothing', but then pretends that it is from Edgar. Gloucester reads its contents, which suggest that Edgar and Edmund should murder Gloucester and split the inheritance. Edmund manipulates Gloucester, who is easily persuaded that Edgar is an 'unnatural' villain. Edmund pretends to plead on Edgar's behalf and arranges that Gloucester will overhear a conversation between them. Gloucester exits, blaming all the problems in family and state on 'These late eclipses in the sun and moon'.

Lines 119–177: Edmund is scornful of those who believe that destiny is decided by the stars and blame their 'evil' on 'a divine thrusting on', thus raising a debate between free will and fate, as he claims that the stars have no influence on his personality or fortune. Edgar interrupts and Edmund changes behaviour on 'cue', suggesting his directorial role in the action. He persuades Edgar that Gloucester is angry with him and suggests that they avoid meeting. Giving Edgar the key to his lodging, he promises to help.

ACT 1 SCENE 3

Goneril and her steward Oswald discuss Lear's irrational temper. She gives instructions to say that she is ill and cannot see Lear and that the servants are to ignore him.

ACT 1 SCENE 4

Lines 1–91: Kent is disguised, but while his appearance has changed, his nature has not – he is still an 'honest-hearted fellow'. Not recognizing him, Lear employs Kent and asks Oswald for

Goneril, but is ignored. One of Lear's knights says that Oswald refuses to come back, that Goneril is unwell, and points out that Lear has been neglected recently. When Oswald reappears, he is disrespectful and Lear loses his temper. Kent trips Oswald up and insults him, earning Lear's thanks.

Lines 92–179: Lear's Fool delivers a series of jokes, riddles, nonsense and rhymes. These have comic effect, but they are also ambiguous, providing perceptive comment on Lear's circumstances and reinforcing some key themes such as cruelty, division and folly. In the Quarto text, Kent comments that 'This is not altogether fool my lord'.

Lines 180–302: Goneril lists her grievances. Lear's temper and language become wilder, suggesting the growing disquiet of his mind. The interjections of the Fool, combining nonsense and wisdom, contribute to the growing disorder. Albany ineffectually attempts to calm Lear, who curses Goneril with either sterility or the future birth of a 'child of spleen'. He leaves. Goneril ignores Albany, showing where the power lies in their relationship. Lear returns, having discovered that Goneril has reduced his train of knights by fifty. Despite uncontrollable anger, his tears suggest weakness. He decides to go to Regan, saying she will 'flay' Goneril's 'wolfish visage' – an example of the animal imagery associated with the two sisters.

Lines 303–330: Goneril claims it is unwise to allow Lear to enforce the whims of his old age, and calls Oswald to take a letter to Regan. She criticizes Albany for his 'milky gentleness'.

ACT 1 SCENE 5

Lear sends letters to Gloucester with Kent, then struggles against madness as he talks to his Fool.

ACT 2 SCENE 1

Lines 1–91: Edmund urges Edgar to escape, suggesting that Cornwall believes Edgar is plotting against him, and that Gloucester is in pursuit. Edmund directs Edgar's flight, pretending that he is helping, but convincing Gloucester's party that he is trying to stop him. He wounds his own arm and tells Gloucester that Edgar stabbed him when he refused to help Edgar. Gloucester tells 'Loyal and natural' Edmund that he will make him his heir.

Lines 92–140: Gloucester confirms Cornwall and Regan's queries about Edgar. Cornwall praises Edmund, takes him into his service, then begins to explain their arrival. Regan interrupts, showing her dominance, and claims that she wanted Gloucester's advice on letters from Lear and Goneril.

ACT 2 SCENE 2

Lines 1–151: Outside Gloucester's castle, Oswald claims not to know the disguised Kent, who insults and beats him. While Cornwall attempts to establish how the quarrel started, Kent continues to insult Oswald, who explains that Kent (who calls himself 'Caius') is in Lear's service. Cornwall comments on Kent's plain-spoken nature, but ironically assumes that his 'plainness / Harbour[s] more craft and more corrupter ends' and places him in the stocks. In the Quarto text, Gloucester argues stocks are for 'basest and 'temnest wretches' and it is insulting to Lear to punish his messenger in them.

Lines 152–173: Gloucester apologizes and says that he will plead for Kent's release, but Kent says not to. Kent's soliloquy reveals that he has a letter from Cordelia.

Lines 174–194: Edgar intends to disguise himself as a mad beggar from Bedlam. Edgar's soliloquy and the following sequence are sometimes edited and played as separate scenes, but the action continues uninterrupted in that Kent remains onstage asleep in the stocks.

Lines 195–280: Lear will not believe that Regan and Cornwall have put Kent in the stocks – it is an 'outrage' 'upon respect'. Fighting his rising anger, Lear goes to confront them. The Fool comments on Kent's folly in continuing to serve Lear.

Lines 281–393: Enraged that Regan and Cornwall will not speak with him, Lear sends Gloucester to summon them. His language reflects his growing disturbance, which he fights to suppress – 'my rising heart! But, down!' When they arrive, Lear pours out his grievances against Goneril. Regan responds in a reasoned but insulting manner, saying that Lear is old and needs to be 'ruled and led', and suggests that he ask Goneril's forgiveness. Lear's pride and anger rise, but he thinks Regan will acknowledge the 'dues of gratitude' that he has bought with 'half o'th'kingdom'.

Lines 394–525: Goneril and Regan unite against Lear, gradually reducing his number of knights – a symbol of his power – until he has nothing. He reminds them of what they owe him – 'I gave you all'. When Regan asks whether Lear needs even one follower, he replies 'O, reason not the need! Our basest beggars / Are in the poorest things superfluous: / Allow not nature more than nature needs, / Man's life is cheap as beast's.' The encounter of king and beggar, the question of 'superfluity' and the stripping down from courtly accoutrements to raw nature are at the core of the play. Lear asks the heavens for patience, but the growing storm reflects his turbulent mind and he leaves in 'high rage' to go out onto the heath. Goneril, Regan and Cornwall tell Gloucester to shut his doors against Lear and the storm.

ACT 3 SCENE 1

In this act, the relatively brief and fast-paced scenes move between different locations and characters. This, combined with the evocation of the storm, creates a sense of chaos that mirrors the breakdown of Lear's reason and kingdom.

Kent learns that Lear is on the heath in the storm with the Fool. He reveals that the French have spies in the courts of Cornwall and Albany, between whom dissension is growing. Kent gives the Gentleman a ring to show to Cordelia as confirmation of his true identity.

ACT 3 SCENE 2

Lear's disordered speech reflects his mental state as he invokes nature to destroy mankind and 'Strike flat the thick rotundity o'th'world'. In his chaotic speeches there are recurrent references to children, ingratitude and justice as he blames his daughters for his situation. The Fool encourages Lear to shelter, commenting that the 'night pities neither wise men nor fools', drawing attention to the blurred distinctions between wisdom and folly, sanity and insanity. Lear rages about justice, still denying any responsibility and asserting that he is 'a man / More sinned against than sinning'. Kent persuades him to take shelter in a nearby hovel while he begs Goneril and Regan for shelter. Alone, the Fool speaks a rhymed 'prophecy' that perhaps transcends the context of the play, warning against the injustices and corruption of 'Albion' (Britain).

ACT 3 SCENE 3

Gloucester has been refused permission to help Lear and has lost control of his castle. He reveals that Edmund has a letter concerning Cornwall and Albany locked in his closet, and that he intends to help Lear. He asks Edmund to tell Cornwall that he is ill, to prevent his assistance of Lear being discovered. Once alone, Edmund reveals his intention to betray Gloucester.

ACT 3 SCENE 4

Lines 1–110: Kent tries to persuade Lear to enter the hovel out of the storm, but Lear is more concerned with the 'tempest' in his mind and remains outside, dwelling on 'Poor naked wretches' who, 'houseless' and 'unfed', have no defence against the elements. In a moment of brief self-awareness he declares: 'O, I have ta'en / Too little care of this!' The Fool is frightened out of the hovel by Edgar, in disguise as the near-naked 'Poor Tom'. In a pitiful and ironic contrast to the genuine insanity of Lear, 'Tom' feigns madness through fragmented speech. Like the Fool's nonsense, however, there are recognizable themes, pertinent to the play, such as lust, devilishness and nakedness. Lear continues to dwell on his troubles, insisting that 'nothing' but 'unkind daughters' could have 'subdued nature / To such a lowness' in Tom. Asking 'Is man no more than this?', Lear removes his clothes, approaching the raw condition of 'the thing itself: unaccommodated man'.

Lines 111–188: In a confused conversation which evokes the external storm and the 'tempest' inside Lear's head, Gloucester and Kent attempt to persuade Lear to enter Gloucester's castle. Tom interjects with 'insane' comments that focus on demons and witchcraft, but are taken by Lear to be the words of a 'philosopher' and 'learned Theban'. Ironically, Gloucester talks of Edgar and 'poor banished' Kent.

ACT 3 SCENE 5

Edmund has betrayed Gloucester. Cornwall swears that he will have revenge and rewards Edmund by giving him his father's title. Edmund pretends to be distressed at having to betray Gloucester, but plans to make it worse by discovering him 'comforting the king'.

ACT 3 SCENE 6

Gloucester shows Kent, Lear, Tom and the Fool into a farmhouse adjoining his castle. The dialogue is fragmented as Lear continues to focus on injustice, the Fool continues to produce sense in nonsense and Edgar acts his part as madman. Kent's voice of reason is unable to prevail. In a Quarto-only sequence, Lear insists on holding a 'trial' of Goneril and Regan, seeing them before him in his madness. With Tom and the Fool as judges, this episode highlights the distorted nature of justice so far in the play. Edgar's pity for Lear makes it hard to sustain his 'counterfeiting', and after Gloucester leads the others away, he rejects his disguise.

ACT 3 SCENE 7

Cornwall sends Goneril to tell Albany that France has landed, instructing Edmund to accompany her. Oswald informs Cornwall that Lear has gone to Dover. Gloucester is brought for questioning. Regan cruelly encourages the servant to bind Gloucester 'hard' and disrespectfully plucks his beard. He admits that he sent Lear to Dover to protect him from Regan's 'cruel nails' and Goneril's 'boarish fangs'. Cornwall puts out one of Gloucester's eyes. A servant tries to help Gloucester, but as Cornwall fights him, Regan seizes a sword – a symbol of her 'unwomanly' power – and stabs the servant. Cornwall takes Gloucester's other eye as Regan reveals that it was Edmund who betrayed him. Gloucester thus gains metaphorical 'sight' as he is literally blinded. Regan orders Gloucester to be put out onto the heath to 'smell / His way to Dover'. She leads the mortally injured Cornwall away. In the Quarto text, the remaining servants discuss Regan's lack of womanly feeling, offer first aid to Gloucester and vow to get 'the Bedlam' (Tom) to lead him to Dover.

ACT 4 SCENE 1

Edgar argues that even the 'most dejected thing of fortune' can still have hope, but then he sees his blinded father and realizes he is 'worse than e'er'. Gloucester shows self-awareness when he says that he 'stumbled' when he saw, and ironically talks of his 'dear son Edgar'. Gloucester blames the gods, to whom men are 'As flies', and who 'kill us for their sport'. The old man leading Gloucester recognizes 'Poor Tom' and Edgar realizes that he must remain disguised and 'play fool to sorrow'. Gloucester wishes Tom to lead him to Dover, despite the old man's protests, arguing that ''Tis the times' plague, when madmen lead the blind'. Edgar's pity for Gloucester means that he struggles to maintain his deception. Gloucester asks to be taken to the edge of Dover's cliffs.

ACT 4 SCENE 2

Lines 1–31: Goneril wonders why Albany did not meet her. Oswald informs her that Albany has changed – he 'smiled' to hear of the French army's arrival and said 'The worse' at Goneril's return. He refuses to believe Gloucester's treachery or Edmund's loyalty. Goneril sends Edmund back, blaming Albany's change on his 'cowish terror'. She gives him a love token and kisses him, telling him to wait for 'A mistress's command'.

Lines 32–77: Albany and Goneril quarrel. In a Quarto-only sequence, Albany shows new strength as he berates Goneril for her treatment of her father, calling her and Regan 'Tigers, not daughters'; she accuses him of cowardice, describing him as 'a moral fool'. In the Folio's edited version of their exchange, Goneril calls her husband a 'Milk-livered man'. A messenger brings news of Cornwall's death and Gloucester's blinding; he delivers Goneril a letter from Regan. Albany is horrified and swears revenge on Edmund for his betrayal of Gloucester. Goneril shows mixed feelings at Cornwall's death – Regan is less powerful as a widow, but she is also free to marry Edmund.

ACT 4 SCENE 3

In a Quarto-only scene, Kent and a Gentleman inform the audience that France has returned to his kingdom, leaving Cordelia in England. Kent asks for Cordelia's reaction to his letter. The natural imagery – 'Sunshine and rain at once: her smiles and tears' – shows her goodness and contrasts with the darker images of nature associated with Goneril and Regan. Kent comments that the differences between the sisters can only be accounted for by 'the stars above' who 'govern our conditions', recalling the comments made about fate and free will by Gloucester and Edmund in Act 1 scene 2. Lear is in Dover, but refuses to see Cordelia because of his 'burning shame' at his treatment of her.

The Folio text moves straight to a scene in which Cordelia marches onstage at the head of her army, informing the audience that Lear has been sighted, still mad, crowned with wildflowers and weeds. Cordelia sends soldiers to find him. A Gentleman (Doctor in Quarto) says that sleep will help Lear and that there are medicinal herbs that will achieve this – a benevolent image of nature that contrasts with the violent storm. A messenger brings news that the British are marching towards them and Cordelia makes it clear that France's armies are not fighting for 'blown ambition' – unlike Goneril and Regan – but for love of Lear.

ACT 4 SCENE 4

Albany's army has set out, although Oswald says that it took 'much ado' for Albany himself to join them and that Goneril 'is the better soldier'. Oswald has a letter from Goneril to Edmund that Regan wishes to read, but Oswald refuses. Regan expresses concern at Goneril's interest in Edmund and argues that he is better suited to her, because she is a widow. She asks Oswald to remind Goneril of this and tells him there is a reward for whoever kills Gloucester.

ACT 4 SCENE 5

Lines 1–93: Edgar persuades Gloucester that they are at a cliff top. Gloucester comments that Edgar's 'voice is altered'. With truthful irony, Edgar responds that he is changed in nothing but his garments. Gloucester delivers a suicide speech and then throws himself forward. Edgar pretends to have found him at the bottom of the cliff, claiming that it is a miracle he survived the fall. He asks who was with Gloucester at the cliff's head, suggesting that 'It was some fiend', but that he has been spared by the gods. Gloucester resolves to 'bear / Affliction'.

Lines 94–215: Lear appears dressed in flowers and talking nonsense, still fixated on his daughters. Gloucester recognizes his voice, but Lear does not recognize him, taking him for 'Goneril with a white beard'. In a pitifully ironic exchange Lear claims to remember Gloucester's eyes, and demands that he read an imaginary challenge. Lear excoriates women for their sexual indulgence. He shows 'reason in madness' as he talks of justice and how it is useless against sin that is plated 'with gold'. Lear runs away from Cordelia's attendants.

Lines 216–306: Edgar is leading Gloucester to safety, but Oswald finds them and tries to kill Gloucester. Under yet another persona, Edgar fatally wounds Oswald, who begs him to deliver a letter to Edmund. Edgar reads the letter from Goneril, urging Edmund to kill Albany so that she may marry him. Edgar buries Oswald, keeps the letter to show Albany, and leads Gloucester away.

ACT 4 SCENE 6

Cordelia thanks Kent and asks him to change out of his disguise. Kent replies that he has a reason to remain as he is. A Gentleman (Doctor in Quarto) asks Cordelia's permission to wake Lear. Cordelia kisses Lear and laments her sisters' treatment of him. When he wakes, she addresses him with respect fitting for a 'royal lord'. Lear is disorientated and humbled, in contrast to his earlier pride and calls himself a 'foolish fond old man'. He recognizes Cordelia and assumes that she hates him, acknowledging that she has 'some cause'. She refutes this and leads him away. Kent reveals that Edmund is leading Cornwall's army.

ACT 5 SCENE 1

Lines 1–31: Edmund describes Albany's 'alteration' and 'self-reproving'. Regan questions Edmund about Goneril and accuses him of adultery with her. Edmund denies this as Albany and Goneril arrive, bringing news that Lear and Cordelia are reunited. Albany is divided between his role as a leader who must defend his country and his personal reluctance to fight Lear. Goneril and Regan are both reluctant to leave Edmund alone with each other.

Lines 32–66: Disguised, Edgar hands Albany the letter and leaves. Edmund informs Albany that 'The enemy's in view'. Alone, Edmund contemplates the two sisters, coldly observing that 'Neither can be enjoyed / If both remain alive'. He resolves to let Goneril kill Albany if he survives the battle and swears that there will be no mercy for Lear and Cordelia.

ACT 5 SCENE 2

Edgar leaves Gloucester in safety and goes to fight for Lear. He returns to report that Lear and Cordelia have been defeated and captured. Gloucester wishes to remain where he is to be captured or to die, but Edgar says that men must 'endure' until their appointed time.

ACT 5 SCENE 3

Lines 1–114: Cordelia thinks that they will see her sisters now they are captives, but Lear does not wish to, constructing a fantasy where he and Cordelia will live happily and safely in prison. Edmund orders them to be taken away and gives the captain instructions to kill them. Albany, Goneril and Regan arrive, and Albany praises Edmund's 'valiant strain', asking for the captives. Edmund says that he has sent Lear away so that he will not 'pluck the common bosom on his side'. Albany reproves Edmund for taking authority, but Regan claims that he has proved himself Albany's 'brother' by leading her armies. Goneril and Regan begin to fight over Edmund and Regan claims him as her 'lord and master'. Albany arrests Edmund for treason, and ironically bars Regan's claim on Edmund as he is 'subcontracted' to Goneril. As Albany challenges Edmund, Regan is taken ill, poisoned by Goneril. The trumpet sounds to summon a champion for Albany who will maintain that Edmund, supposed Earl of Gloucester, is 'a manifold traitor'.

Lines 115–265: Edgar answers the summons, but does not identify himself, except that he is 'as noble' as Edmund. They fight and Edmund is mortally wounded, but Goneril argues that he is not defeated because he was not bound to fight 'An unknown opposite'.

Albany demonstrates the shift in power between them as he tells her to 'Shut [her] mouth' and produces her letter to Edmund. Goneril flees. Edmund admits the charges and wishes to know his killer, as he will forgive him if he is noble. Edgar reveals his identity and says that they should 'exchange charity'. He argues that 'The gods are just', perhaps a response to Gloucester's lament in Act 4 scene 1. Edgar relates how Gloucester died on being told of the true identity of the man who has led him in his blindness: his heart was too weak to support the extremes of 'joy and grief' provoked by the knowledge. A messenger brings news that Goneril has poisoned Regan and stabbed herself. Their bodies are brought onstage as Kent arrives, seeking Lear. Edmund resolves to do 'some good' before dying, and reveals that Lear and Cordelia are condemned to death, and that Cordelia's hanging will be made to look like suicide. He sends his sword as a 'token of reprieve' and is carried out.

Lines 266–349: Howling, Lear carries in Cordelia's body. He tries to revive her, ignoring Kent's attempts to speak to him, and reveals that he killed the executioner, remembering 'the day' that he 'would have made [them] skip', a brief return to his previous, regal self before he disintegrates once more. He dies believing that he sees Cordelia breathe, and Kent begs his own heart to break. Edmund's death is reported and Albany asks Kent and Edgar to rule and sustain 'the gored state', but Kent refuses, feeling death is near. Despite Albany's assertion that 'All friends shall taste / The wages of their virtue, and all foes / The cup of their deservings', any sense of justice, human or divine, seems scant and the play's resolution is bleak.

KING LEAR IN PERFORMANCE: THE RSC AND BEYOND

The best way to understand a Shakespeare play is to see it or ideally to participate in it. By examining a range of productions, we may gain a sense of the extraordinary variety of approaches and interpretations that are possible – a variety that gives Shakespeare his unique capacity to be reinvented and made 'our contemporary' four centuries after his death.

We begin with a brief overview of the play's theatrical and cinematic life, offering historical perspectives on how it has been performed. We then analyse in more detail a series of productions staged over the last half-century by the Royal Shakespeare Company. The sense of dialogue between productions that can only occur when a company is dedicated to the revival and investigation of the Shakespeare canon over a long period, together with the uniquely comprehensive archival resource of promptbooks, programme notes, reviews and interviews held on behalf of the RSC at the Shakespeare Birthplace Trust in Stratford-upon-Avon, allows an 'RSC stage history' to become a crucible in which the chemistry of the play can be explored.

Finally, we go to the horse's mouth. Modern theatre is dominated by the figure of the director. He or she must hold together the whole play, whereas the actor must concentrate on his or her part. The director's viewpoint is therefore especially valuable. Shakespeare's plasticity is wonderfully revealed when we hear directors of highly successful productions answering the same questions in very different ways.

FOUR CENTURIES OF *KING LEAR*: AN OVERVIEW

The first Lear was Richard Burbage, the leading actor with Shakespeare's company, the King's Men. He was described by an anonymous elegist listing his best-known roles as 'Kind Lear'.[1] Little is known otherwise of the earliest performances. The Fool is thought to have been played by Robert Armin, the company's leading comic actor after the departure of Will Kempe. A talented singer and musician, Armin was noted for his witty paradoxical fooling. Some scholars have, however, suggested that Armin may have played Edgar, since Tom o'Bedlam speaks a kind of fool's language and Armin was equally capable of the multiple role-changes that the character puts himself through. This casting would have opened up the possibility for a boy-actor to double the roles of Cordelia and the Fool, who never appear on stage together. Such doubling would give added poignancy to the line 'And my poor fool is hanged', but it remains counter-intuitive to suppose that Armin was cast in any role other than that of the Fool.

There is a record of a court performance at Whitehall on St Stephen's night, 26 December 1606. It was a bold choice to play the mad king and the image of a 'dog obeyed in office' before the court. A play of 'king Lere' was performed at Gowthwaite Hall in Yorkshire in 1610. This was probably Shakespeare's version, not the old *Leir* play (which recently scholarship has ascribed to Thomas Kyd, author of the highly successful *Spanish Tragedy*). A company of English actors in Dresden in 1626 played the 'Tragoedia von Lear, König in Engelandt', probably also Shakespeare's version.

The play was revived briefly after the Restoration of the monarchy in 1660 and subsequent reopening of the theatres, but in 1681 Nahum Tate staged a production using a text which he himself had adapted. In his dedicatory epistle Tate emphasized the idea of the rough and unfinished nature of Shakespeare's work. It was a 'heap of jewels' that needed to have order, regularity and polish applied to it for its true beauty to be revealed. Tate simplified language, plot and character, eliminating the Fool and much of the play's complexity. He included a love story between Edgar and

Cordelia, together with a confidante for Cordelia, Arante. The play's
happy ending concludes with Lear restored, handing his throne over
to Edgar and Cordelia. Tate's *Lear* and various revised forms of the

2. William Charles Macready as Lear in 1838, with the dead Cordelia: until
this revival, the stage was dominated by Nahum Tate's reworking with a
happy ending in which Cordelia survives and marries Edgar.

adaptation, including one by David Garrick, replaced the original on stage, except possibly in Dublin, where the Smock Alley prompt-books are based on Shakespeare's printed text. The authentically Shakespearean original was not performed on the London stage again, save for a handful of performances by Edmund Kean in the early nineteenth century, until Macready's restored (if heavily cut) production of 1838.

Thomas Betterton had been Tate's Lear. David Garrick, the most celebrated actor-manager of the eighteenth century, restored parts of Shakespeare's text in his own production at Drury Lane but retained Tate's ending. His performance was acclaimed for its pathos and humanity. In his diary James Boswell records: 'I was fully moved, and I shed abundance of tears.'[2] The Shakespearean editor George Steevens, after confessing his view that 'Tate's alteration ... had considerably improved the great original', went on to extol the virtues of Garrick's acting: 'Were we to enquire in what particular scene Mr Garrick is preeminently excellent it would be a difficult circumstance to point it out.' He did, though, single out Garrick's 'mode of speaking the curse at the end of the first act of the play'. In his view Garrick 'gives it additional energy, and it is impossible to hear him deliver it without an equal mixture of horror and admiration'.[3] John Philip Kemble (Theatre Royal, Drury Lane, 1788) played Lear with his tragedian sister, Sarah Siddons, as Cordelia. The critic and poet Leigh Hunt was disappointed: 'He personated the king's majesty perfectly well, but not the king's madness ... he is always stiff, always precise, and he will never, as long as he lives, be able to act any thing mad unless it be a melancholy mad statue.'[4]

During the Regency period, when old King George III was mad, the London theatre managers tactfully abstained from staging the play. Soon after the king's death in 1820, the fiery Romantic actor Edmund Kean played the role at Drury Lane later to mixed reviews. The London *Times* objected that the storm scene 'was less effective than many others' chiefly because it was 'exhibited with so much accuracy that the performer could scarcely be heard amidst the confusion', but the reviewer was better pleased by the fifth act in which 'there was scarcely a dry eye in the theatre'.[5] William Hazlitt felt that 'Mr Kean chipped off a bit of the character here and there: but he did not pierce the solid substance, nor move the entire mass.'[6] Hazlitt reviewed Junius Brutus Booth's production at Covent Garden in the same year more favourably: 'There was no feebleness, and no vulgarity in any part of Mr Booth's acting, but it was animated, vigorous, and pathetic throughout.'[7]

When Macready, who had played Edmund to Booth's Lear, restored Shakespeare's text in his Covent Garden production of 1838, the Fool, reintroduced for the first time in more than a hundred and fifty years, was played by a young woman, Priscilla Horton. Macready set the play in a pagan Saxon Britain replete with Druidic stone circles. Critics were generally enthusiastic:

> Mr Macready's Lear, remarkable before for a masterly completeness of conception, is heightened by this introduction of the Fool to a surprising degree. It accords exactly with the view he seeks to present of Lear's character ... Mr Macready's representation of the father at the end, broken down to his last despairing struggle, his heart swelling gradually upwards till it bursts in its closing sigh, completed the only perfect picture that we have of Lear since the age of Betterton.[8]

It may be asked how someone writing a century and a half after the event could have known that Betterton's was a 'perfect picture' of Lear, but the point here is to stress how much the characterization of Lear gains from the restoration of his foil, the Fool.

Samuel Phelps produced the play at Sadler's Wells in 1845 using simpler staging and a fuller version of the text than that of Macready, which had remained heavily cut despite the rejection of Tate. The naturalism of Phelps' performance was praised but the storm was thought excessive: 'it is not imitation, but realization'.[9] Charles Kean staged a successful production at the Princess's Theatre in 1858. Set in Anglo-Saxon Britain, it boasted a strong supporting cast including Kate Terry as Cordelia. Meanwhile in New York, Edwin Booth, son of Junius Brutus, revived the play using Shakespeare's text, giving a performance described by William Winter as 'the fond father and the broken old man. It was the great heart, shattered by cruel unkindness, that he first, and most of all, displayed.'[10] The great Italian actor, Tommaso Salvini, also won praise for his performances at Boston's Globe Theatre in 1882 and London's Covent Garden in 1884, despite the fact that he spoke in Italian whilst the rest of the cast spoke in English, a proceeding that the novelist Henry James described as 'grotesque, unpardonable, abominable'.[11] Henry Irving's elaborately staged production at the Lyceum in 1892 was set in a Britain of Roman ruins with Druidic priests and Viking warriors. Using a heavily cut text that reduced the play's violence and sexuality, Irving emphasized Lear's age and paternalism in a performance that attracted mixed notices, although Ellen Terry's Cordelia was widely praised.

At the end of the nineteenth century directors such as William Poel and Harley Granville Barker promoted the simple staging of Shakespeare's plays, attempting to recreate the conditions of the Elizabethan playhouse, with its fast continuous action in contrast to the spectacular staging of the Victorians which involved lengthy scene changes. In his *Prefaces to Shakespeare* (1927), Granville Barker argued vigorously against critical prejudice towards the play in performance and insisted on its theatrical viability, a judgement borne out by the many productions since. The twentieth and twenty-first centuries have produced a number of distinguished Lears but have also concentrated on more balanced productions which give greater weight and opportunity to lesser roles.

John Gielgud first played Lear in Harcourt Williams' production at the Old Vic in 1931 at the age of twenty-six. Despite his obvious talent, critics thought him too young for the part. In 1940 Gielgud had a second opportunity to play the part, again at the Old Vic, in a production set in early modern Europe, based on the ideas of Granville Barker, who oversaw the early rehearsals and personally coached Gielgud. In an essay of 1963 Gielgud claimed that the ten days in which Barker worked with the company 'were the fullest in experience that I have ever had in all my years upon the stage'.[12] The production was a success, although the noted critic James Agate concluded that Gielgud's performance was 'a thing of great beauty, imagination, sensitiveness, understanding, executive virtuosity, and control. You would be wrong to say – this is not King Lear! You would be right to say that this is Lear every inch but one.'[13]

In 1936 the director-designer Theodore Komisarjevsky staged a memorable and radical production at the Shakespeare Memorial Theatre in Stratford-upon-Avon. There was a simple but effective set, consisting mainly of a grand staircase, illuminated by a cyclorama which changed colour to reflect the mood of the scene. As the London *Times* review put it:

> On this simple stage of steps and platforms, where every movement is sharp and significant and the light-borne colour keeps pace with the changing character of the scene, Mr Randle Ayrton has complete freedom to act Lear.[14]

A decade later Laurence Olivier played Lear at the Old Vic as 'a whimsical old tyrant who takes this way of dividing his kingdom simply as a jest, until the joke turns serious because Cordelia refuses to play'.[15] His performance was not to all tastes but Alec Guinness as the Fool was widely praised. Sir Donald Wolfit, an

3. Expressionist design in the 1930s: the opening scene of the Komisarjevsky production.

old-style actor-manager, toured his own production between 1947 and 1953 – Ronald Harwood's experience as Wolfit's backstage dresser inspired his play *The Dresser* (1980).

Gielgud played Lear for a third time in 1950, in a production which he co-directed with Anthony Quayle. Although his performance had developed in a number of ways, it was still largely influenced by his work with Granville Barker. He played the part again in 1955 in a production directed by George Devine and designed by Isamu Noguchi. This time Gielgud aimed for psychological realism in his performance but it was generally agreed that while the stylized set worked, the heavy costumes were problematic.

In 1956 Orson Welles directed and starred in a production at the New York City Center. Falling and breaking one ankle and spraining the other during rehearsals, Welles, undeterred, played the part in a wheelchair, pushed around by the Fool. In 1959 Charles Laughton played Lear in a production at the Shakespeare Memorial Theatre, directed by Glen Byam Shaw. Critics were divided, especially about Laughton's conception of the role. One of them, Alan Brien, complained that Laughton developed 'from boyishness to senility without even an intervening glimpse of maturity'.[16]

Three years later Peter Brook directed his groundbreaking production starring Paul Scofield (discussed in detail below). There have been numerous distinguished productions since: in 1968 Trevor Nunn directed with Eric Porter playing Lear; in 1974 Buzz Goodbody directed a pared-down version for the RSC's small studio theatre, The Other Place; in 1976 Trevor Nunn directed Donald Sinden as Lear; in 1979 Peter Ustinov played Lear in a production directed by Robin Phillips at Stratford, Ontario; Adrian Noble's 1982 production with Michael Gambon is discussed below. In 1989 Jonathan Miller directed Eric Porter at the Old Vic; 1990 saw The Renaissance Theatre company's production, directed by Kenneth Branagh with Richard Briers as Lear and Emma Thompson as the Fool; in the same year Nicholas Hytner directed John Wood at Stratford; in 1993 Noble directed the play at Stratford again, this time with Robert Stephens as Lear (discussed below). In 1997 in the (London) National's intimate Cottesloe studio, Richard Eyre directed

4. John Gielgud as Lear in the hovel (1950 production), with Fool and Poor Tom in the foreground, the disguised Kent behind.

a production (his swansong as Artistic Director) with Ian Holm playing Lear – a highly acclaimed production that was later recorded for television; in the same year Peter Hall directed Alan Howard at the Old Vic; and in 1999 Yukio Ninagawa directed Nigel Hawthorne for the RSC; in 2001 Julian Glover played Lear in Barry Kyle's production at the Globe and the following year Jonathan Kent directed Oliver Ford-Davies at the Almeida, a performance much-admired for its intelligence; Jonathan Miller again directed the play, this time for the 2002 Stratford Festival, Ontario, with Christopher Plummer in the lead; in 2004 Bill Alexander directed Corin Redgrave in a production that used a full conflated text and ran for nearly four hours; in 2007 the RSC's Complete Works Festival in which all Shakespeare's plays were performed closed with Trevor Nunn's production at the Courtyard Theatre with Ian McKellen as King Lear (see interview with Nunn, below). Powerful small-scale productions include a touring one by Kaboodle Theatre Company (1991–94), which made very strong use of a mix of Oriental-imperial costumes and modernity (a feisty Cordelia in Doc Marten boots).

The tradition of adapting the play has been continued in the theatre with versions such as Edward Bond's radical rewriting, *Lear* (1972) and the Women's Theatre Group and Elaine Feinstein's feminist *Lear's Daughters*, as well as Jane Smiley's novel, *A Thousand Acres* (1997). On film, there were early silent versions in America and Italy (1909–10). A number of stage productions have been filmed, including Peter Brook's, shot in a stark black-and-white style that intensified the existential bleakness of his stage version. Grigori Kozintsev (1970) produced a beautiful, deeply moving version featuring the sufferings of Russian peasants. It was based on a translation by Boris Pasternak and used haunting music by Dmitri Shostakovich. Akira Kurosawa's *Ran* (1985), set in feudal Japan, substantially reworked Shakespeare's play so as to eliminate Gloucester but incorporate the sub-plot material in a version in which Lear's daughters become his married sons. It played a major part in stimulating renewed western interest in epic eastern cinema.

AT THE RSC

Lears for Our Time

> Our own century seems better qualified to communicate and respond to the full range of experience in King Lear than any previous time, save possibly Shakespeare's own.[17]

In post-Second World War England, *King Lear* has been performed more times than in its entire prior performance history. The play speaks with special power to the contemporary psyche. In a violent age where atrocities, murders, poverty and acts of self-destruction are commonly seen on television, the violence in the play, and its concerns about human rights, seem particularly apposite. However, *Lear* is so vast in its conception that, as well as societal concerns, it deals with very fundamental philosophical thoughts about what it is to be human in a godless world, or in a world where faith plays little part in the absurdity of human behaviour.

Jan Kott's influential book entitled *Shakespeare Our Contemporary* (1964) was of great inspiration to late twentieth-century directors. His thoughts about *King Lear* as a play about 'the disintegration of the world' prompted a landmark production of the play by Peter Brook, which would alter the way the play was conceived and the characters performed to this day:

> In the 1950s it became apparent that the world might destroy itself through accidental nuclear warfare, and the plays of Samuel Beckett achieved international fame: *Waiting for Godot* (1953) showed a world of absurdity, *Endgame* (1957) a world without meaning at all. Soon afterwards the Polish critic Jan Kott wrote an influential essay, 'King Lear, or Endgame,' which viewed Shakespeare through the spectacles or blinkers of Beckett and emphasized the element of grotesque tragicomedy in the play.[18]

Brook was also heavily influenced by the dramatic theories of Bertolt Brecht, with his desire to 'alienate' the audience by breaking down the illusions of realism. Brecht's influence was especially evident in the bare staging of *Lear*. Two large flats at either side of the stage moved in and out at angles to create internal and external spaces. The storm was created by three large rusty thunder sheets with a vibrating motor behind creating a hint of rumbling thunder. The lighting was deliberately bright and constant, only dimming for the storm scene and Gloucester's blinding. Everything was seen with clarity, leaving no room for the dramatic signalling which darkness evokes. There was no background music. Brook firmly believed that *Lear* should be staged with no music at all. Music almost always controls our emotional reaction to a scene, and Brook was particularly keen to block any easy audience response.

J. C. Trewin described the set:

> Visually we are taken to a terrifying world, a place of abstract symbols, a rust-flaking world, harsh and primitive. There are tall, coarse grey-white screens; metal shapes that might have been dredged from the sea-bed: things ancient, scaled with rust. As the night moves on, the stage grows barer and barer until nothing is left but the screens, and Lear and Gloucester play out their colloquy on a bleak infinity of stage; two voices at the world's end.[19]

Brook wanted this *Lear* to be a *Lear* of its time. He designed the production himself and wanted to create a totally believable society, both barbaric and sophisticated. It is notable that this production took place just after the Cuban missile crisis. He wished to create a nihilistic vision, to remove the sympathetic responses of the audience and blur the lines between good and evil in the play. As a result of this he was accused of distorting Shakespeare's tragedy to enhance his own directorial viewpoint.

Brook's interpretation meant that productions of *Lear* would never be the same after this point. Indeed, there have been very few productions since which have not followed his lead in some regard, whether their focus be political, metaphysical or domestic.

> Critics and directors of the Left have been quick to seize on Lear's demand that the ruling class expose themselves 'to feel what wretches feel, / That thou mayst shake the superflux to them' and

5. 'What, art mad? A man may see how this world goes with no eyes': the bleakness of Peter Brook's 1962 production with Paul Scofield (left) as Lear and Alan Webb as the blinded Gloucester.

Gloucester's wish that 'distribution should undo excess, / And each man have enough' as evidence of the play's critique of existing political structures, and much recent criticism has discussed *King Lear* as a political drama reflecting the ideological concerns that were to divide England during the seventeenth century.[20]

This trend in recent criticism has been reflected in performance. Set pre-First World War, the RSC's 1976 production made reference to the conditions of those disenfranchised by war. One page of the programme featured hundreds of faces of workhouse children; on another there was a bleak landscape with two figures in the distance, presumably working a land that yields little or nothing. In this production Donald Sinden's acclaimed performance as Lear:

> chronicles the process by which suffering turns self-pity and self-love into outward versions of themselves. In practice this means that Lear learns to identify with the poor and downtrodden, classes never far from the drab, pockmarked, nineteenth century face of this production. Indeed, the three-man directorate of Trevor Nunn, John Barton and Barry Kyle ... do all they can to bring period penury to our attention, gratuitously introducing a troupe of vagrants to trot round the stage between scenes, and transforming Michael Williams's Fool into a bald scrofulous relic, a seedily eccentric song-and-dance man who might have stumbled out of *Bleak House* ... determined to stress that *Lear* is a social as well as an elemental play.[21]

The setting for the 2004 production directed by Bill Alexander was of a post-war world in which the country was in a flux of insecurity, distinctly modern in feel but without reference to a specific time:

> This *Lear* appears at times to be set in a crumbling mental home, backed by the scaffolding and half-destroyed brick walls of Tom Piper's bleak setting. It suggests that a nuclear bomb has already fallen on Lear's kingdom and the survivors are left wandering about trying to work out – post-Apocalypse – who they are and what has happened and above all where the hell they are supposed to be going next ... There is a bizarre timelessness here – so that in a post-Victorian world, when the old King comes on dressed like a mad deserter from the First World War, there is no real surprise, just the feeling that Alexander and his cast have

had yet another disturbing thought about the many insights into madness and identity-crisis offered in the play.[22]

Of the setting, designer Tom Piper explained:

> Bill [Alexander] felt very strongly that you can't set this play in one particular place, it has to be an invented world, so we're aiming to create parallel worlds: the Victorian married with strange bits of technology... I wanted to include a broken element, to convey a sense of a world that could be in decay or on the edge of industrialisation.[23]

Corin Redgrave, a noted left-wing campaigner as well as a member of a distinguished acting dynasty, played Lear in this production. He saw the play as 'modern, topical and relevant because it so vividly portrays a country divided by an almost impassable fault-line between those who have enough and those who don't. Any attempt I make to build up an idea of Lear the man, Lear the ruler, is still very strongly influenced by that thinking.'[24]

Again, although not overtly political in the actors' focus, Adrian Noble's 1993 production infused the political implication of Lear's decision into the setting:

> This production turned the map into paper flooring whose divisions the Fool (a gag over his mouth emphasizing his obvious outrage) was made to mark with red paint. It was then gradually reduced to tatters until the ground beneath, which was covered with a great blood-red stain, was wholly revealed.[25]

There are numerous references in *King Lear* to the stars, gods, and the fates. Setting the play in a non-Christian era endows the play with an adaptable metaphysical stance that has international appeal. In 1999, Japanese director Yukio Ninagawa of the Sainokuni Shakespeare Company undertook a joint production with the RSC. This production focused on the elemental nature of the play, the dark forces of nature which emerge from the void created by Lear's misjudgements:

This is a hauntingly but savagely beautiful production. Yukio Horio's set is dominated by a huge black wooden walkway sloping gently towards you and widening into an immense platform. At the back the walkway seems to disappear into black darkness, whence the actors emerge like mythological figures, both real and remote. All this suggests the structure of the classical Noh stage, where the curtained entrance also leads somewhere indeterminate: a primeval darkness that holds no moral secrets ... this reinforces the uncomfortable Shakespearian vision of a world where you are left without the consolation or guidance of a moral order.[26]

The handling of the storm scene was particularly controversial. Boulders of various sizes were choreographed to drop onto the stage as Lear raged against the storm. Most audience members and reviewers were more concerned about the safety of the actors than the director's vision, which 'conjures a world in which Nature's moulds are cracked'.[27]

The breakdown in family relationships is, of course, central to *King Lear* and modern directors have often used this as an accessible focal point in productions. Initially produced as a touring production for schools, Buzz Goodbody's small cast chamberpiece version of *Lear* in 1974

was performed by a cast of nine, with one musician playing gong, trumpet, snare and kettle drum. An all-purpose servant was added, while one sub-plot was cut (losing Albany, Cornwall, Oswald, and the French King) ... The acting area was empty, except for a few props, like a rug and banners which unfurled when Lear appeared ... Scenes were set simply, using props and, as with the storm, music and lights, which at key moments in the production underscored the director's point ... *Lear* was not seen as epic in terms of great public scenes of wide-open spaces peopled with a huge cast ... Its focus was on two families, in which the personal as well as the age differences played a more important part than is usually recognised.[28]

In this powerful, intimate production, 'the play as a whole became an intense study of private griefs of their two families, with Kent and the Fool both reduced to appalled outsiders, helplessly looking on'.[29]

Described by critic Irving Wardle as 'an all-too-familiar story of family life',[30] Nicholas Hytner's 1990 production also turned *Lear* into a tale of dysfunctional family neurosis. He encoded his very cerebral reading in the set design of David Fielding, creating an enclosed space for the staging of *Lear* that took the form of a cube:

> Open on one side with its outer walls painted to look like heavy steel, the cube simply revolves and stops, to present a succession of interiors and exteriors. Sometimes it will stop with a corner pointing towards the audience so that actors can stand out of sight of each other while Shakespearian eavesdropping can take place. In the storm scene, it will revolve continuously – the idea being that, as a metaphor for the world of the play (as well as Lear's mental world), it is spinning out of control.[31]

The effect of the cube was to reduce the scale of the play – something apparently deliberate in the director's interpretation. Psychological and domestic, Lear's world became both a mental ward and the interior of his mind, a controlled civilized space allowed to go mad through neglect and misjudgement. John Wood's very human and neurotic Lear went on an inner and outer journey of physical suffering and mental awareness: 'We are left with an interpretation which is as much medical as moral. The geriatric ward slugs it out with the psychiatric wing. There is little sense of hubris on the one hand, or of concentrated evil on the other.'[32] The emphasis on Lear's genuine insanity stemming from the family reflected the wider world of the play and the state of Britain. Michael Billington described it as 'an exploration of the insane contradictions of a world where the gods are seen as both just and wantonly cruel, where Nature is both purifying and destructive'.[33]

Fools and Madmen

Real and assumed madness play an essential part in the plot of *King Lear*. In a programme note by Michael MacDonald, author of an historical study called *Mystical Bedlam: Madness, Anxiety and Healing in Seventeenth Century England* (1983), Adrian Noble's 1993 production was contextualized by means of the suggestion that the audience

> is presented with three kinds of madness: real in Lear himself, assumed in Tom/Edgar, and professional in the Fool. To its original audience, in a population largely uneducated, unable to distinguish between epilepsy, demonic possession and a skilful beggar on the make, the spectacle of an old man and a half-naked creature railing at the weather and babbling about demons would not have been especially unusual: like the unemployed and other vagrants the countryside teemed with, they were a fact of life.[34]

Lear is very rarely played as being driven mad exclusively by the cruelty that is inflicted on him, but is often portrayed as being dangerously unhinged from the start. In Nicholas Hytner's production,

> The early household scenes are honeycombed with ... micro-sequences, which take you inside Lear's head, showing his hunger for affection, his need to play the strong man, his short attention span, and his helpless descents into blind rage. These are an embarrassment to the court and they give the sisters every pretext for saying something to keep the old man happy. But it is only when they try to draw the line that you really see what they have had to put up with. At the suggestion that he should shed a few knights, all hell breaks loose in the Albany dining room, with Lear emptying his gun into the ceiling, crushing Goneril to the ground like a blubbering child, clearing the space for carnage by hanging the Fool on a coat-hook: and finally vanishing into the night leaving his shaken hosts facing each other down a long table for their solitary dinner.[35]

Very clearly a man with no control over his own emotions, John Wood's Lear was also an emotional vandal to his daughters, and his influence could be seen in their learnt behaviour.

In Buzz Goodbody's 1974 production, to be a sane man in a cruel world was to be part of that cruelty. Lear's madness became the transitional stage from cruelty to humanity:

> Tony Church did not play Lear as a virtuoso acting part, but as a down-to-earth king, a patriarch who got his pleasure from hunting. He is out in the cold because of who he is – not a mighty monarch fallen from grace, but an old man on the point of death, facing himself and his life ... When he is 'sane', he represents the cruel world, arbitrary and aggressive, and only when he is 'mad' does he embody human values.[36]

In the stunning visual sequence which started Adrian Noble's 1982 production, lunacy not only led to virtue but was linked to it through the characters of the Fool and Cordelia:

> On Lear's throne the Grock-like Fool and Cordelia sit facing each other, with their necks at opposite ends of a taut halter (resembling a noose), as if lunacy and virtue were inseparable ... What follows is a delirious descent into a world of barbarism in which farce and tragedy are umbilically linked.[37]

Antony Sher played the Fool as 'Lear's alter-ego, the visible mark of his insanity. His Master's Voice as he perches on his lap like a ventriloquist's doll, the conscience of the King.'[38] In the words of the reviewer in the *Jewish Chronicle*, 'There is a strong sense in which, just as the great comic double acts are like watching a schizophrenic trying to pull himself together, Antony Sher's red-nosed clown and Michael Gambon's violent old man are two warring parts of one psyche.'[39] The poet and critic James Fenton, writing in the London *Sunday Times*, pushed the point further:

> Michael Gambon's Lear was a man all too willing to cast off his role as king, and his relationship to the Fool pointed to this uneasiness.

Lear's foolishness and his love for his Fool are the points of departure for the interpretation. In all his madness, his anger and his suffering, we do not forget this. Indeed, I wonder if Lear has ever fooled around so enthusiastically.

Imagine a production in which the King, though condemned to kingship, would clearly love to have been a comedian, while the Fool, although unable to stop jesting, is transfixed by the horror of his true perception of the tragedy. This is the version which Adrian Noble has directed ... This is not the Fool of criticism, not an A-level 'assess-the significance-of-the-Fool' fool. This is your genuine professional fool. Inside whom is a man in a panic, the Cassandra of the play, whose raving prophesies terrify the prophet himself.[40]

Sher described how in rehearsals they came up with a solution to the disappearance of the Fool after the arrival of Tom o'Bedlam.[41] During the mock trial scene the Fool picked up a pillow to represent Regan. On the words 'anatomize her', Lear stabbed the pillow in a frenzy of rage. In his insane and violent outburst he fatally stabbed the Fool accidentally. With all the attention on Lear leaving the hovel, the others did not realize what had happened. The Fool slumped down dead into a barrel in which he stood.

The emphasis put on the Fool in this production (the programme cover featured a fool's face with a red nose that appeared to be an amalgam of Lear and the Fool), along with Sher's magnificent performance, led many critics to feel that the play became unbalanced, losing impetus in the final acts after the Fool was killed.

At the end of the hovel scene Edgar has replaced the Fool as Lear's spiritual mentor. Lear takes Edgar off in one direction as the Fool exits in another. According to director Adrian Noble,

That happens accidentally. He doesn't plan that ... For some reason he decides to take on the sins of others ... in exactly the same way as a pilgrim, monk or nun ... dedicate their lives in a particular way that enables other people to have a richer spiritual life. It is a gift of humanity to God. This is exactly the same thing with Edgar.[42]

Lear's journey into his own fooldom takes him from the enclosed mental space of the court out into the world and the secrets of humanity, to emotions denied and hidden from him by dint of his position in society. This awakening by the Fool and Poor Tom leads to a political and spiritual epiphany that is life-changing and possibly world-changing. Many directors have seen the following lines – often quoted in their programme notes – as the core of the play:

Poor naked wretches, wheresoe'er you are,
That bide the pelting of this pitiless storm,
How shall your houseless heads and unfed sides,
Your lopped and windowed raggedness, defend you
From seasons such as these? O, I have ta'en
Too little care of this! Take physic, pomp,
Expose thyself to feel what wretches feel,
That thou mayst shake the superflux to them
And show the heavens more just.

The political dimensions of *King Lear* are most clearly evidenced in the king's interaction with the mad beggar. Edgar, the abused son and Poor Tom, the forgotten citizen of Lear's England, embodies both familial and national neglect. Edgar's disguise as Bedlam beggar is also crucial to Lear's spiritual journey. In Noble's second production of the play for the RSC in 1993:

[Lear's] growing obsession with this emblem of 'unaccommodated man' causes the displacement of the Fool . . . was brilliantly visualized in the image of Ian Hughes clinging forlornly to Poor Tom's hand at the end of a human chain that Gloucester led across the stage.[43]

Visually Edgar has variously appeared as a Caliban-type figure, the poor bare-forked animal spouting obscenities but in need of the world's pity, as Christ-like with a crown of thorns, bloodied and suffering for the world's sins, or alternatively as demonic, as in the RSC's 1982 production when 'Jonathan Hyde's Edgar as a virtually naked Poor Tom [burst] through the splintering floor like some infernal demon born on to Lear's "great stage of fools".'[44] 'It was the modern equivalent of the entrance of a devil from the pit of Hell, and Tom's demonic side, which actors so often miss as they go for shivering pathos, was established at once.'[45]

Thrown to the wilderness by his family, Edgar evolves from 'worm' to potential king. His suffering appears as a barbaric initiation rite designed by the toughest of gods. It is a trial of cruelty fitting for the evil world that is unleashed in the play.

The Absence of Humanity

King Lear is a play rich with vicious bestial images, all symbolic of the barbaric capabilities of man and woman. Goneril, for instance, is described as having a 'wolfish visage'. Edward Topsell's *Historie of Foure-footed Beastes* (1607) mixed scientific fact, folklore and classical allusions to animals and mythological creatures, giving them often exotic and fantastic attributes. It describes the customary attributes associated with the wolf in animal lore: treachery, deceit, hypocrisy, ravenousness and cruelty. These associations gave Shakespeare's audience an accurate idea of Goneril's character and her subsequent behaviour. However, for modern directors, 'Another interpretative decision that must be faced . . . is whether to accept the moral polarity of Lear's daughters as a fact of the story or to suggest more naturalistic reasons for their behaviour.'[46]

In recent years patriarchal repression and child abuse of one form or another have often been regarded as the defining reasons for evil in children. Lear has accordingly been portrayed as physically and mentally abusive or neglectful, demanding, cantankerous, a bully who has created so much pent-up anger in his two elder daughters that it erupts when they are given the opportunity to release their feelings without recrimination; that is to say, when they are in power.

In the influential 1962 production, Peter Brook portrayed Lear's knights as rowdy and destructive, while Irene Worth's Goneril was self-contained and cool, remonstrating with Lear in measured tones, speaking as somebody with cause to complain. Some critics thought such a treatment a distortion of the text, but most modern directors have followed this interpretation to some degree. Though it helps to humanize Goneril, it does make the descent into evil very difficult to portray.

Janet Dale, who played the part in 1993, admitted that 'I am trying to play her with a conscience, but I suspect the lines won't support it.' Rather than an outright evil woman, she wished to portray her as a woman 'of moral degeneration'.[47]

By focusing on the psychology of these extremely dysfunctional families, the violence in Nicholas Hytner's 1990 production became rooted in explainable terms:

The production is about confused people destroyed by their incomprehensible emotions or, as with Wood's massively erratic Lear, struggling through new ones ... The effects of long abuse are evident in his daughters. Alex Kingston's Cordelia has become rebellious, bloody-minded and rejects Lear almost more than he does her. Estelle Kohler's Goneril and Sally Dexter's Regan, seem still to want the love of this old, impossible man ... It is fashionable nowadays to allow us to see the 'bad' daughters' point of view, but rarely as strongly as here. Both of them seem badly in need of Valium, psychoanalysis, or both. They are frustrated, exhausted, at the end of a tether which finally breaks, liberating all that suppressed anger and barely contained madness. Their evils proliferate, but they, like Goneril and Regan themselves, are ultimately Lear's fault.[48]

Order opens up to reveal chaos. And the same pattern is visible in erratic human behaviour. Lear, having cursed Goneril with sterility, rushes back to embrace her. Astonishingly, Regan first conspires in the blinding of Gloucester and then tenderly asks him, rather than her wounded husband, 'How dost my lord?' Mr Hytner ushers us into a morally topsy-turvy universe in which good and evil frequently cohabit within the same person.[49]

One cannot escape the fact that what Regan and Goneril do is evil and unnatural. In Buzz Goodbody's 1974 production, which cut the role of Cornwall, 'Regan put out Gloucester's eyes unaided, with a broach.'[50] Modern stagings of the blinding scene nearly always show Regan's active participation in the mutilation of Gloucester. Emily Raymond, who played Goneril in 2004, felt that Goneril and Regan 'had a brutal upbringing – [with] smacks of physical violence and mental abuse. I think Lear probably took his daughters to hangings and taught them the brutal way to deal with traitors – you don't hang them, you pluck out their eyes and let them live, to serve as a deterrent to others.'[51]

What impact does it have to turn the violence and evil in *Lear* into something psychological instead of metaphysical? Does the implication that it is somehow the 'natural' result of a bad, neglected upbringing, diminish the epic nature of the play and the horrific impact of the sisters' monstrous acts? Lear's world is thrown out of order by his inability to be an adequate father *and king*. James I, in his publication *The True Law of Free Monarchies*, underlined the divine right of kings and the duty of all monarchs to treat their subjects as a caring father would do his children. Lear's misunderstanding of his role as a fixed point in the natural order of things and his irresponsibility in relation to his position in society unleash unnatural chaos.

In 1993 Adrian Noble emphasized violent cosmic forces prevalent in the play by use of an abstract but symbolic set:

When David Bradley's superlative Gloucester, his eyes gouged out, staggers away from the scene of atrocity and from Simon Dormandy's chillingly, psychopathic Cornwall, the focus clears at last. Noble used the Folio edition of the text, so cutting the aid of Gloucester's servants after the blinding. The sightless Bradley gazes in the direction of a blue and white model of the globe, fixed above the stage. As he stares, a crack runs across the globe's circumference and the sands of time begin to pour out of it. The society of King Lear, with family life collapsing in warfare and inhuman cruelty . . . is ominous of all civilised human life ruined and coming to an end.[52]

In this bleak vision,

Noble's most original stroke is to suggest that the cruelty unleashed by Lear's folly spreads to even the conventionally good characters. The chief beneficiary is Simon Russell Beale's extra-ordinary Edgar who starts as goody-two shoes and who is turned by the horrors he has witnessed into a symbol of revenge. In this production he doesn't just kill Oswald; he batters his face with a staff as if in retaliation for the blinding of his father. The most unplayable major role in Shakespeare suddenly acquires a specific identity: a man forever tainted by the contagion of violence.[53]

In his final battle with Edmund, Russell Beale as Edgar tried 'to rip out the dying Edmund's eyes in reprisal'.[54] Similarly, Bill Alex-ander's 2004 production included 'chilling touches that alert you afresh to the barbarism of its world. For example, in the climactic duel between Edmund and Edgar, it's only chance that stops the virtuous brother from exacting primitive "eye for an eye" justice'[55] – 'In order to force Edmund to drop his arms, [Edgar] grabbed him by either side of his face and pushed his thumbs into his eyes. This reference to the blinding of Gloucester was eerily resonant.'[56]

Our opinion of Edgar will determine how we consider the end of the play. His spiritual journey, which echoes Lear's, provides him with a unique understanding of humanity and the preciousness of life. But he is also a very human avenger who has to set the world right and provide hope for the future. To overbalance his character with deliberate malicious and violent action furthers a nihilistic vision of the play by removing the certainty of redemption for a lost and barbaric world. Adrian Noble in 1982 stressed this element of unredeemed cruelty. *Guardian* critic Michael Billington explains:

> Edgar slays Oswald by breaking his back with a staff, and the fraternal duel between Edgar and Edmund is a bare-chested, bloody, unchivalric combat that ends with Edmund's head being dumped in water. Even at the last the characters look out into the future in a spirit of sceptical uncertainty.[57]

In Peter Brook's vision of the play chaos was part of the natural order. His production emphasized the inhumanity and disinterested-ness of the forces that annihilate Lear. There was no moral structure beneath the surface of civilization: 'Everywhere one looks, one sees only the facades and emblems of a world and, ironically, as characters acquire sight, it enables them to see only into a void.'[58]

Brook removed key moments of redemption and humanity: the servants did not tend Gloucester after he has been blinded but callously bumped into him as they cleared away the stage. Edmund's attempt to redeem himself and stop the order that will see the death of Cordelia was cut. As Lear died, his final words 'Look there' were spoken as he stared ahead into nothingness. We were not left with the usual tableau of survivors grieving over Lear and Cordelia. The cast left, carrying out their dead bodies, leaving Edgar and the dead Edmund on stage alone. Edgar moved centre-stage, and then went to his brother. As he dragged his brother's corpse up towards the back of the stage a distant rumble of thunder sounded in the background, leaving the audience with the impression that worse was to follow. '[W]e that are young / Shall never see so much nor live so long' took on a genuinely apocalyptic meaning. This was an image of the horror of 'the promised end' of the world.

Where Brook's production succeeded was in making the audience grieve for humanity, or more specifically for the absence of humanity. It seemed a fitting statement for its time, and it is one that still touches us today. Lear's speech in the hovel is central to Brook's vision – it is not by chance that he used this quote in the programme for the production's world tour: 'Expose thyself to feel what wretches feel.' Corin Redgrave, who played King Lear in 2004, also took this line:

> The play investigates how, in a dying or decaying world, we can live better and be better towards one another. It can't produce any conclusions to that because the world as Shakespeare saw it at that time was dying, just as our world as we see it is dying. Shakespeare was writing in a world which he sees going to hell on wheels and writing a text book in case the world should ever recover. So it is the most bleak of plays, but it is a very salutary play, a very necessary play ... you could not possibly lose *King Lear* without impoverishing ourselves terribly.[59]

THE DIRECTOR'S CUT: INTERVIEWS WITH ADRIAN NOBLE, DEBORAH WARNER AND TREVOR NUNN

Adrian Noble, born in 1950, arrived at the RSC from the Bristol Old Vic, where he had directed several future stars in productions of classic plays. His first production on the main stage of the Royal Shakespeare Theatre in Stratford was the acclaimed 1982 *Lear*, discussed here, with Michael Gambon as the king and Antony Sher as an extraordinarily powerful Fool. Two years later his *Henry V* sowed the seed for Kenneth Branagh's film. Among his other major productions during his two decades at the RSC were *Hamlet*, again with Branagh in the title role, *The Plantagenets*, based on the *Henry VI/Richard III* tetralogy, and the two parts of *Henry IV*, with Robert Stephens as Falstaff. Stephens returned in 1993 to play Lear in a second production of the tragedy, also discussed here. Noble's 1994 *Midsummer Night's Dream* was made into a film. He was Artistic Director from 1991 to 2003, since when he has been a freelance director. His production style is characterized by strong use of colours and objects (such as umbrellas), and fluid scenic structure.

Deborah Warner, born in 1959, trained in stage management at the Central School of Speech and Drama. At the age of twenty-one she formed her own 'fringe' company, Kick Theatre, imaginatively staging stripped-down productions of the classics, including *King Lear* (1985, discussed here), at the Edinburgh Festival. In 1987 she made her RSC debut with a rigorously simple but deeply moving *Titus Andronicus*, starring Brian Cox, on the intimate stages of the Swan at Stratford and The Pit at London's Barbican. A *King John* in a similar style followed the next year and in 1990 she directed *King Lear*, again with Brian Cox, on the proscenium Lyttelton stage of the National Theatre in London (also discussed here). She has subsequently specialized in Samuel Beckett and opera, but has returned to Shakespeare with a *Richard II* at the National, featuring her collaborator Fiona Shaw cross-dressed in the title role, and a large-scale *Julius Caesar* at the Barbican.

Sir Trevor Nunn is the most successful and one of the most highly regarded of modern British theatre directors. Born in 1940, he was a brilliant student at Cambridge, strongly influenced by the literary close reading of Dr F. R. Leavis. At the age of just twenty-eight he succeeded Peter Hall as Artistic Director of the RSC, where he remained until 1978. He greatly expanded the range of the company's work and its ambition in terms of venues and touring. He also achieved huge success in musical theatre and subsequently became Artistic Director of the National Theatre in London. His productions are always full of textual insights, while being clean and elegant in design. Among his most admired Shakespearean work has been a series of tragedies with Ian McKellen in leading roles: *Macbeth* (1976, with Judi Dench, in the dark, intimate space of The Other Place), *Othello* (1989, with McKellen as Iago and Imogen Stubbs as Desdemona), and *King Lear* (2007, in the Stratford Complete Works Festival, on world tour, and then in London).

One of the first questions one always wonders about with *King Lear* is: what do you decide on as a setting for the play? We've seen everything from a Stonehenge-like world to contemporaneity by way of Samurai Japan. So what kind of a world did you and your designer seek to create?

AN: There are two or three driving forces in relation to the setting. First of all there is the need to create a series of credible family units, because the dynamic of the play emanates from damaged families; in particular Lear's and Gloucester's two parallel families. So one needs to be able to create a domesticity and parallel familial worlds. The second thing one needs to be able to explore is an epic quality, by which I mean the fact that the reality we live in fractures and splinters as the reality inside Lear's head fractures and splinters. Shakespeare quite deliberately expresses the horrors and the madness that are happening inside the human being through the physicality of it.

In both productions I sought for a setting and a world that could fragment and start behaving in an almost independent way. With both productions the walls started splitting and almost exploded apart. In 1993 with Robert Stephens as Lear I found an image at the very end of the first act which I felt was rather telling: the moon started bleeding sand. That seemed to me an exquisitely painful image, with the moon's very strong connection with the eye. The milk of human kindness had completely disappeared.

I found myself eschewing a completely modern, contemporary world, because it seemed to me that would quite swiftly become a highway to nowhere. In a similar way I eschewed the old Stonehenge version which seemed to me as silly as setting it in Wapping. So we found a world that probably related to Europe a hundred and fifty years ago, with greatcoats, where people still hunted, where the motor vehicle hadn't taken over our world. Neither myself, Bob Crowley, who designed the first, or Anthony Ward, who designed the second, would I think be able to place it within fifty years of a particular date.

DW: My interest in both my productions was to release the characters through their language and their relationships. What the play does is to take the audience into the interior of themselves. It is a mirror of the desolation of the human spirit, how lost it is, how far we fall in families and how hard sought are the conditions that prompt personal change. That's why the setting of any given production has little connection to the key that may unlock the scenes and acts. The play has to flow through our imaginations and then it has to lodge, and that is why I used such a pared-down aesthetic so that the space is clear for that to happen. All great plays do this but each must be met in their particular. With Kick Theatre in 1985 we were in a church hall in Edinburgh with three ladders and a bucket of water for the heath scene. With the NT [National Theatre] we were on the wide open stage of the Lyttelton Theatre where different aesthetic choices needed to be made before we began. Hildegard Bechtler's set was poetic and beautiful but bare, and the 'world' was not precisely named by it. It was not the 'Stone Age *Lear*', or the 'Third Reich *Lear*' but the Brian Cox, David Bradley, Ian McKellen, Susie Engel and Clare Higgins *Lear*. It was actor-led and actor-inspired and I still believe that that is a very good way with Shakespeare. Belief in casting and the group creation of the world is what matters.

TN: Shakespeare says that King Lear is the king of Ancient Britain. On the other hand, Shakespeare includes scenes involving duelling with swords, there are references to a graced palace, to women wearing gorgeous clothes that scarcely keep them warm and Gloucester refers to wearing spectacles. Shakespeare is making clear that he doesn't mind breaking the rules as far as historical accuracy goes. It's very likely that *King Lear* was performed at the Globe, or indeed at court performances, with the actors wearing a mixture of contemporary Elizabethan/Jacobean clothing, with some additional elements of cloak and robe that would indicate an earlier period.

I think Shakespeare was interested in the idea that a history play should apply acutely and precisely to the age that the *audience* lives in, so he was keen to have it both ways. I've seen Stonehenge-based productions of *King Lear*, and frankly it does seem very odd that Lear should make such a fuss about being out on a heath in a storm when his normal domestic condition appears to be open to the elements.

Shakespeare is presenting the huge contrast between a man who has been encouraged to believe that he is the closest thing to a god in human terms, and the man who comes to perceive he is like a beggar 'no more but this'. Lear is a conduit of the gods and he's in totally autocratic authority. His smallest whisper is converted into law, and nobody, such as Kent, can question him. So, in this production, I have elected to set the play in a seemingly nineteenth-century environment with resonances of the tsarist order in Russia and/or the Austrian autocracy of Franz Joseph. The intention is to stress that Lear's power is total and dictatorial like a tsar or an emperor, in all matters, political and social, and that it derives from god with whom he communicates. This, I think, allows us to encompass the requirements of the social structure of the play and, what's more, the anachronisms make complete sense. Lear's journey takes him from that autocratic power to somebody who, in the storm, asks himself for the first time, 'How do wretches survive in conditions like these, if they cannot keep warm because they have no proper clothing?' And then, wanting to embrace that houseless situation, he meets Tom o'Bedlam (who happens to be a man going through the same crisis, another man who's been used to comfort and is now, in order to survive, turning himself into a crazed beggar), and as he studies the beggar's naked exposure, Lear urgently wants to place himself in that condition, so he can experience being the 'forked animal' for himself.

Shakespeare had long been fascinated with the philosophical idea that a king can journey through the guts of a beggar. He has used the notion of king to beggar on a number of previous occasions, but in *Lear* he takes it to the extreme. I think *Richard II* is almost a sketch for *King Lear*; here we have a godlike king who in the end is sobbing, 'I need friends and since I am ordinary like you – how can you say I am a king?' Shakespeare takes that king to a small prison cell, and then, alone and the lord of nothing, he grants him extraordinary self-knowledge. But in *King Lear*, the journey of the king is to a yet more extreme destination.

Why did your Lear react so extremely to Cordelia's refusal to play the game of quantifying her love in words (or perhaps of quantifying her love all too literally – if I marry, my father will have 50 per cent of my love and my husband the other 50 per cent)?

AN: In a way you have to go back a step from that to ask yourself why Lear loves Cordelia so much more than the other two girls. There are dozens of reasons why, and I think most families could find their own reason why one child is, or appears to be, more beloved than the other. If the character in question is an obsessive like Lear than it starts getting potentially dangerous. His little girl has grown up and defies him, and he can't deal with that at all. He can't deal with retiring, he can't deal with getting old, he can't deal with not being in control any more. And as a consequence of all these things poor Cordelia gets it in the neck. And he regrets it almost immediately. Within a day he regrets it – probably within hours.

6. Ian McKellen as Lear in Trevor Nunn's 2007 production, in the opening scene with quasi-military 'Ruritanian' regalia.

DW: My Lear was a spoilt Lear, a vain Lear – a man who wants to hear what he wants to hear. His foolish gung-ho confidence is to wrap and disguise his need – a desire for a public show of affection – in a party game. He makes light of something that is weighty and important to him so that nobody suspects his underlying vulnerability. He demands that his daughters play out in public something that is private, and he claims this right because the prizes are high and marvellous. However, he knows who will take which prize because the 'game' is rigged – the parcels of land are already named, signed and sealed by king and court. The whole extravagant business is a contrivance to feed his vanity, to continue to make him feel that he holds the centre even in old age. We are witnessing a grotesque public massage of ego. Lear is a man used to getting what he wants, but he gets badly burnt. He discovers that love is not a commodity, that it must be given freely. It may be that he has lost sight of what love is a long time before the play begins. He's getting the answer he wants in two cases from the very daughters he did not treat well – if their behaviour later in the piece is anything to go by – and seems to barely know the character of his favourite – Cordelia – whose reaction is a huge surprise to him. There is a lot we do not know about this mysterious man, but his short-sightedness is placed on the table at the very opening of the play. Here is a man who will need to travel far to begin to gain the gift of personal insight. His friend Gloucester will literally lose his sight: blind men both.

And why didn't your Cordelia, or why *couldn't* she, put her love into words?

AN: That's a much more difficult question to answer. It's a young person's thing, whereby the spoken truth is more important than making your mum and dad happy. It's the moment of leaving home. The domestic psychological detail is very precise in the play. In Lear's household, Cordelia is at the point of leaving home to go and get married. That's a huge moment in every family, although it's very often not recognized. Some daughters never leave home. They are still at home, in the thrall of their parents, when they're seventy. Cordelia

7. The opening scene in Deborah Warner's 1990 production: a party game goes horribly wrong, with Brian Cox as Lear in wheelchair and paper crown.

leaves home and Lear can't deal with that. But she knows she has to do it, especially with a father like him.

DW: Cordelia does not want to play this extravagant and obscene party game. She is young, she is shy and she is about to be married, perhaps even the public nature of this serious business of land division is difficult for her. Anyhow, extravagant party game or not, it is the wrong moment for her to speak of her love to her father, and she certainly does not want to talk about such matters in public. When her sisters speak she is appalled by their preparedness to speak on cue, and especially so since she knows they are being dishonest. Cordelia wants to hold to her own truth. Horrified by what is happening around her, she wants to stop the game, and that is just what she does. It goes horribly wrong because she won't play, and she advertently or inadvertently humiliates her father in public. She is young and she believes with stern clarity in the virtues of honesty, truth and love. She is earnest – some might say over-earnest in this context, and she causes an atomic explosion.

Lear is both a king and a father. That often seems to be a choice that directors and actors have to make – are you going to give the primary emphasis to Lear's journey as a king giving up his crown, or is the primary emphasis going to be on the family relationships? Or do you actually think that the essence of the play is that the two are inextricably intertwined?

AN: Without question they are entwined. I didn't find that a choice. It isn't a choice that I recognize.

DW: The father relationship is the most interesting, he is a father who happens to be a king; but since all fathers are kings then, yes, all is intertwined. There is a lot we don't know about him, about his reign – but we know that he owns the land of his country and chooses to divide that up in such a way that will benefit his retirement most comfortably. He is a king/father heading towards retirement, a dangerous time in all families and in all monarchies.

TN: You won't be surprised to hear that your 'third way' alternative is the one this production goes for. Shakespeare is frighteningly brilliant at doing 'family breakup'. He does it superbly – in *Hamlet*, for example. I would say he does it equally shockingly in *The Merchant of Venice*, and in *Macbeth* we watch a marriage coming apart at the seams. There are small insights in *King Lear* into how the king's family has been pushed apart by events and attitudes. Lear is eighty years old. He has three daughters, and there is no Mrs Lear. The older daughters are married to powerful men and live in their own palaces. The youngest daughter is only just of marriageable age. Hidden behind the play, is there a story that he was a king who had two wives? – the first wife producing two daughters, Goneril and Regan, and then after her death (as we can frequently see in modern complex family histories) there is the child of a second marriage, the late child (as far as that father is concerned) who then dominates the father's affections. There's sufficient evidence in the play to suggest that jealousies and rifts within the family derive from such a back-story.

But I don't think exploration of a family feud is where Shakespeare wants matters to stop. It's not where his focus is. Routinely at the start of rehearsals, I say we have to first uncover the *theme* of a Shakespeare play. If you're a director, you must X-ray the play to find out what its bone structure is and where its vital organs are. A production shouldn't work from the outside, it must proceed from a sense of what the *internal* structure is, and thereby discover how everything contained in the play is meaningful because it is contiguous to that thematic structure.

In the case of *Lear*, it being one of the greatest plays of Shakespeare's maturity, the investigation is not going to be easy and the wellspring is not going to lie very close to the surface. Those who have written about *Lear* as Shakespeare's study of Nature are, to my thinking, somewhere near the mark, in the sense that Shakespeare is certainly inquiring into *human* nature in *Lear*, and he often uses the term 'nature' to encompass human behaviour and its contradictions. But let's take that definition of a theme just a little bit further. I would say Shakespeare is wanting to look at the human being, both sublime and ridiculous; I think he is asking, 'What is the human condition?' Why do humans say to themselves they are close to being angels, aspiring towards those qualities that are spiritual and godlike? And yet, why are they, in much of their action, so close to behaving like animals? Why, as it were anthropologically, do they have animal instincts that the species appears not to be able to get rid of?

I think it's no surprise that in this play Shakespeare doesn't define exactly who the god or gods are. There's a shadowy Apollo or Jupiter, and the sun is sacred, but the largely anonymous gods are referred to, as a sort of necessity for human beings to believe in, so that somehow humans can feel their actions are predestined, or governed by forces above and beyond themselves. Everything is under the control or the will of the gods.

But then, close to the centre of the play, there's a young man who says: 'Thou, nature, art my goddess: to thy law / My services are bound' – a young man who seems to be saying, 'I don't believe in the gods above, it's human nature that I am influenced by.' At the end of that first soliloquy, Edmund says, I sense almost in mockery: 'Now gods, stand up for bastards.' Well, he implies, you 'gods' have supposedly stood up for everybody else, it's high time you let bastards have a go. It's an extremely dangerous bit of comedic dramaturgy, but atheistical Edmund creating mayhem in his world, is placed in sharp contrast to the majority who genuinely beg the gods to intervene, at times almost obsessively. And I think Shakespeare makes it clear that 'the gods' don't. Repeatedly they are deaf or callous or non-existent. They do nothing, even when their intervention would be an affirmation of 'the good' in opposition to what is evil; they don't utter, they don't move a muscle. Are the heavens empty?

An actor who has played Lear has said that the real difficulty in playing the part is deciding how much to let rip how soon – if you give too much to the anger in the first half you're too exhausted for the madness in the second half, but if you have too much control to begin with, the transition into madness can seem too sudden and extreme to be convincing. Do you recognize that difficulty? And as a director, what can you do to help your Lear through it?

AN: I think that's very true. Most Lears I've talked to find the second half much easier than the first half, because the first half requires such a level of energy and a very skilful control of your resources. The truth is, it's almost unplayable – the pain is so great, the vocal demands so much. I've seen people cop out of it and say I'm going to do it quite quietly, but that's complete crap. They are selling the part and the audience short. It gets actors down a lot actually, because it magnifies your failures. The same is true for directors. It's like Everest, it's an unforgiving mountain, and people die on the way up, or they get badly hurt. It is like singing Wagner, and not everybody can sing Wagner.

DW: You need all your energy and all your fight to play Lear, just as an opera singer needs theirs for Tristan, Wotan or Siegfried. You cannot leave it too late. Brian Cox was forty-four when he played it for me. The first scene demands that the actor hit raw and engulfing fury within minutes. Throughout the opening scenes this anger is

8. 'The oldest hath borne most': Robert Stephens (right) as Lear and David Bradley as Gloucester, finding a human bond in their anguish, in Adrian Noble's 1993 production.

further released until it lets fly and the play climbs from there. You have to risk exhaustion to play it well. This play is not gentle on its lead actor, but where Shakespeare is brilliant and kind is in letting the evening be shared and there is, of course, the famous break at the start of the second half for a rest in the dressing room. Shakespeare always acts as helpful assistant to the director and he supports the actors by graphing and arcing their evening. Actors must follow him for their physical well-being, but they must follow what he asks for too. Real anger, real madness ... or, no play.

How did your production deal with the part of the Fool and his disappearance halfway through the action?

AN: In the first production in 1982 with Michael Gambon and Tony Sher it became quite famous. We did an improvisation in rehearsal, and I said just hold that a fraction longer, and the net result was that

King Lear accidentally stabbed the Fool, and he died. I had teachers coming in to say 'You have to write in your programme that that is not what Shakespeare wrote!' Because it is completely logical. Just before this, there's: 'The little dogs and all, Trey, Blanch and Sweetheart, see, they bark at me' and there's 'lie here and rest awhile'; 'draw the curtains'. And so we had the Fool using a cushion and Lear chasing him, and in stabbing the cushion he accidentally stabs the Fool. And then the little feathers became dogs. It was very beautiful and completely logical.

The Fool's function in life is entirely tied up with the king. He's like a soldier's batman. There's no logic for him to exist once the master's dead, or mad.

DW: My National Theatre Fool (David Bradley) died during the interval of exhaustion and cold. He went to sleep in a wheelbarrow somewhere in the dark interior of the hovel and never woke again. A sad and quiet death that went practically unnoticed. In my Kick Theatre production the actress Hilary Townley played both Cordelia and the Fool (a doubling I am sure Shakespeare intended), which

9. Michael Gambon as Lear and Antony Sher as the Fool, with mask, in Adrian Noble's 1982 production.

solves so many issues so very easily. For example, 'my poor fool is hanged' draws effortless and painful meaning from such casting.

One striking feature of Shakespeare's reworking of the old anonymous *Leir* play is his removal of its Christian frame of reference (that was one of the reasons why Tolstoy perversely said he preferred the old play!). The characters are always appealing to the gods, but not getting the response they want. And then there is Edmund appealing to Nature as his goddess. What was your thinking about religion in the play?

AN: The first time I did it I quite consciously sought a godless universe. I was very influenced by Brecht and Beckett. I sought a godless universe and a quite vengeful, spiteful universe. I made heavy cuts at the end of the play to highlight that fact.

The second time I imagined a universe that was not godless, but in which the gods sat back and refused to interfere. The choice is as much to do with the director or interpreter as the writing.

DW: The removal of any uniting Christian frame makes this text all the more available to us now. The characters are struggling away as we are all struggling away, and have ever been struggling away for centuries. From the seventeenth century to the twenty-first, Shakespeare allows us no simple answers, and that is why productions should beware of giving them.

TN: Remember, in the old *Leir* play, the king is restored to his throne and Cordelia lives. By changing the ending, Shakespeare deliberately violates a seemingly fundamental rule of drama, namely that plays serve as a moral or cautionary influence on their audience, because they show, regardless of trial and vicissitude, that the good will triumph in the end. In *King Lear* we're surely expecting just that, but Shakespeare won't allow it. I think this is proof positive that Shakespeare's intentions were very different from those of the old play. Shakespeare's investigation of the extremes of human behaviour, into the nature of man the species, concludes that life *isn't* like a morality play. When everything in our religious and cultural history requires us to believe that ultimately the gods will intervene on the side of virtue, Shakespeare says emphatically that they don't. It's more than the conclusion that his play is not Christian, it's that he moves to a conclusion that is, at the very least, agnostic.

For me, it is centrally important that there is no sense of divine justice in this tragedy. I'm wondering whether any other writer during the Elizabethan age ever ventured to question whether or not the heavens might be empty? In the early scenes, as I said, Shakespeare's play sets up the fundamental belief in his characters that human actions are overseen by the gods. Lear seems to believe that, like him, the gods are old men, that they are intelligent and that they're watching, and he clearly sees himself as in privileged contact with the gods. But as the play progresses, Shakespeare shows us more people praying for the intervention of the gods, to no avail. The battle at the climax of the story will determine whether or not the 'good' will triumph. Gloucester is urged by Edgar to 'Pray that the right may thrive.' He does. They don't. Finally, as it's realized that a death sentence is on both Lear and Cordelia, Albany leads all present in a final prayer as soldiers run to the prison – 'The gods defend her!' The first word of the next line is 'Howl'. Cordelia is dead. No intervention. The gods aren't mentioned again.

So yes, I think Edmund is placed before us early on as evidence of a solitary, dangerous, atheistical intelligence. Then as Lear's journey takes him increasingly towards challenging the behaviour of the gods, arriving at his epiphany in the 'unaccommodated man' speech, his more fundamental questions begin. 'What is the *cause* of thunder?' 'Is there any *cause* in nature that makes these hard hearts?' His questions now seem to be reaching towards Darwinian rather than divine explanations, and his belief in the gods begins to evaporate.

What about Edgar? He's quite an actor, performing in different voices, isn't he? He's Poor Tom, but then after that, after the cliff fall, he's the man on the beach and after that he's the peasant with the accent who kills Oswald – why does Edgar have all these different languages and voices and play all

these different roles? Why doesn't he much sooner just say, 'Look, Dad, I'm sorry. You should be sorry, you got the wrong son, I'm the good one. You're blind, this is me ...' So many opportunities in so many different roles ... until he finally gets around to telling his father the truth, by which time he's left it so late that all Gloucester can do is die of a heart attack.

AN: I think he takes upon himself the sins of others, in particular the sins of the father, in order to redeem himself. It's a profoundly religious, spiritual journey that Edgar goes on and a very tough regime that he imposes upon himself. The disguises, flagellation and infliction of misery are all part of that. Through the course of the play he cleanses himself. He's like a character out of a George Herbert poem.

TN: Edgar does say, at a crucial moment of the play, at the moment where he could cease to be the Tom o'Bedlam character at last, 'I cannot daub it further', and then in the very next instant, 'And yet I must'. In this production we've tried to identify something specific about that change of mind. There are men on Gloucester's orders scouring the country on the hunt to capture and kill Edgar if they find him. We have a troop of those soldiers passing at that point, so Edgar's 'yet I must' is clearly justified as self-preservation, and by association the preserving of his father.

But there's a deeper explanation that Edgar himself also provides when he takes Gloucester, who is suicidally bent, to an imaginary cliff edge. Just before the death plunge moment, Edgar has an aside to the audience, 'Why I do trifle thus with his despair / Is done to cure it'. This is fundamental in Edgar's journey. He observes that his father is now only full of resentment and hatred for the world, of believing that there was never anything worth believing in. Edgar, still clinging to his belief in divine justice, cannot allow his misguided, misled father to die a bad death or an unredeemed death. Therefore he makes it his mission to bring his father beyond suicidal thoughts to a different, reconciled set of attitudes. The gods seem to be unwilling to back up that reconciliation and continue to rain down horror, but Edgar's changes of identity are entirely to bring his father to a better spiritual place.

There's something of a fairytale quality to the play, isn't there? Goneril and Regan as the ugly sisters, Cordelia as a Cinderella with an unhappy ending. But, especially since Peter Brook's famous production and film, there's also an approach to the play that emphasizes Lear's unreasonable rage, the chaos caused by his riotous knights, and the sense that his daughters, Goneril especially, aren't villains through and through?

AN: It's hard to really admire anybody in the play actually. You can like them all a lot, and you can feel for them a lot, but it is hard to admire anybody. You can admire Gloucester, and probably Edgar's morality. As for the sisters, Shakespeare always writes what is needed. It can be very frustrating, especially for actresses, because it often happens with the female parts, that Shakespeare sees no point in showing you the bits of the iceberg under the water. He thinks that is a complete waste of scenes. It doesn't mean that the bit that is revealed does not have a complete world of which it is a part. Exactly the same thing applies to Gertrude and Lady Macbeth, whereby when the function ceases to have a crucial element or a driving force, Shakespeare just stops. Lady Macbeth and Gertrude just stop. Actresses tend to think there must be a missing or lost scene, but there isn't. Like the Fool in the second half of the play, it isn't there because there's no need for it. It doesn't mean you can't make it completely real, but you have to come at it from his time, not like a movie. The actor may have a back story, but you can only show so much because you don't need any more.

TN: I think it would be wholly wrong for a production to suggest that Goneril and Regan are of evil disposition at the beginning of the play; but there is a degree of ambition in their behaviour, and there is a degree of competition between them, and possibly there is that element of hidden resentment of how their much-the-younger sister has become the favourite of their old father.

Traditionally, late nineteenth-century and early twentieth-century versions of *Lear* did indeed go very strongly for the interpretation that Lear himself was always to be seen as kind and gentle and white-haired and frail. And therefore a delightful old man goaded intolerably by two wicked sisters. When Peter Brook did his production in 1962, there was a sense that an extraordinary revolution had taken place because Brook, absolutely honest to the text, said: 'Lear is behaving entirely unjustifiably, now he's behaving appallingly, and now he's behaving absolutely beyond the limit to the point where no father can expect to get away with that.' It was a production that tried explicitly to exonerate the sisters. I remember that, at that time, the impact of revealing Lear's behaviour as frequently unacceptable hit home very strongly. Now, of course, any production trying to propose that Lear is a close relative of Father Christmas would be laughed off the stage. The Brook view has become the standard view.

However, we do still have to explain how Goneril and Regan get to a condition of alarming ruthlessness in the second half of the play. All I will say is – especially if anybody hasn't seen the play before – watch out for the moment when Lear utters his curse on Goneril, and particularly his curse on Goneril's womb – a curse more bloodcurdling than I hope any lady in the audience will ever hear in her life. We all know that when dreadful things are said in rage, those words can never be unsaid. This is a major turning point of the play, and causes Goneril to become vengeful, regardless of consequence.

The blinding of Gloucester is perhaps the most horrific moment in all Shakespeare. How did you stage that and did it have contemporary resonances for you? In Trevor Nunn's 2007 production Regan behaves with sadistic glee that's also a kind of fear – it inevitably conjured up the American soldiers in Abu Ghraib gaol in Iraq. Torture in times of war is something that just doesn't go away …

AN: Yes, it had resonances in the sense that it confronts you with the most shocking things that humanity can do to humanity, but I almost never make references to contemporary events, because in my view it's a blind alley. Scenes like that talk directly to the audience and their souls and hearts. You don't need people coming on in flak jackets and dressed as Iraqis.

It is a dangerous scene for a number of reasons. It's dangerous because the blinding is done to an old man, and secondly, it's completely plugged in to this extraordinarily dangerous sexual relationship between Cornwall and Regan. It's plugged into the scheme of the play in terms of the breakdown of order and the dawn of chaos. It's a wild, very, very unpleasant scene.

DW: The theatre is a very safe place to explore the taboo and the pornographic. That safe place of examination may be the very point of theatre. As a theatre director, if you have to do a blinding you want to make it as ghoulish as you can. The audience is then left working it through in the safety of the evening, and a live and engaged audience will inevitably draw contemporary parallels. All great plays have the power to do this and the greater the performances the greater that power to prompt connection. This brings us back to what I said about these plays flowing through our imaginations. Few of us experience directly something like the horror of Abu Ghraib, but the theatre allows us to imagine such a reality, to process it and to question it from every angle. The Greek theatre was a public debate where the audience tested their response to the barbaric and nudged towards a legal system and the founding of modern democracy. Shakespeare's theatre took this debate into the new-found world of the seventeenth century and put up on stage every single human emotion, so that we could have a place to go where we might discuss ourselves. Sometimes one can view Shakespeare's legacy as the complete human emotional encyclopaedia. A place to go to study each and every human experience – to map ourselves in the safety of the theatre.

TN: As you know, this is not a production that is trying to say 'Here we are in the Middle East in the twenty-first century.' But it is hoping that all the things that are part of our experience now will be brought to bear on a contemporary audience watching and receiving the play.

Shakespeare's play was almost certainly heavily censored when it was first performed. It was probably first performed at court and so it is likely that quite a number of cuts were applied to the text because statements were being made that would not be acceptable to a royal ear, and possibly shouldn't be heard by anybody. There are a host of things that Lear says about human institutions, 'justice' – 'which is the justice, which is the thief?'; 'authority' as in the police or governmental authority – 'a dog's obeyed in office' – getting its power from name or uniform, but not by standards of behaviour. He talks about 'politicians' – 'Get thee glass eyes, / And like a scurvy politician seem / To see the things thou dost not'. Lear goes through a list of modern and to our ears, highly recognizable contemporary institutions and says so many of them are corrupt and therefore worthless. But Shakespeare had the perfect reply to the censors. The man saying these terrible things is mad. Who knows, if he had not had that defence, Shakespeare might have done a spell in jail.

Over previous generations the blinding scene has been cut down or merely 'suggested', as something taking place in the dark. Such bowdlerization of Shakespeare is based on the judgement that these things are not for civilized people to watch, or hear. In the twentieth century, believing that Shakespeare should be very much like Samuel Beckett (who was so obviously greatly influenced by the play), the blinding scene became increasingly essential to the play. As we watch, Shakespeare is saying, 'Face up to the fact that human beings are capable of unspeakably animal behaviour towards each other.' These days, as we read of torture, of the callousness of the suicide bomber who blows up children, we ask how any group of people can say they are justified by any cause whatsoever in doing such things to another group of people? But Shakespeare tells us that it is in us. We humans do it. We do it as a species, and we must face the truth that it's in human nature to be inhuman.

Academics get very exercised about the variants between the Quarto and Folio texts of the play – the fact that Lear has different dying words in each version, that a different person inherits the gored state at the end of each version (Albany speaks the final lines in Quarto, Edgar in Folio), and so on. Did you concern yourself with these textual matters or do you feel that the director is free to pick and mix, cut and paste, his or her own version of the play?

AN: I think the director is free to do what he wants to do, but he must also be answerable for what he does. I've never been very interested in the textual variations. What I did, particularly in the first production, was skin the last three hundred or four hundred lines – I was absolutely brutal with the cuts there. And the impact of it was that, at the very moment of repentance, it was too late. There was no time to save Lear and Cordelia's lives, because the people on stage had been chatting, talking all the time. That was all very much to do with the fact that it was a godless universe. The truth is on both occasions I created a world that seemed to me to be logical from all the different versions. I would then be responsible for that and I would stand by that.

TN: I don't think that in 1968 when I first directed the play anybody was yet saying 'The Quarto and the Folio are two quite different plays.' I remember at the time consulting John Barton, and arriving at a 'best of both worlds' conflated text. That text became the basis of the text I used in 1976 with Donald Sinden, but then when I started out this time with Ian McKellen I did read a number of scholars who were telling me that I *should* be making a choice between Quarto and Folio. Alas, I found myself unwilling to lose rich and evocative material from either version, and so I worked with a slightly different conflation, but a conflation nonetheless. For me, the more important change since I first directed the play is not in scholarship, but in the simple fact that I am thirty years older now. Shakespeare's engagement with ultimate questions about mortality, what we construct for ourselves to explain or to accept our mortality, of course speaks more potently to me now. The play, as I have said, is very hard on organized human society and institutions of every kind. There is very little Lear and Gloucester have left to believe in, before they must endure their going hence. Edgar is left to conclude the play, and I think deliberately, it is a conclusion of a man who has nothing really to say. He offers no positive, no beliefs, no journey to a better future. He is by then almost the only character left standing, and in the bleakest of all Shakespeare's endings, he seems to know that all we can determine on is to 'endure'.

SHAKESPEARE'S CAREER IN THE THEATRE

BEGINNINGS

William Shakespeare was an extraordinarily intelligent man who was born and died in an ordinary market town in the English Midlands. He lived an uneventful life in an eventful age. Born in April 1564, he was the eldest son of John Shakespeare, a glove-maker who was prominent on the town council until he fell into financial difficulties. Young William was educated at the local grammar in Stratford-upon-Avon, Warwickshire, where he gained a thorough grounding in the Latin language, the art of rhetoric and classical poetry. He married Ann Hathaway and had three children (Susanna, then the twins Hamnet and Judith) before his twenty-first birthday: an exceptionally young age for the period. We do not know how he supported his family in the mid-1580s.

Like many clever country boys, he moved to the city in order to make his way in the world. Like many creative people, he found a career in the entertainment business. Public playhouses and professional full-time acting companies reliant on the market for their income were born in Shakespeare's childhood. When he arrived in London as a man, sometime in the late 1580s, a new phenomenon was in the making: the actor who is so successful that he becomes a 'star'. The word did not exist in its modern sense, but the pattern is recognizable: audiences went to the theatre not so much to see a particular show as to witness the comedian Richard Tarlton or the dramatic actor Edward Alleyn.

Shakespeare was an actor before he was a writer. It appears not to have been long before he realized that he was never going to grow into a great comedian like Tarlton or a great tragedian like Alleyn. Instead, he found a role within his company as the man who patched up old plays, breathing new life, new dramatic twists, into tired repertory pieces. He paid close attention to the work of the university-educated dramatists who were writing history plays and tragedies for the public stage in a style more ambitious, sweeping and poetically grand than anything which had been seen before. But he may also have noted that what his friend and rival Ben Jonson would call 'Marlowe's mighty line' sometimes faltered in the mode of comedy. Going to university, as Christopher Marlowe did, was all well and good for honing the arts of rhetorical elaboration and classical allusion, but it could lead to a loss of the common touch. To stay close to a large segment of the potential audience for public theatre, it was necessary to write for clowns as well as kings and to intersperse the flights of poetry with the humour of the tavern, the privy and the brothel: Shakespeare was the first to establish himself early in his career as an equal master of tragedy, comedy and history. He realized that theatre could be the medium to make the national past available to a wider audience than the elite who could afford to read large history books: his signature early works include not only the classical tragedy *Titus Andronicus* but also the sequence of English historical plays on the Wars of the Roses.

He also invented a new role for himself, that of in-house company dramatist. Where his peers and predecessors had to sell their plays to the theatre managers on a poorly-paid piecework basis, Shakespeare took a percentage of the box-office income. The Lord Chamberlain's Men constituted themselves in 1594 as a joint stock company, with the profits being distributed among the core actors who had invested as sharers. Shakespeare acted himself – he appears in the cast lists of some of Ben Jonson's plays as well as the list of actors' names at the beginning of his own collected works – but his principal duty was to write two or three plays a year for the company. By holding shares, he was effectively earning himself a royalty on his work, something no author had ever done before in England. When the Lord Chamberlain's Men collected their fee for performance at court in the Christmas season of 1594, three of them went along to the Treasurer of the Chamber: not just Richard Burbage the tragedian and Will Kempe the clown, but also Shakespeare the scriptwriter. That was something new.

The next four years were the golden period in Shakespeare's career, though overshadowed by the death of his only son Hamnet, aged eleven, in 1596. In his early thirties and in full command of both his poetic and his theatrical medium, he perfected his art of comedy, while also developing his tragic and historical writing in new ways. In 1598, Francis Meres, a Cambridge University graduate with his finger on the pulse of the London literary world, praised Shakespeare for his excellence across the genres:

> As Plautus and Seneca are accounted the best for comedy and tragedy among the Latins, so Shakespeare among the English is the most excellent in both kinds for the stage; for comedy, witness his *Gentlemen of Verona*, his *Errors*, his *Love Labours Lost*, his *Love Labours Won*, his *Midsummer Night Dream* and his *Merchant of Venice*: for tragedy his *Richard the 2*, *Richard the 3*, *Henry the 4*, *King John*, *Titus Andronicus* and his *Romeo and Juliet*.

For Meres, as for the many writers who praised the 'honey-flowing vein' of *Venus and Adonis* and *Lucrece*, narrative poems written when the theatres were closed due to plague in 1593–94, Shakespeare was marked above all by his linguistic skill, by the gift of turning elegant poetic phrases.

PLAYHOUSES

Elizabethan playhouses were 'thrust' or 'one-room' theatres. To understand Shakespeare's original theatrical life, we have to forget about the indoor theatre of later times, with its proscenium arch and curtain that would be opened at the beginning and closed at the end of each act. In the proscenium arch theatre, stage and auditorium are effectively two separate rooms: the audience looks from one world into another as if through the imaginary 'fourth wall' framed by the proscenium. The picture-frame stage, together with the elaborate scenic effects and backdrops beyond it, created the illusion of a self-contained world – especially once nineteenth-century developments in the control of artificial lighting meant that the auditorium could be darkened and the spectators made to focus on the lighted stage. Shakespeare, by contrast, wrote for a bare platform stage with a standing audience gathered around it in a courtyard in full daylight. The audience were always conscious of themselves and their fellow-spectators, and they shared the same 'room' as the actors. A sense of immediate presence and the creation of rapport with the audience were all-important. The actor could not afford to imagine he was in a closed world, with silent witnesses dutifully observing him from the darkness.

Shakespeare's theatrical career began at the Rose Theatre in Southwark. The stage was wide and shallow, trapezoid in shape, like a lozenge. This design had a great deal of potential for the theatrical equivalent of cinematic split-screen effects, whereby one group of characters would enter at the door at one end of the tiring-house wall at the back of the stage and another group through the door at the other end, thus creating two rival tableaux. Many of the battle-heavy and faction-filled plays that premiered at the Rose have scenes of just this sort.

At the rear of the Rose stage, there were three capacious exits, each over ten feet wide. Unfortunately, the very limited excavation of a fragmentary portion of the original Globe site, also in 1989, revealed nothing about the stage. The first Globe was built in 1599 with similar proportions to those of another theatre, the Fortune, albeit that the former was polygonal and looked circular, whereas the latter was rectangular. The building contract for the Fortune survives and allows us to infer that the stage of the Globe was probably substantially wider than it was deep (perhaps forty-three feet wide and twenty-seven feet deep). It may well have been tapered at the front, like that of the Rose.

The capacity of the Globe was said to have been enormous, perhaps in excess of three thousand. It has been conjectured that about eight hundred people may have stood in the yard, with two thousand or more in the three layers of covered galleries. The other 'public' playhouses were also of large capacity, whereas the indoor Blackfriars theatre that Shakespeare's company began using in 1608 – the former refectory of a monastery – had overall internal dimensions of a mere forty-six by sixty feet. It would have made for a much more intimate theatrical experience and had a much smaller capacity, probably of about six hundred people. Since they paid at least sixpence a head, the Blackfriars attracted a more select or 'private' audience. The atmosphere would have been closer to that of an indoor performance before the court in the Whitehall Palace or at Richmond. That Shakespeare always wrote for indoor production at court as well as outdoor performance in the public theatre should make us cautious about inferring, as some scholars have, that the opportunity provided by the intimacy of the Blackfriars led to a significant change towards a 'chamber' style in his last plays – which, besides, were performed at both the Globe and the Blackfriars. After the occupation of the Blackfriars a five-act structure seems to have become more important to Shakespeare. That was because of artificial lighting: there were musical interludes between the acts, while the candles were trimmed and replaced. Again, though, something similar must have been necessary for indoor court performances throughout his career.

Front of house there were the 'gatherers' who collected the money from audience members: a penny to stand in the open-air yard, another penny for a place in the covered galleries, sixpence for the prominent 'lord's rooms' to the side of the stage. In the indoor 'private' theatres, gallants from the audience who fancied making themselves part of the spectacle sat on stools on the edge of the stage itself. Scholars debate as to how widespread this practice was in the public theatres such as the Globe. Once the audience were in place and the money counted, the gatherers were available to be extras on stage. That is one reason why battles and crowd scenes often come later rather than early in Shakespeare's plays. There was no formal prohibition upon performance by women, and there certainly were women among the gatherers, so it is not beyond the bounds of possibility that female crowd members were played by females.

The play began at two o'clock in the afternoon and the theatre had to be cleared by five. After the main show, there would be a jig – which consisted not only of dancing, but also of knockabout comedy (it is the origin of the farcical 'afterpiece' in the eighteenth-century theatre). So the time available for a Shakespeare play was about two and a half hours, somewhere between the 'two hours' traffic' mentioned in the prologue to *Romeo and Juliet* and the 'three hours' spectacle' referred to in the preface to the 1647 Folio of Beaumont and Fletcher's plays. The prologue to a play by Thomas Middleton refers to a thousand lines as 'one hour's words', so the likelihood is that about two and a half thousand, or a maximum of three thousand lines made up the performed text. This is indeed the length of most of Shakespeare's comedies, whereas many of his tragedies and histories are much longer, raising the possibility that he wrote full scripts, possibly with eventual publication in mind, in the full knowledge that the stage version would be heavily cut. The short Quarto texts published in his lifetime – they used to be called 'Bad' Quartos – provide fascinating evidence as to the kind of cutting that probably took place. So, for instance, the First Quarto of *Hamlet* neatly merges two occasions when Hamlet is overheard, the 'Fishmonger' and the 'nunnery' scenes.

The social composition of the audience was mixed. The poet Sir John Davies wrote of 'A thousand townsmen, gentlemen and whores, / Porters and servingmen' who would 'together throng' at the public playhouses. Though moralists associated female play-going with adultery and the sex trade, many perfectly respectable citizens' wives were regular attendees. Some, no doubt, resembled the modern groupie: a story attested in two different sources has one citizen's wife making a post-show assignation with Richard Burbage and ending up in bed with Shakespeare – supposedly eliciting from the latter the quip that William the Conqueror was before Richard III. Defenders of theatre liked to say that by witnessing the comeuppance of villains on the stage, audience members would repent of their own wrongdoings, but the reality is that most people went to the theatre then, as they do now, for entertainment more than moral edification. Besides, it would be foolish to suppose that audiences behaved in a homogeneous way: a pamphlet of the 1630s tells of how two men went to see *Pericles* and one of them laughed while the other wept. Bishop John Hall complained that people went to church for the same reasons that they went to the theatre: 'for company, for custom, for recreation ... to feed his eyes or his ears ... or perhaps for sleep'.

Men-about-town and clever young lawyers went to be seen as much as to see. In the modern popular imagination, shaped not least by *Shakespeare in Love* and the opening sequence of Laurence Olivier's *Henry V* film, the penny-paying groundlings stand in the yard hurling abuse or encouragement and hazelnuts or orange peel at the actors, while the sophisticates in the covered galleries appreciate Shakespeare's soaring poetry. The reality was probably the other way round. A 'groundling' was a kind of fish, so the nickname suggests the penny audience standing below the level of the stage and gazing in silent open-mouthed wonder at the spectacle unfolding above them. The more difficult audience members, who kept up a running commentary of clever remarks on the performance and who occasionally got into quarrels with players, were the gallants. Like Hollywood movies in modern times, Elizabethan and Jacobean plays exercised a powerful influence on the fashion and behaviour of the young. John Marston mocks the lawyers who would open their lips, perhaps to court a girl, and out would 'flow / Naught but pure Juliet and Romeo'.

THE ENSEMBLE AT WORK

In the absence of typewriters and photocopying machines, reading aloud would have been the means by which the company got to know a new play. The tradition of the playwright reading his complete script to the assembled company endured for generations. A copy would then have been taken to the Master of the Revels for licensing. The theatre book-holder or prompter would then have copied the parts for distribution to the actors. A partbook consisted of the character's lines, with each speech preceded by the last three or four words of the speech before, the so-called 'cue'. These would have been taken away and studied or 'conned'. During this period of learning the parts, an actor might have had some one-to-one instruction, perhaps from the dramatist, perhaps from a senior actor who had played the same part before, and, in the case of an apprentice, from his master. A high percentage of Desdemona's lines occur in dialogue with Othello, of Lady Macbeth's with Macbeth, Cleopatra's with Antony and Volumnia's with Coriolanus. The roles would almost certainly have been taken by the apprentice of the lead actor, usually Burbage, who delivers the majority of the cues. Given that apprentices lodged with their masters, there would have been

10. Hypothetical reconstruction of the interior of an Elizabethan playhouse during a performance.

ample opportunity for personal instruction, which may be what made it possible for young men to play such demanding parts.

After the parts were learned, there may have been no more than a single rehearsal before the first performance. With six different plays to be put on every week, there was no time for more. Actors, then, would go into a show with a very limited sense of the whole. The notion of a collective rehearsal process that is itself a process of discovery for the actors is wholly modern and would have been incomprehensible to Shakespeare and his original ensemble. Given the number of parts an actor had to hold in his memory, the forgetting of lines was probably more frequent than in the modern theatre. The book-holder was on hand to prompt.

Backstage personnel included the property man, the tire-man who oversaw the costumes, call-boys, attendants and the musicians, who might play at various times from the main stage, the rooms above and within the tiring-house. Scriptwriters sometimes made a nuisance of themselves backstage. There was often tension between the acting companies and the freelance playwrights from whom they purchased scripts: it was a smart move on the part of Shakespeare and the Lord Chamberlain's Men to bring the writing process in-house.

Scenery was limited, though sometimes set-pieces were brought on (a bank of flowers, a bed, the mouth of hell). The trapdoor from below, the gallery stage above and the curtained discovery-space at the back allowed for an array of special effects: the rising of ghosts and apparitions, the descent of gods, dialogue between a character at a window and another at ground level, the revelation of a statue or a pair of lovers playing at chess. Ingenious use could be made of props, as with the ass's head in *A Midsummer Night's Dream*. In a theatre that does not clutter the stage with the material paraphernalia of everyday life, those objects that are deployed may take on powerful symbolic weight, as when Shylock bears his weighing scales in one hand and knife in the other, thus becoming a parody of the figure of Justice who traditionally bears a sword and a balance. Among the more significant items in the property cupboard of Shakespeare's company, there would have been a throne (the 'chair of state'), joint stools, books, bottles, coins, purses, letters (which are brought on stage, read or referred to on about eighty occasions in the complete works), maps, gloves, a set of stocks (in which Kent is put in *King Lear*), rings, rapiers, daggers, broadswords, staves, pistols, masks and vizards, heads and skulls, torches and tapers and lanterns which served to signal night scenes on the daylit stage, a buck's head, an ass's head, animal costumes. Live animals also put in appearances, most notably the dog Crab in *The Two Gentlemen of Verona* and possibly a young polar bear in *The Winter's Tale*.

The costumes were the most important visual dimension of the play. Playwrights were paid between £2 and £6 per script, whereas Alleyn was not averse to paying £20 for 'a black velvet cloak with sleeves embroidered all with silver and gold'. No matter the period of the play, actors always wore contemporary costume. The excitement for the audience came not from any impression of historical accuracy, but from the richness of the attire and perhaps the transgressive thrill of the knowledge that here were commoners like themselves strutting in the costumes of courtiers in effective defiance of the strict sumptuary laws whereby in real life people had to wear the clothes that befitted their social station.

To an even greater degree than props, costumes could carry symbolic importance. Racial characteristics could be suggested: a breastplate and helmet for a Roman soldier, a turban for a Turk, long robes for exotic characters such as Moors, a gabardine for a Jew. The figure of Time, as in *The Winter's Tale*, would be equipped with hourglass, scythe and wings; Rumour, who speaks the prologue of *2 Henry IV*, wore a costume adorned with a thousand tongues. The wardrobe in the tiring-house of the Globe would have contained much of the same stock as that of rival manager Philip Henslowe at the Rose: green gowns for outlaws and foresters, black for melancholy men such as Jaques and people in mourning such as the Countess in *All's Well that Ends Well* (at the beginning of *Hamlet*, the prince is still in mourning black when everyone else is in festive garb for the wedding of the new king), a gown and hood for a friar (or a feigned friar like the duke in *Measure for Measure*), blue coats and tawny to distinguish the followers of rival factions, a leather apron and ruler for a carpenter (as in the opening scene of *Julius Caesar* – and in *A Midsummer Night's Dream*, where this is the only sign that Peter Quince is a carpenter), a cockle hat with staff and a pair of sandals for a pilgrim or palmer (the disguise assumed by Helen in *All's Well*), bodices and kirtles with farthingales beneath for the boys who are to be dressed as girls. A gender switch such as that of Rosalind or Jessica seems to have taken between fifty and eighty lines of dialogue – Viola does not resume her 'maiden weeds', but remains in her boy's costume to the end of *Twelfth Night* because a change would have slowed down the action at just the moment it was speeding to a climax. Henslowe's inventory also included 'a robe for to go invisible': Oberon, Puck and Ariel must have had something similar.

As the costumes appealed to the eyes, so there was music for the ears. Comedies included many songs. Desdemona's willow song, perhaps a late addition to the text, is a rare and thus exceptionally poignant example from tragedy. Trumpets and tuckets sounded for ceremonial entrances, drums denoted an army on the march. Background music could create atmosphere, as at the beginning of *Twelfth Night*, during the lovers' dialogue near the end of *The Merchant of Venice*, when the statue seemingly comes to life in *The Winter's Tale*, and for the revival of Pericles and of Lear (in the Quarto text, but not the Folio). The haunting sound of the hautboy suggested a realm beyond the human, as when the god Hercules is imagined deserting Mark Antony. Dances symbolized the harmony of the end of a comedy – though in Shakespeare's world of mingled joy and sorrow, someone is usually left out of the circle.

The most important resource was, of course, the actors themselves. They needed many skills: in the words of one contemporary commentator, 'dancing, activity, music, song, elocution, ability of body, memory, skill of weapon, pregnancy of wit'. Their bodies were as significant as their voices. Hamlet tells the player to 'suit the action to the word, the word to the action': moments of strong emotion, known as 'passions', relied on a repertoire of dramatic gestures as well as a modulation of the voice. When Titus Andronicus has had his hand chopped off, he asks 'How can I grace my talk, / Wanting a hand to give it action?' A pen portrait of 'The Character of an Excellent Actor' by the dramatist John Webster is almost certainly based on his impression of Shakespeare's leading man, Richard Burbage: 'By a full and significant action of body, he charms our attention: sit in a full theatre, and you will think you see so many lines drawn from the circumference of so many ears, whiles the actor is the centre . . . .'

Though Burbage was admired above all others, praise was also heaped upon the apprentice players whose alto voices fitted them for the parts of women. A spectator at Oxford in 1610 records how the audience were reduced to tears by the pathos of Desdemona's death. The puritans who fumed about the biblical prohibition upon cross-dressing and the encouragement to sodomy constituted by the sight of an adult male kissing a teenage boy on stage were a small minority. Little is known, however, about the characteristics of the leading apprentices in Shakespeare's company. It may perhaps be inferred that one was a lot taller than the other, since Shakespeare often wrote for a pair of female friends, one tall and fair, the other short and dark (Helena and Hermia, Rosalind and Celia, Beatrice and Hero).

We know little about Shakespeare's own acting roles – an early allusion indicates that he often took royal parts, and a venerable tradition gives him old Adam in *As You Like It* and the ghost of old King Hamlet. Save for Burbage's lead roles and the generic part of the clown, all such castings are mere speculation. We do not even know for sure whether the original Falstaff was Will Kempe or another actor who specialized in comic roles, Thomas Pope.

Kempe left the company in early 1599. Tradition has it that he fell out with Shakespeare over the matter of excessive improvisation. He was replaced by Robert Armin, who was less of a clown and more of a cerebral wit: this explains the difference between such parts as Lancelet Gobbo and Dogberry, which were written for Kempe, and the more verbally sophisticated Feste and Lear's Fool, which were written for Armin.

One thing that is clear from surviving 'plots' or story-boards of plays from the period is that a degree of doubling was necessary. *2 Henry VI* has over sixty speaking parts, but more than half of the characters only appear in a single scene and most scenes have only six to eight speakers. At a stretch, the play could be performed by thirteen actors. When Thomas Platter saw *Julius Caesar* at the Globe in 1599, he noted that there were about fifteen. Why doesn't Paris go to the Capulet ball in *Romeo and Juliet*? Perhaps because he was doubled with Mercutio, who does. In *The Winter's Tale*, Mamillius might have come back as Perdita and Antigonus been doubled by Camillo, making the partnership with Paulina at the end a very neat touch. Titania and Oberon are often played by the same pair as Hippolyta and Theseus, suggesting a symbolic matching of the rulers of the worlds of night and day, but it is questionable whether there would have been time for the necessary costume changes. As so often, one is left in a realm of tantalizing speculation.

THE KING'S MAN

The new king, James I, who had held the Scottish throne as James VI since he had been an infant, immediately took the Lord Chamberlain's Men under his direct patronage. Henceforth they would be the King's Men, and for the rest of Shakespeare's career they were favoured with far more court performances than any of their rivals. There even seem to have been rumours early in the reign that Shakespeare and Burbage were being considered for knighthoods, an unprecedented honour for mere actors – and one that in the event was not accorded to a member of the profession for nearly three hundred years, when the title was bestowed upon Henry Irving, the leading Shakespearean actor of Queen Victoria's reign.

Shakespeare's productivity rate slowed in the Jacobean years, not because of age or some personal trauma, but because there were frequent outbreaks of plague, causing the theatres to be closed for long periods. The King's Men were forced to spend many months on the road. Between November 1603 and 1608, they were to be found at various towns in the south and Midlands, though Shakespeare probably did not tour with them by this time. He had bought a large house back home in Stratford and was accumulating other property. He may indeed have stopped acting soon after the new king took the throne. With the London theatres closed so much of the time and a large repertoire on the stocks, Shakespeare seems to have focused his energies on writing a few long and complex tragedies that could have been played on demand at court: *Othello, King Lear, Antony and Cleopatra, Coriolanus* and *Cymbeline* are among his longest and poetically grandest plays. *Macbeth* only survives in a shorter text, which shows signs of adaptation after Shakespeare's death. The bitterly satirical *Timon of Athens*, apparently a collaboration with Thomas Middleton that may have failed on the stage, also belongs to this period. In comedy, too, he wrote longer and morally darker works than in the Elizabethan period, pushing at the very bounds of the form in *Measure for Measure* and *All's Well that Ends Well*.

From 1608 onwards, when the King's Men began occupying the indoor Blackfriars playhouse (as a winter house, meaning that they only used the outdoor Globe in summer?), Shakespeare turned to a more romantic style. His company had a great success with a revived and altered version of an old pastoral play called *Mucedorus*. It even featured a bear. The younger dramatist John Fletcher, meanwhile, sometimes working in collaboration with Francis Beaumont, was pioneering a new style of tragicomedy, a mix of romance and royalism laced with intrigue and pastoral excursions. Shakespeare experimented with this idiom in *Cymbeline* and it was presumably with his blessing that Fletcher eventually took over as the King's Men's company dramatist. The two writers apparently collaborated on three plays in the years 1612–14: a lost romance called *Cardenio* (based on the love-madness of a character in Cervantes' *Don Quixote*), *Henry VIII* (originally staged with the title 'All is True'), and *The Two Noble Kinsmen*, a dramatization of Chaucer's 'Knight's Tale' These were written after Shakespeare's two final solo-authored plays, *The Winter's Tale*, a self-consciously old-fashioned work dramatizing the pastoral romance of his old enemy Robert Greene, and *The Tempest*, which at one and the same time drew together multiple theatrical traditions, diverse reading and contemporary interest in the fate of a ship that had been wrecked on the way to the New World.

The collaborations with Fletcher suggest that Shakespeare's career ended with a slow fade rather than the sudden retirement supposed by the nineteenth-century Romantic critics who read Prospero's epilogue to *The Tempest* as Shakespeare's personal farewell to his art. In the last few years of his life Shakespeare certainly spent more of his time in Stratford-upon-Avon, where he became further involved in property dealing and litigation. But his London life also continued. In 1613 he made his first major London property purchase: a freehold house in the Blackfriars district, close to his company's indoor theatre. *The Two Noble Kinsmen* may have been written as late as 1614, and Shakespeare was in London on business a little over a year before he died of an unknown cause at home in Stratford-upon-Avon in 1616, probably on his fifty-second birthday.

About half the sum of his works were published in his lifetime, in texts of variable quality. A few years after his death, his fellow-actors began putting together an authorized edition of his complete *Comedies, Histories and Tragedies*. It appeared in 1623, in large 'Folio' format. This collection of thirty-six plays gave Shakespeare his immortality. In the words of his fellow-dramatist Ben Jonson, who contributed two poems of praise at the start of the Folio, the body of his work made him 'a monument without a tomb':

> And art alive still while thy book doth live
> And we have wits to read and praise to give …
> He was not of an age, but for all time!

SHAKESPEARE'S WORKS:
A Chronology

1589–91	*? Arden of Faversham* (possible part authorship)
1589–92	*The Taming of the Shrew*
1589–92	*? Edward the Third* (possible part authorship)
1591	*The Second Part of Henry the Sixth*, originally called *The First Part of the Contention betwixt the Two Famous Houses of York and Lancaster* (element of co-authorship possible)
1591	*The Third Part of Henry the Sixth*, originally called *The True Tragedy of Richard Duke of York* (element of co-authorship probable)
1591–92	*The Two Gentlemen of Verona*
1591–92 perhaps revised 1594	*The Lamentable Tragedy of Titus Andronicus* (probably co-written with, or revising an earlier version by, George Peele)
1592	*The First Part of Henry the Sixth*, probably with Thomas Nashe and others
1592/94	*King Richard the Third*
1593	*Venus and Adonis* (poem)
1593–94	*The Rape of Lucrece* (poem)
1593–1608	*Sonnets* (154 poems, published 1609 with *A Lover's Complaint*, a poem of disputed authorship)
1592–94/ 1600–03	*Sir Thomas More* (a single scene for a play originally by Anthony Munday, with other revisions by Henry Chettle, Thomas Dekker and Thomas Heywood)
1594	*The Comedy of Errors*
1595	*Love's Labour's Lost*

1595–97	*Love's Labour's Won* (a lost play, unless the original title for another comedy)
1595–96	*A Midsummer Night's Dream*
1595–96	*The Tragedy of Romeo and Juliet*
1595–96	*King Richard the Second*
1595–97	*The Life and Death of King John* (possibly earlier)
1596–97	*The Merchant of Venice*
1596–97	*The First Part of Henry the Fourth*
1597–98	*The Second Part of Henry the Fourth*
1598	*Much Ado about Nothing*
1598–99	*The Passionate Pilgrim* (20 poems, some not by Shakespeare)
1599	*The Life of Henry the Fifth*
1599	'To the Queen' (epilogue for a court performance)
1599	*As You Like It*
1599	*The Tragedy of Julius Caesar*
1600–01	*The Tragedy of Hamlet, Prince of Denmark* (perhaps revising an earlier version)
1600–01	*The Merry Wives of Windsor* (perhaps revising version of 1597–99)
1601	'Let the Bird of Loudest Lay' (poem, known since 1807 as 'The Phoenix and Turtle' (turtle-dove))
1601	*Twelfth Night, or What You Will*
1601–02	*The Tragedy of Troilus and Cressida*
1604	*The Tragedy of Othello, the Moor of Venice*
1604	*Measure for Measure*
1605	*All's Well that Ends Well*
1605	*The Life of Timon of Athens*, with Thomas Middleton
1605–06	*The Tragedy of King Lear*
1605–08	? contribution to *The Four Plays in One* (lost, except for *A Yorkshire Tragedy*, mostly by Thomas Middleton)
1606	*The Tragedy of Macbeth* (surviving text has additional scenes by Thomas Middleton)
1606–07	*The Tragedy of Antony and Cleopatra*
1608	*The Tragedy of Coriolanus*

1608	*Pericles, Prince of Tyre*, with George Wilkins
1610	*The Tragedy of Cymbeline*
1611	*The Winter's Tale*
1611	*The Tempest*
1612–13	*Cardenio*, with John Fletcher (survives only in later adaptation called *Double Falsehood* by Lewis Theobald)
1613	*Henry VIII (All is True)*, with John Fletcher
1613–14	*The Two Noble Kinsmen*, with John Fletcher

THE HISTORY BEHIND THE TRAGEDIES: A Chronology

Era/Date	Event	Location	Play
Greek myth	Trojan war	Troy	*Troilus and Cressida*
Greek myth	Theseus King of Athens	Athens	*The Two Noble Kinsmen*
c.tenth–ninth century BC?	Leir King of Britain (legendary)	Britain	*King Lear*
535–510 BC	Tarquin II King of Rome	Rome	*The Rape of Lucrece*
493 BC	Caius Martius captures Corioli	Italy	*Coriolanus*
431–404 BC	Peloponnesian war	Greece	*Timon of Athens*
17 Mar 45 BC	Battle of Munda: Caesar's victory over Pompey's sons	Munda, Spain	*Julius Caesar*
Oct 45 BC	Caesar returns to Rome for triumph	Rome	*Julius Caesar*
15 Mar 44 BC	Assassination of Caesar	Rome	*Julius Caesar*
27 Nov 43 BC	Formation of Second Triumvirate	Rome	*Julius Caesar*
Oct 42 BC	Battle of Philippi	Philippi, Macedonia	*Julius Caesar*
Winter 41–40 BC	Antony visits Cleopatra	Egypt	*Antony and Cleopatra*
Oct 40 BC	Pact of Brundisium; marriage of Antony and Octavia	Italy	*Antony and Cleopatra*
39 BC	Pact of Misenum between Pompey and the triumvirs	Campania, Italy	*Antony and Cleopatra*
39–38 BC	Ventidius defeats the Parthians in a series of engagements	Syria	*Antony and Cleopatra*

34 BC	Cleopatra and her children proclaimed rulers of the eastern Mediterranean	Alexandria	*Antony and Cleopatra*
2 Sep 31 BC	Battle of Actium	On the coast of western Greece	*Antony and Cleopatra*
Aug 30 BC	Death of Antony	Alexandria	*Antony and Cleopatra*
12 Aug 30 BC	Death of Cleopatra	Alexandria	*Antony and Cleopatra*
Early first century AD	Cunobelinus/ Cymbeline rules Britain (and dies before AD 43)	Britain	*Cymbeline*
During the reign of a fictional (late?) Roman emperor		Rome	*Titus Andronicus*
c.ninth–tenth century AD	Existence of legendary Amleth?	Denmark	*Hamlet*
15 Aug 1040	Death of Duncan I of Scotland	Bothnguane, Scotland	*Macbeth*
1053	Malcolm invades Scotland	Scotland	*Macbeth*
15 Aug 1057	Death of Macbeth	Lumphanan, Scotland	*Macbeth*
7 Oct 1571	Naval battle of Lepanto between Christians and Turks	The Mediterranean, off the coast of Greece	A context for *Othello*

FURTHER READING AND VIEWING

CRITICAL APPROACHES

Booth, Stephen, *King Lear, Macbeth, Indefinition and Tragedy* (1983). Not for beginners, but very penetrating.

Bradley, A. C., *Shakespearean Tragedy* (1904). Still worth reading a century after publication.

Cavell, Stanley, 'The Avoidance of Love', in *Disowning Knowledge in Seven Plays of Shakespeare* (1987). A sceptical philosopher's reading; still less for beginners, but so full of deep insight that it has claims to be among the best pieces ever written on the play.

Colie, Rosalie L., and F. T. Flahiff, *Some Facets of 'King Lear': Essays in Prismatic Criticism* (1974). An unusually strong collection of critical essays.

Danby, J. F. *Shakespeare's Doctrine of Nature* (1949). Contexts for Edmund.

Dollimore, Jonathan, '*King Lear* and Essentialist Humanism', in *Radical Tragedy: Religion, Ideology and Power in the Drama of Shakespeare and his Contemporaries* (1984). Inflected by neo-Marxist cultural politics.

Elton, William R., *King Lear and the Gods* (1966). Useful contextualization in the intellectual history of Shakespeare's time.

Empson, William, 'Fool in *Lear*', in *The Structure of Complex Words* (1951). Superb essay on a key word.

Goldberg, S. L., *An Essay on King Lear* (1974). Consistently thoughtful.

Greenblatt, Stephen, 'Shakespeare and the Exorcists', in *Shakespeare Negotiations: The Circulation of Social Energy in Renaissance England* (1988). Inventive account of why Shakespeare used an anti-Popish treatise for the mad language of Poor Tom.

Heilman, R. B., *This Great Stage: Image and Structure in King Lear* (1963). Good account of image patterns.

Kermode, Frank, ed., *King Lear: A Casebook* (1969). Fine collection of studies from the nineteenth and early twentieth centuries.

Kott, Jan, *Shakespeare Our Contemporary* (1964). The chapter on *King Lear* as a bleak, absurd drama analogous to Samuel Beckett's *Endgame* has been hugely influential; Peter Brook saw an early version, which did much to shape his 1962 production.

Mack, Maynard, *King Lear in Our Time* (1966). Remains valuable in our time.

Taylor, Gary, and Michael Warren, eds, *The Division of the Kingdoms: Shakespeare's Two Versions of King Lear* (1983). Groundbreaking collection of essays on Quarto and Folio variants.

THE PLAY IN PERFORMANCE

Brooke, Michael, 'King Lear on Screen', www.screenonline.org.uk/tv/id/566346/index.html. Overview of film versions.

Chambers, Colin, *Other Spaces: New Theatre and the RSC* (1980). Includes fine account of the powerfully intimate Buzz Goodbody production.

Jackson, Russell and Robert Smallwood, eds, *Players of Shakespeare 2* (1988). Interviews with actors, including Antony Sher on playing the Fool in Adrian Noble's production.

Leggatt, Alexander, *King Lear*, Shakespeare in Performance (1991). Good survey.

Ogden, James and Scouten, Arthur H., eds, *Lear from Study to Stage: Essays in criticism* (1997). Contains several illuminating essays.

Rosenberg, Marvin, *The Masks of King Lear* (1972). Many fascinating details of performances down the ages.

AVAILABLE ON DVD

King Lear, directed by Peter Brook (1970, DVD 2005). Bleak interpretation with magisterial performance by Paul Scofield.

King Lear (*Korol Lir*), directed by Grigori Kosintsev (1970, DVD 2007). Powerful Russian version.

King Lear, directed by Jonathan Miller (BBC Television Shakespeare, 1982, DVD 2004). Michael Hordern as Lear in a reworking (with fuller, perhaps overlong text) of an earlier television version by Miller, based ultimately on a stage production at Nottingham.

King Lear, directed by Michael Elliott (Channel 4 Television, 1983, DVD 2007). Laurence Olivier's last Shakespearean performance.

Ran, directed by Akira Kurosawa (1985, DVD 2006). Epic Japanese adaptation in Samurai setting.

A Thousand Acres, directed by Jocelyn Moorhouse (1997, DVD 2006). Jessica Lange, Michelle Pfeiffer and Jennifer Jason Leigh in a film version of a novel by Jane Smiley that transposes the story to the American Midwest and tells it from the point of view of the three daughters.

King Lear, directed by Richard Eyre (BBC2 Television 1998, DVD 2006). Filming of Eyre's exemplary small-scale National Theatre production.

My Kingdom, directed by Don Boyd (2001, DVD 2005). Richard Harris' last role: the *Lear* plot transposed to the world of a twenty-first-century Liverpool drug baron.

REFERENCES

1 Gamini Salgado, *Eyewitnesses of Shakespeare: First Hand Accounts of Performances 1590–1890* (1975), p. 38.
2 James Boswell, in a diary entry on 12 May 1763, in *Boswell's London Journals: 1762–1763*, ed. Frederick A. Pottle (1950), pp. 256–7.
3 George Steevens, review dated 16–18 February 1773, quoted in *Shakespeare, The Critical Heritage*, ed. Brian Vickers, vol. 5, *1765–1774* (1979), pp. 501–2.
4 Leigh Hunt in an originally unsigned review of *King Lear* in *The Examiner*, No. 21, 22 May 1808, pp. 331–3.
5 *The Times*, Review of *King Lear*, 25 April 1820.
6 William Hazlitt, in a *London Magazine* review of June 1820.
7 William Hazlitt, in a *London Magazine* review of May 1820.
8 John Forster, 'The Restoration of Shakespeare's Lear to the Stage,' *The Examiner*, No. 1566, 4 February 1838, pp. 69–70.
9 'Review of *King Lear*', *The Athenaeum*, No. 1066, 1 April 1848, p. 346.
10 William Winter, 'The Art of Edwin Booth: King Lear', in his *Life and Art of Edwin Booth* (1893), pp. 177–85.
11 Henry James, 'Tommaso Salvini', *The Atlantic Monthly*, Vol. LI, No. CCCV, March 1883, pp. 377–86.
12 John Gielgud, 'Granville Barker Rehearses *King Lear*', in his *Stage Directions* (1963, repr. 1979), pp. 51–5.
13 James Agate, review of *King Lear* in *Brief Chronicles: A Survey of the Plays of Shakespeare and the Elizabethans in Actual Performance* (1943, repr. 1971), pp. 201–3.
14 *The Times*, Review of *King Lear*, 21 April 1936.
15 W. A. Darlington, 'Old Vic at Home', *New York Times*, 13 October 1946.
16 Alan Brien, 'Simulation in the Fields', *The Spectator*, Vol. 203, No. 6843, 21 August 1959, pp. 223–4.
17 Maynard Mack, *King Lear in our Time* (1966).
18 James Ogden, 'Introduction', in *Lear from Study to Stage: Essays in Criticism*, ed. James Ogden and Arthur H. Scouten (1997).
19 *Illustrated London News*, Vol. 241, No. 6433, 17 November 1962.
20 Stephen J. Philips, 'Akira Kurosawa's *Ran*', in *Lear from Study to Stage*, p. 102.
21 Benedict Nightingale, *New Statesman*, 3 December 1976.
22 Sheridan Morley, *Daily Express*, 2 July 2004.
23 Tom Piper, *King Lear*, RSC Online Playguide, 2004.
24 Corin Redgrave, *King Lear*, RSC Online Playguide, 2004.
25 Benedict Nightingale, 'Some Recent Productions', in *Lear from Study to Stage*, p. 236.
26 John Peter, *Sunday Times*, 31 October 1999.
27 Michael Billington, *Guardian*, 30 October 1999.
28 Colin Chambers, *Other Spaces: New Theatre and the RSC* (1980), p. 71.
29 Nightingale, 'Some Recent Productions', p. 232.

30 Irving Wardle, *Independent*, 15 July 1990.
31 David Fielding, designer of the 1990 production, in interview with Lynne Truss, *Independent*, 8 July 1990.
32 John Gross, *Sunday Telegraph*, 15 July 1990.
33 Michael Billington, *Guardian*, 13 July 1990.
34 Note in *King Lear*, RSC programme, 1993.
35 Irving, *Independent*, 15 July 1990.
36 Chambers, *Other Spaces*, p. 69.
37 Michael Billington, *Guardian*, 30 June 1982.
38 Billington, *Guardian*, 30 June 1982.
39 David Nathan, *Jewish Chronicle*, 9 July 1982.
40 James Fenton, *Sunday Times*, 4 July 1982.
41 Antony Sher, 'The Fool in King Lear', in *Players of Shakespeare 2*, ed. Russell Jackson and Robert Smallwood (1988).
42 Adrian Noble, interview for *King Lear*, RSC Education Pack, 1993.
43 Robert Wilcher, 'King Lear', in *Shakespeare in Performance*, ed. Keith Parsons and Pamela Mason (1995), p. 91.
44 Gordon Parsons, *Morning Star*, 5 July 1982.
45 Alexander Leggatt, *King Lear*, Shakespeare in Performance (1991), p. 55.
46 Wilcher, 'King Lear', p. 93.
47 Janet Dale, in RSC Education Pack, 1993.
48 Benedict Nightingale, *The Times*, 12 July 1990.
49 Billington, *Guardian*, 13 July 1990.
50 Nightingale, 'Some Recent Productions', p. 231.
51 Emily Raymond, *King Lear*, RSC Online Playguide, 2005.
52 Nicholas de Jongh, *Evening Standard*, 21 May 1993.
53 Michael Billington, *Guardian*, 22 May 1993.
54 Nightingale, 'Some Recent Productions', p. 239.
55 Paul Taylor, *Independent*, 5 July 2004.
56 Peter J. Smith, in *Cahiers Élisabéthains*, No. 66 (2004).
57 Billington, *Guardian*, 30 June 1982.
58 Charles Marowitz, 'Lear Log', *Tulane Drama Review*, Vol. 8, No. 2 (Winter 1963), pp. 103–21.
59 Redgrave, *King Lear*.

ACKNOWLEDGEMENTS AND PICTURE CREDITS

Preparation of '*King Lear* in Performance' was assisted by a generous grant from the CAPITAL Centre (Creativity and Performance in Teaching and Learning) of the University of Warwick for research in the RSC archive at the Shakespeare Birthplace Trust. The Arts and Humanities Research Council (AHRC) funded a term's research leave that enabled Jonathan Bate to work on 'The Director's Cut'.

Picture research by Helen Robson, Jan Sewell and Kevin Wright. Grateful acknowledgement is made to the Shakespeare Birthplace Trust for assistance with picture research (special thanks to Helen Hargest) and reproduction fees.

Images of RSC productions are supplied by the Shakespeare Centre Library and Archive, Stratford-upon-Avon. This Library, maintained by the Shakespeare Birthplace Trust, holds the most important collection of Shakespeare material in the UK, including the Royal Shakespeare Company's official archive. It is open to the public free of charge.

For more information see www.shakespeare.org.uk.

1. Robert Armin © Bardbiz Limited
2. Mr Macready (1838) Reproduced by permission of the Shakespeare Birthplace Trust
3. Directed by Theodore Komisarjevsky (1936) Reproduced by permission of the Shakespeare Birthplace Trust
4. Directed by John Gielgud and Anthony Quayle (1950) Angus McBean © Royal Shakespeare Company
5. Directed by Peter Brook (1962) Angus McBean © Royal Shakespeare Company

6. Directed by Trevor Nunn (2007) Manuel Harlan © Royal Shakespeare Company
7. Directed by Deborah Warner (1990) © Donald Cooper/Photostage
8. Directed by Adrian Noble (1993) © John Bunting
9. Directed by Adrian Noble (1982) Joe Cocks © Shakespeare Birthplace Trust
10. Reconstructed Elizabethan Playhouse © Charcoalblue

"**Thanks to Bate and Rasmussen, we now have a rendering of the complete works that, in a rare publishing achievement, would also give complete satisfaction to the author himself.**"
- *Robert McCrum, The Observer*

Also Available:

A Midsummer Night's Dream	978-0-230-21789-8
Antony and Cleopatra	978-0-230-57618-6
Hamlet	978-0-230-21787-4
King Lear	978-0-230-57614-8
Love's Labour's Lost	978-0-230-21791-1
Macbeth	978-0-230-57620-9
Othello	978-0-230-57622-3
Richard III	978-0-230-22111-6
Sonnets and Other Poems	978-0-230-57624-7
The Tempest	978-0-230-21785-0
The Winter's Tale	978-0-230-57616-2
The RSC Complete Works	
Hardback	978-0-230-00350-7
Paperback	978-0-230-20095-1
Leather-bound	978-0-230-00351-4

www.rscshakespeare.co.uk

CPI Antony Rowe
Eastbourne, UK
February 12, 2019